faith beyond resentment

'A terrific book. James Alison is one of the really fresh and original voices in Catholic theology. These "Fragments" provide insight, inspiration and challenge for the sympathetic and attentive reader.'

ENDA McDONAGH

'James Alison's many admirers will find in this book much that is new, but also all that they will be used to – wit, clarity, depth and surprises.'

ROWAN WILLIAMS

'Like all James Alison's books, *Faith Beyond Resentment* is almost frighteningly profound. Alison, as he tells us a girardian must, reads texts. Not just any texts, but the texts of Scripture. Alison's readings train us to undertake the slow and painful work of living free of resentment. So taught we discover how debates about "homosexuality" can be repositioned from the stance of "us" versus "them" to "us" versus "us". So positioned we may even learn to accept the salvation that is ours in Christ.'

STANLEY HAUERWAS

'To touch the nerve of life and find the only words that say it, is exceptional. To do it again and again is more like genius. And Alison does just this. The blazing truth is that fear of desire creates a "moral" world, of good people (who keep the fear going) and bad people (who dangerously relax it). The two worlds, of the good and the bad, keep one another alive and well. Jesus is free of the fear of desire, and seeks by his teaching and actions to awaken this freedom in people so that desire can be in them what it really is: love trying to happen. This got Jesus crucified – and still gets him crucified. The world does not like what Jesus shows us God is like.

'The gay question urges upon the Church as nothing else does the implication of Jesus' comfortableness with desire, for in no other moral area is the fear of desire so operative, so that the supreme authority has come as close as it can (in spite of a Tridentine anathema) to naming desire in the homosexual person as evil. Homophobia is at root erophobia.'

SEBASTIAN MOORE

faith beyond resentment:

fragments catholic and gay

———◄◦►———

James Alison

A Herder & Herder Book
The Crossroad Publishing Company
New York

The Crossroad Publishing Company
481 Eighth Avenue, New York, NY 10001

First published in the UK in 2001 by Darton, Longman and Todd Ltd.
First published in the United States in 2001 by The Crossroad Publishing Company.

For the purposes of conversation regarding *Faith Beyond Resentment*, James Alison
can be reached at cgfragments@btinternet.com

Printed and bound in the United Kingdom by Page Bros, Norwich, Norfolk
Designed by Sandie Boccacci
Phototypeset in 11¾/13½ pt Perpetua by Intype London Ltd

Library of Congress Cataloguing-in-Publication Data

Alison, James 1959–
    Faith beyond resentment: fragments Catholic and gay / James Alison
    p. cm.
    Includes bibliographical references.
    ISBN 0–8245–1922–1 (alk. paper)
      1. Catholic gays—Religious life.   2. Catholic Church—Doctrines.
I. Title.
    BX1795.H66 A45   2001
    261.8′35766′08822—dc21

                                                            2001000789

2 3 4 5 6 7 8 9 10   10 09 08 07 06

CONTENTS

——◄◦►——

Chapter One is a modified version and translation of a talk written in Chicago, Illinois and given in Costa Rica in May 1995. It has since appeared in English in *Contagion* 4 (Spring 1997) and *Theology and Sexuality* no 7 (September 1997), and appears here by kind permission of both Editors.

Chapter Two is a modified version and translation of a talk written in Shreveport, Louisiana and given in Mexico City in November 1997. It was first published, in slightly different form, in the journal *Theology and Sexuality* no 11 (September 1999), and appears here by kind permission of the Editor.

Chapter Three was written in Chicago, Illinois in January 1997 and substantially expanded in Rio de Janeiro, Brazil in July 2000.

Chapter Four is a modified version of a talk written and given in London in March 1999. It was published in *Contagion* 7 (Spring 2000) and appears here by kind permission of the Editor.

Chapter Five is a modified version of a talk written in Santiago de Chile and given at St Gregory of Nyssa Church, San Francisco, California in October 1999.

Chapter Six is a modified version of a talk written in Santiago de Chile and given in Edinburgh, Scotland in May 2000.

Chapter Seven is a modified version of a presentation prepared in Santiago de Chile for the meeting of the Colloquium on Violence and Religion held at Boston College, Massachusetts in May/June 2000.

Chapter Eight was written in London in August 1999 and substantially expanded in Rio de Janeiro, Brazil in August 2000.

Chapter Nine was written in Santiago de Chile and presented in a forum on violence in Woodside, California in October 1999.

Chapter Ten was written in Rio de Janeiro, Brazil in August 2000.

The quotation from p. 224–5 of René Girard's *Je vois Satan tomber comme l'éclair* (Paris: Grasset, 1999) which appears in translation on pp. 165–6 is used here by kind permission.

The quotation from the Council of Trent on pp. 226–7 is a modified form of the translation appearing in N.Tanner (ed.), *Decrees of the Ecumenical Councils* (London: Sheed & Ward/Washington DC: Georgetown University Press, 1990).

'How' Joseph must have thought, as he donned his Egyptian vizier's robe, 'am I going to enable my brothers to share all this abundance which has been given me? They think I'm probably dead, and effectively that's what they wanted. They are a long way away, and even if, by the sort of miracle usually confined to Bible stories, they were to wend their weary way across the desert from Canaan to Egypt, they are probably still just as jealous and fratricidal as ever they were, and thus would be frightened of me. They would think me likely to be plotting revenge and so wouldn't open up enough to be able to receive all the things I want to give them. To tell them that we were wrong is to play tit for tat. Not to tell them anything is to treat them as incorrigible and deprive them of the joyous breaking of heart which will enable us to become real brothers. What on earth am I to say?'

I am not sure that any lesser starting point is worthy of gay people who are becoming able to speak the gift of faith. The position of the effectively dead man who, after losing any belonging, after struggling through an unsatisfactory apprenticeship and a prison sentence in a realm he did not know, without any support from his own, has found himself given a position of such favour and abundance that his task is to imagine generosity for others. This is what I mean by calling this book 'Faith beyond resentment'. Joseph exercised Pharaoh's generosity as though he had never undergone any of the experiences which led him to his position. He was so entirely free of any sort of resentment that he was able to imagine an entirely generous and sustained programme for the reconciliation of his brothers, and act it out in such a way that they were eventually able to get the point, overcome their fratricide and be reconciled.

In the pages that follow, it is to just such a making available of abundance from a complete lack of resentment that I aspire. And yet the reality falls far short of the aspiration. I don't suppose that Joseph was free from resentment as he was sold into slavery by his brothers. He had time for meditation as he was dragged off to Egypt, meditation which could easily have turned into bitterness, resentment and despair. He had cause for more of the same when his seemingly safe job got turned into a trap by the wife of his master Potiphar. And in whose entrails would the worm not have turned during a long and undeserved jail-sentence? Yet it was in the midst of these experiences that Joseph developed an awareness of being loved such that he recognised that none of the people against whom he might justly feel resentment were really worthy of his dedicating to them that weight of emotional involvement. And he moved beyond even that, to a position of such freedom that he began to be able to plot not vengeance, but sustained forgiveness as the gift of humanising others.

The reason I have called these pages 'fragments' is that they inhabit the process of losing resentment. The freedom from resentment which I have described is aspirational, but the process of losing it is real. The chapters upon which you are embarking mark my failure to write the book which I once planned, a symphonically elegant treatise on the unbinding of the gay conscience. I have instead been given to dwell within the process of the unbinding of that conscience. Each chapter is perhaps a pit stop on the camel route to Egypt, a few hours stolen from my duties in Potiphar's mansion, an idling away of time in prison.

'Fragments' is a pretty word – the sort of word that theologians and others like to use out of a certain professional modesty. It is the same with titles beginning 'Towards a . . .' (new understanding of this, radical rewrite of that). But the word hides something which is not pretty: it means things broken. Broken words. A broken ability to find sense. And professional modesty is merely playful if the brokenness is not real. To come across broken pieces and try to put them together is one thing. To discover oneself among the broken pieces which are being put together is quite another.

These pages are written out of brokenness. This is something for which neither my theological training nor my pretensions of literacy could have prepared me. If I had escaped being broken, I would indeed have written my 'symphonically elegant work on the unbinding of the gay conscience'. And it would have been false. There is nothing elegant about inhabiting a space which has historically, socially and theologically been regarded at best as risible and at worst as evil. Any elegance in the pages that follows is, I fear, a sign of a failure to inhabit that space and speak from it, to let go of a residual veneer of sophisticated denial, to allow words to arise instead from the unspeakable, the unacceptable, the abominable. To speak prettily from a space that is littered with murder, with suicide, and with lies is perhaps simply presumptuous. And yet not to speak at all, not to try to do homage to the wastage and the pain by stammering the forgiveness that those deprived of words cannot articulate, even when, time after time, I miss the pathos and the depth of the forgiveness that is required, is to render too much tribute to despair.

The background to these texts is not that of a lifelong struggle with the oppressive force of Catholic teaching. I was brought up in a conservative middle-class English evangelical Protestant environment. The gift of Catholic faith, which I received at the age of eighteen, was never a movement towards the exotic, the liturgical, the aesthetic. It was, and is, the gift of enabling me to be wrong, and not to worry about it, of letting go of being right so as to receive being loved. I have never experienced Catholicism as itself creating the great annihilation of being which has accompanied same-sex desire throughout the monotheistic world and beyond, however much Catholicism has pandered to, succumbed to and institutionalised the forces of that annihilation, and however little it has been brave enough to resist them when it should have known better. Until I received the gift of Catholic faith I dwelt in that annihilation wordlessly, imagelessly. I experienced it as a void created and maintained by silent voices of righteous hatred. For hatred can only create a void; and hatred is incapable of being wrong. But my void was that of the thoroughly English, respectable, hatred which seemed normal as I grew up in the 1960s and 70s; and it was this that formed the being which faith has interrupted unalterably. For while hatred itself is incurably righteous, even self-righteous haters like myself can be given a heart.

Not only did the gift of Catholic faith keep me from killing myself, but little by little it has given me the tools, the structure and the words with which to sink into, to inhabit, and to begin to detoxify, at least for myself, and I hope for others, the great annihilation of being. This gift has made it possible for me to begin to discover what it might mean to be rejoiced in as being gay, and how to love and share a dignity which the centuries have denied us. A discovery which will, I suspect, become more and more common. So you will not find a protest against the Catholic faith in these pages. Though you may find yourself sharing my amazement at how all the deepest and most resilient elements of the faith seem to point in exactly the opposite direction to that so tensely insisted on by the stewards of its formulas.

What I want to share with you is a story neither of protest nor of heroism. It is something much more like an unfinished journey into discovery of being. A journey in which Catholic faith provides the wherewithal to make the discovery possible, both because of and in spite of its own structure. Various gifts have contributed to turning this hater, who could so easily have become a self-hating clergyman, or a closet homophobic politician, into the author of these pages. After the gift of Catholic faith, there was the gift of being associated with a religious order which took me in when I was on the brink of despair, taught me theology and gave me the basic theological tools which set me free to discover that faith is not given us so as to enable us to 'belong to the Church' but so that we may understand and love being human. Then there came the gift of the thought of René Girard, which has given me the structure and eventually the courage to reimagine the Christian faith in what turns out to be an unexpectedly orthodox way. It is his thought, which underpins all the chapters of this book, which allowed me not to be frightened of dwelling in the space of the hatred from which I had always run away. Not frightened, because becoming aware that by dwelling peacefully in this space, the

Word would come. Then, as courage grew, there was the gift of being repudiated by the South American branch of the religious order with which I lived. It was in the midst of this repudiation that I discovered that God has nothing to do with religious violence. It was time to let go of the shelter to which I clung and dare to be what I had never dared to be all along.

Even after the repudiation I lingered on for a few months, which was when I received the most destabilising gift of all. The death from AIDS of the man I loved. More shocking than the speed and surprise of his death was the realisation which dawned on me in the days immediately after it, that there was nothing evil or distorted or silly or pretend about the love between us. It was the real thing. And that meant that I had no shelter, could not consent to cowardice any more. Could not be complicitous with the denigration of love. Had to move forward.

These pages start here. They have been written over the six years that have passed since Laércio's death. These are years in which I have stumbled, at first with dismay, and gradually with delight, into adult life, into being unemployed, trying to find work, holding jobs and losing them, having a bank account, falling into debt, working my way out of it, attempting to settle in a country, being unable to, trying again. They are years in which I have tried to learn how to be faithful to a theologian's vocation without any institutional belonging, academic or ecclesiastical. Years in which I have tried to imagine what it is to exercise priesthood in exile. That is another reason why I can offer you only fragments: in six years I have moved countries seven times, and have had access to my own books only for one eight-month interlude. The result is many fewer footnotes than is normal in a book of theology.

Of the ten chapters, seven were written for specific audiences, and the remainder were either written or adapted for this book. I have kept them in roughly the order in which they were written because I hope that you will detect something of progress in them, something of a gradual daring to sink into and personally to inhabit texts and experiences which it is too easy to read from outside. Something of a development of voice. I have divided the chapters into two parts. The first contains a series of attempts to dwell in biblical texts in such a way that they fuel imagination and spark off recognitions which enable us to engage in a re-creation of being. The second part emerged as I began to dare to think that I must learn to speak for myself, something which I suspect is going to be increasingly important for theology written by gay people as our consciences do indeed become free. The uncertain tenor, the tentative nature of these rehearsals of a voice will be self-evident.

What do I hope you will get from these pages? I hope that you will find your faith less easily scandalised, that you are more easily able to relax into being loved, that you will become more aware of the earth-shaking mercy behind God becoming incarnate and dwelling among us, a mercy whose implications maybe it is especially gay and lesbian people who can make alive at this time.

When, in this book, I say 'Catholic' I'm not sure whether I mean 'Roman Catholic' or simply Christian. When I say 'Church' I am not sure whether I mean 'juridical structure' or simply 'God's faithful people'. When I say 'gay' I'm not sure whether or not 'lesbian' is included – and sometimes whether or not 'straight' isn't included as well. In each case, I am complicit with my belonging, and the limits of my freedom from circumstance are for others to discern. My rare uses of the word 'homosexual' appear almost invariably in inverted commas. There is something ineradicably 'they'-ish about the word, and these are 'we'-seeking pages.

Because I have had little access to books over the last six years, my debts to the people who have sustained me are much greater than my debts to other authors. There are those who, by inviting me to talk, in some cases putting their own reputation at risk, have kept my vocation alive: Amando Robles OP, Carlos Mendoza OP, Martin Pendergast, Mark Lodico, Rev. Donald Schell, Robert Hamerton-Kelly, Rev. Richard Kirker, Robert Daly SJ. There are the friends who have sustained me with conversation, hospitality and financial help when it seemed that I was adrift on a towering sea: Fr Sebastian Moore OSB, David Otto, Don and Marina Dupree, Miko and Dorothee Giedroyc, Dr Jillian Vites, Fr Peter Harris, Rev. Roger Royle, Desirée Howells, Rev. Robert Wiggs,

Jim Davis, Rev. Eric James, Rev. Kanley McHayle, Alfredo Dorea SJ. Other collaborators have given me constant feedback, shared their stories, and inspired me with their work and love: Julie Shinnick, Peter McGlynn, Marie-Charlotte Bouësseau, Angel Méndez OP, Daniel Ulloa OP, Jerry Cleator OP, Nelson González, Rev. Paul Nuechterlein, Marcelo Iturrieta, Hector Tapia. Other friends have allowed this book to happen, helping to edit its chapters in such a way as not to make the author's chronic lack of self-confidence any worse: Andrew and Kathleen McKenna, in whose home one chapter was written, and many others corrected, Mary Grove, Eugene Rogers, Angela West, Bruce Williams OP, Linda Hogan, Diana Culbertson OP and, with special grace, Michael Kelly. Glenn Brooks and José Lugo Reyes have done more than either of them could know to teach me the fraternity which I have tried to pass over into these pages. None of these can be held responsible for any of the deficiencies in what you are about to read.

I owe a particular burden of thanks to Brendan Walsh and Barbara James, my friends, and frequently my hosts. In religious publishing, resentment sells, conspiracy theories sell, scandal sells. Because of this, a book which combines theology, Catholicism, priests, gay people, the Vatican and so on should surely be a money-spinner. Yet Brendan and his team at Darton, Longman and Todd have been confronted with these best-selling ingredients cooked up by an author who doesn't believe in conspiracy theories, seeks to undo scandal, and thinks his own work valueless in exactly the degree to which it is resentful. In short, the very reverse of a commercial proposition. They haven't blinked.

These pages are dedicated to the memory of my friend and classmate, Fr Benjamin O'Sullivan, monk of Ampleforth Abbey who died by his own hand in 1996. May his prayers bring something of his infectious joy to those who most need it, and most hope that these pages will not disappoint them.

Rio de Janeiro, *August 2000*

PART ONE

inhabiting the text

CHAPTER ONE

the man blind from birth and the Creator's subversion of sin

introduction

I would like to undertake with you a reading of Chapter 9 of John's gospel. The reading will not be a simple commentary, but an attempt to experiment with the perspective of the reading. That is to say, we're asking 'Who is reading this passage?', 'With whom do we identify?' And the reason for this approach is to nudge us into beginning to raise certain questions of fundamental morals, how we talk about them, or live them in a more or less coherent and convincing way. I can't promise you any great conclusions, because this is an experimental approach to the subject. I should also begin by saying that my intention is not to cause scandal, but to provoke a discussion which allows a fuller way of living a Christian life. In this sense what I'm trying out is an attempt at a search for a theological method which I have not yet mastered and which, if developed, will, I hope, prove somewhat emancipatory for all of us.

miracle or theological debate?

Let us begin our reading of John 9. At first sight we have an account of a miraculous healing. It is the story of a man blind from birth who receives his sight from Jesus one Sabbath, and then of the consequences of this healing among the people who witness, or hear about, the matter. If the account were to be found in one of the synoptic gospels, perhaps it might remain at that – there is

3

no shortage of such stories. I have no doubt that, in the background to the story, we're dealing with an historical incident of a healing carried out by Jesus on a Sabbath. However, here the 'miraculous healing' element doesn't receive much emphasis, nor does the Sabbath – or rather, the matter of the Sabbath does receive a certain weight, as we will see later on, but with some very idiosyncratically Johannine touches. In any case, the purpose of this chapter is determined by the debate about sin, sight, blindness and judgement within which it is set: these are the jeweller's artwork which show forth, and make sense of, the gem of the healing.

Let us look at the beginning of the story. Jesus sees a man born blind, and his disciples ask him:

> 'Master, who sinned, this man or his parents, that he was born blind?' (9.2)

Jesus answers them:

> 'Neither this man nor his parents. He is blind so that the works of God may be made manifest in him.' (9:3)

That is to say, the whole story which follows comes as an illustration of Jesus' answer to this question of his disciples. Now, I think we've all heard this passage before, and we've probably heard the commentary that is normally made about it, which is that, in those days, people used to attribute moral causes to physical evils (like illnesses) or to natural disasters (like earthquakes or tempests). Jesus would, then, be breaking with this tendency, proper to a primitive religious culture, even though still very present in our own society, and giving instead a divine answer to the problem. Well, this interpretation, while partially correct, doesn't go to the heart of the matter, which seems to me to be much more interesting.

Let's look at the end of the story. We have the former blind man who sees Jesus, and, believing in the Son of Man, worships him. Jesus then comments:

> 'I have come into the world for a judgement (or discernment), that those who do not see may see, while those who see will

become blind.' When they heard this the Pharisees who were with him asked him 'Are we also blind?' Jesus answered them: 'If you were blind, you would have no sin, but since you say that you see, your sin remains.' (9:39–41)

So the whole account has as its frame a discussion about sin. Blindness and sight come to be a way of talking about much more than questions of the health of the eyes. Jesus' final comment is simply enigmatic if we don't follow what has happened meanwhile. Now let us turn to see what has happened in between our two quotes.

the account of an inclusion

What we have is something like two stories intertwined with each other, the story of an inclusion and the story of an exclusion. The story of the inclusion is easy. There was a man who had a defect: he had not finished being created, for when he was born he was lacking sight. This is not only to be excluded from a particular human good, but it is also, by being defective, to be excluded from a fullness of participation in Israel. His physical defect was also a cultic impediment, because only flawless people were permitted to serve God's cult as priests (just as unblemished lambs were needed for sacrifice). A son of Aaron, for example, a member of the priestly caste, could not officiate at worship if he had a physical defect. However, in matters social a purely ritual exclusion doesn't remain at the level of the merely physical. Since ritual has to do with the maintenance of the purity and goodness of the group, so a physical defect which implied a ritual defect also implied a moral defect. In this way, the disciples, as ordinary people of their time and circumstances, deduced from the blind man's physical state some kind of moral problem, whence their question: 'Who sinned that this man be born blind?' (9:2).

Now, please notice the route which the logic follows. The defect excludes; that which excludes from the group also excludes from the way in which the group makes itself good; whence it is deduced that that which excludes has a serious moral cause. In this way, the result of the process, the fact of being excluded from the goodness of the group, is taken as a cause, and by cause, please understand, fault: 'Who sinned?' This is, indeed, a certain sort of logic. It is an absolutely common logic, and we find it in diverse forms round about us without much difficulty: it's called blaming the victim. If someone is assaulted, she must have been doing something to provoke it; if black people have a low socio-economic status, it must be because they are really more stupid or lazy than others; if someone has AIDS, it must be a punishment from God for some form of deviant behaviour. And so think we all in some situations, above all when we're children, and totally dependent on our parents: if something bad happens at home, or our parents are quarrelling, or alcoholic, or are getting divorced, then, in some mysterious way, the fault is ours. If we behave ourselves, making a promise or a vow to God, St Jude, or whomever, then everything will be sorted out. Psychologists call this sort of thinking 'magic', and we all have to grow beyond it somehow.

Well, Jesus' attitude is far removed from magic thinking: not only is it far removed, but he gives us a lesson in the subversion from within of this mentality. He proceeds to carry out an inclusion. First he spits on the earth, and from the clay he makes a paste and anoints the blind man's eyes. Here we have a Hebrew pun, disguised by the Greek of the text. Clay is *adamah*, and it is that from which God originally made 'Adam', mankind, in Genesis 2:7. So, here, what Jesus is doing is the act of finishing creation. The man born blind had palpably not been brought to the fullness of creation, and Jesus finishes off the process by adding the missing clay. The blind man still does not see, and Jesus sends him to a pool where baths of ritual purification took place, and when he comes out, the blind man begins to see. Now, this question of the pool of Siloam is interesting, because it is normally interpreted as a reference to the waters of baptism, and I don't think that there's anything wrong with that, because baptism is (or should be) the rite of inclusion par excellence. However, I think that what is important here is not the allusion to the rite, but to the inclusion: it is from his bathing in a Jewish pool that the blind man comes to be fully included in the Jewish people, and this is beautifully shown in the text. Up until this point the blind man has not said

6

anything. He has not even had voice or name: he has always been a 'him' or a 'that one', recognised by his blindness and his position as a beggar. Even when he begins to see, people carry on talking about 'him', until the moment when the former blind man interrupts to say 'It is I'.

From that moment on, they deign to speak to him, and address him as 'you'. At this point he does not know much about Jesus, for he has not even seen him, since it was only at the pool that he actually began to see. In the rest of the story we see the gradual process by which he becomes aware of who Jesus is. Under interrogation he says that Jesus is a prophet: a perfectly reasonable conclusion. It is as if one of us who received an important cure at the hands of somebody were to call that person a saint. The authorities doubt that he was originally blind, and seek other evidence to determine whether or not he had ever seen before, calling his parents, who point out that their son is an adult, and that he can answer for himself. Another moment of inclusion: now he is an adult, and has the use of the word and responsibility for his actions. Since he knows that he has been cured, he becomes stubborn in the face of his interrogators: his replies get longer, bolder, and more obstinate. He had said that Jesus was a prophet, and of course the Pharisees produce the principal prophet to whom they subscribe: Moses.

> 'We know that God spoke to Moses, but this fellow, we don't know from where he comes.' (9:29)

At this moment the former blind man replies with a formidable lucidity:

> 'Well, isn't that extraordinary, that you don't know from where he comes, when he has opened my eyes. We know that God doesn't listen to sinners, but to those who worship him and do his will. Not since the dawn of time (*ek tou aiōnos*) has it been heard that anybody has opened the eyes of a man born blind. If he didn't come from God, he could do nothing.' (9:30—3)

Now, please notice here an important grammatical game. The

Pharisees use the word 'we' to exclude the former blind man's 'you':

'You are his disciple; we are disciples of Moses.' (9:28)

That is to say their 'we' is defined by contrast with 'you'. However, the former blind man doesn't accept their game, but he answers in terms of an 'us', counting himself in with the Pharisees:

'We know that God doesn't listen to sinners, but to those who worship him and do his will.' (9:31)

That is to say, he is debating in objective terms starting from the common ground of being a son of Moses, along with the Pharisees, and his position is very interesting:

'Not since the dawn of time has it been heard that anybody has opened the eyes of a man born blind.' (9:32)

Please notice John's code: from the dawn of time means: since the creation of the world. Only the Creator could carry out this act of finishing off creation, and if Jesus did not proceed from the Creator, he couldn't have brought about this act of finishing off creation. The former blind man has perceived the full meaning of the clay, the *adamah*: in his person God was finishing off the creation of Adam. From a sub-person without voice or member-ship, he has come to be an included adult, and one who is, furthermore, a fine interpreter of the things of God. Shortly after-wards Jesus comes up to him, and asks him if he believes in the Son of Man. Since the former blind man has still never seen Jesus, he doesn't recognise the one who cured him. Jesus identifies himself, and the former blind man prostrates himself in worship before him. He has moved from a theoretical recognition that this man had to have proceeded from God in order to be able to complete the work of creation, to a full recognition of God in his life. Now he is the complete human, what we would call a Christian: the two things go together. The Christian is one who recognises that it is through Jesus that she is brought to the com-pletion of her creation, and for this reason is progressively inducted, which means included, into the life of God, which is life without end.

the account of an exclusion

Thus far the account of the inclusion. But we're only halfway through the affair. There is also, and the two accounts are intertwined, the account of an exclusion. The blind man begins excluded. So far, no problem. He is merely an occasion for the curiosity of passers-by, allowing them to wonder about the mysteries of the moral causality of physical misfortunes. The established order has no problem with the existence of excluded people. Rather, as we will see, it depends on them. In the degree to which our blind man comes to be included, he provokes first curiosity, and then rejection.

Once cured, the former blind man is taken to the Pharisees. These Johannine figures immediately have a criterion by which to judge if the cure came from God or not. The cure was carried out on a Sabbath, so it cannot come from God. Now the objection is more interesting than it seems. Of God it is said in Genesis that he rested on the Sabbath, after creating everything. So the commandment which obliges people to rest on the Sabbath is a strict injunction to imitate God. And the person who doesn't rest on the Sabbath is a sinner, because he is neither obeying nor imitating God (which comes down to the same thing). Here too we see an element of John's code. In John 5 Jesus cures an invalid on the Sabbath, and the authorities reproach him for this. Jesus declares to them:

'My Father is working up until the present, and I also work.' (John 5:17)

The reply is rather more dense than it seems. It constitutes a formal denial that God is resting on the Sabbath, as well as an affirmation that creation has yet to be completed, and that for this reason Jesus carries on with his work of bringing creation to fulfilment on the Sabbath. Now, back at John 9 we note that when the disciples asked Jesus at the beginning of the story who sinned that this man should have been born blind, he replied that neither he nor his parents had sinned, but that

> 'He is blind so that the *works* of God may be manifest in him.' (9:3)

That is to say, for John the matter of the Sabbath, the healing, and the continuing of creation go absolutely together. The cure on a Sabbath has as its purpose to show God's continued creative power mediated by Jesus. For the same reason, the reaction of the Pharisees is a sign of a profound disagreement with Jesus as to who God is and how God acts. Either the Sabbath serves to bring about a separation between those who observe it, and are thus good, and those who do not and are not, and God is defined, which also means limited, by the Law. Or alternatively the Sabbath is a symbol of creation still unfinished, and is an opportunity for God to reveal his lovingkindness to humans, and God is identified by his exuberant creativity.

Well, it is their realisation that this is what is at stake that produces a schism among the Pharisees. For some of them,

> 'This man does not keep the Sabbath; he cannot come from God.' (9:16)

While for others:

> 'And how could a sinner carry out such signs?' (9:16)

Now the last thing that the Pharisees need has begun to happen: an internal division, which prevents them from taking joint action because there are two diametrically opposed positions in their group. What is the quickest way of overcoming this schism? While there is to be found a man who is incontrovertibly cured, the two possible interpretations of his cure, that it is from God, or that it is not from God (being instead the fruit of some diabolic deception) are bound to persist. And there is no way of resolving such a problem through reasoned discussion. So the problem of the cure has to be dealt with quickly by denying that it ever happened. If the man had never really been blind from birth, then neither has he been cured, and so there is no problem. So, they propose that there was no cure, and the parents of the former blind man are called so as to try to get out of them 'the truth' about their son – that is, that he was not, and never had been, blind.

Well, imagine the reaction of the parents. They know full well that their son had been blind, and that now he is not. However the last thing that they want, they or anybody with a modicum of common sense, is to get caught up in the midst of a group of the indignant just who are showing signs of needing to vent their righteousness. So the parents limit their reply to a minimum: that their son was indeed born blind, and that they have no idea how it is that he now sees. They want to get out as quickly as possible from this potentially violent circle, so they dump their son back into the middle of it, but now with a new status: as an adult who will have to interpret for himself what has happened to him. So they manage to get out of the threat of being victimised by the group of the 'righteous just' by offering their son in their stead.

The first attempt of the group of the Pharisees to get out of the problem by the way of unreality, the denial of the existence of the problem, failed. Now they'll have to get the recipient of the cure to remove their problem for them. They regroup for this new sortie, and call in the former blind man. At this point they adopt a solemn, judicial, tone as befits serious men who must deliberate gravely with knowledge of legal matters. First they present the former blind man with their premise: that man (that is Jesus) is, without any shade of doubt, a sinner. So, they conjure the former blind man with the appropriate legal phrase, 'Give glory to God', meaning: solemnly recognise this fact.[1] Please notice how they proceed. They were unable to recreate their unity by the most convenient means, which would be by the cure turning out never to have happened in the first place. They have to recognise that something did in fact happen. What is important now for them is to produce an unanimous and solemn agreement

---

1. The Johannine irony in the use of this standard legal phrase is exquisite, since it is precisely in refusing to call Jesus a sinner and in being cast out for his pains that the former blind man really does 'give glory to God'.

concerning the interpretation of what did in fact happen. It is as if they were to say: 'You, keep your cure, since we can't get around the fact that you have been cured, but, please, recognise that the cure comes from an evil source. That is, it doesn't matter what has actually happened just so long as you agree with us as to its interpretation. In this way we'll manage to maintain our unity, and you too can form part of the group, you can enter into solidarity with us.'

The former blind man responds with one of the most splendid lines of our religious tradition, and one which we should perhaps take much more seriously:

> 'Whether he is a sinner or not, I do not know; the only thing I know is that before I was blind, and now I see.' (9:25)

That is to say, the former blind man shows a healthy lack of concern for the moral dimension of the issue, a sane agnosticism, and holds on instead only to what is incontrovertibly good: an evident change in his life. By showing this agnosticism he is, at the same time, refusing to participate in solidarity against the one who cured him. And that means he has refused to imitate his parents. They had left him in the centre of the circle, as a probable object of target practice for the righteous just. He could have done the same thing, saying of Jesus 'Yes indeed, he is a sinner.' In that way he'd have managed both to get his sight *and* get out of the centre of the circle, leaving Jesus in his place as sole recipient of the group's ire, making himself instead a member of the club. In order to do this he'd have to give false witness under oath, for he has been solemnly conjured, but there's never been a shortage of people willing to give false witness if the occasion should merit it.

The former blind man refuses to cloak himself with the interpretation demanded by the group, so the group has to find another way out of the problem. Since, owing to his previous status as a blind beggar, he is ignorant, perhaps there was some hint in the concrete way in which the cure was carried out which might allow them to reach the desired interpretation. So they ask him once again what it was that Jesus had done. Perhaps in the description of the act something formally sinful might be detected which would allow them to interpret the act as a sin, now that they can't count on the helpful solidarity of the former blind man. They'd already heard the details before, but perhaps going over the evidence again some elements of witchcraft might be revealed, or anything which would allow them to say: 'You see! He did something evil that something good might come, so the cure cannot come from God.'

At this stage the former blind man begins to ridicule the group's ever more detailed efforts to produce a legal interpretation which allows them to maintain their unity. He asks them if they don't want to become Jesus' disciples themselves. After all, a close investigation of the procedure for carrying out a miracle could be motivated either by a flattering desire to imitate in order to do the same thing, or, as in this case, by the envious desire to get rid of the object of jealousy. It is this remark which produces the detonation of insults. Now, please notice that up until this point they haven't insulted him, and, if we were to take one of the group aside to ask him what they were doing, he would probably have explained that he sympathised with the former blind man. After all, the poor fellow hadn't done anything wrong: he was the victim of the evil of another (in this case Jesus), and doesn't understand the danger that he's in. The crux of the question is this: if he can only be persuaded to interpret what has happened to him with the certainty which they are offering him, then he will be safe, one of the group of the good guys. No problem. They are conducting this interrogation for his own good, and want, up till the last moment, to save him. It's only at the point where they perceive that the former blind man doesn't respect the sincerity of their efforts to lead him down the right path that they begin to mistreat him. That happens when they perceive that, even though he isn't formally one of Jesus' followers, for he doesn't even know him, he's keeping himself independent of the group of the just and their opinions. And it is because of this that he becomes an object of mockery: 'We tried to reason with him; we sought every possible opportunity to show him the right way to go, but he became stubborn in his error.' From sweet reasoning they move to insult.

The first step in this process is their militant affirmation of their group's goodness and their security in their convictions: this is what allows them to become united. The former blind man has managed to resolve their problem of dissension by allowing them to join together in insulting him. Before, they were unable to say 'we' in a convincing way, because there were disagreements of interpretation in their midst. Now they can be united, producing a shining 'we' by contrast with a well-defined 'they':

> 'You may be a disciple of his; *we* are disciples of Moses. We know for a fact . . .' (9:28)

While they are building up to an ever more rabid unity, in their midst the one who is about to be their victim, on whom they will discharge their wrath, is becoming ever more lucid, giving weighty theological arguments, more fitting for a doctor than for a beggar. The eye of the hurricane is a centre of peace and revelation while the expelling rage builds to fever pitch: the former blind man explains very clearly that the source of his cure can be deduced without difficulty. God would not have acted through Jesus if Jesus were a sinner, and of no one has it been heard that they could carry out an act of creation 'ex nihilo' except God alone, whence it can be deduced that:

> 'If this man did not come from God, he could have done nothing.' (9:33)

The logic is perfect, but we're beyond the stage where logic matters. The most explicit revelation happens in the tornado of expulsion. The 'righteous just' are no longer interested in arguments: they've got what they wanted, which is to build up their unity as a group, and they move from casual insults to a straightforward description of the former blind man as absolutely identified with sin. Because of this he is a contaminating element, and they expel him.

Please notice how the thing works. It is not that they reach, independently, the conclusion that the man is absolutely sin, and then, after a long and mature deliberation, decide to throw him out. Rather, the mechanism by which they build their unity issues forth simultaneously in the description of the man as sin and in his expulsion. He couldn't be expelled if he weren't sin, and he wouldn't be sin if it hadn't become necessary to expel him. We're back to magic thought: if someone is excluded, for example, because he's blind, then, somewhere there must be a sin involved. We've advanced not at all.

the subversion of sin

Well, so much for the account of the expulsion. You will have noticed that the accounts of the inclusion and of the exclusion are not independent, but are interwoven, and the account of the inclusion occurs in the middle of, and in a certain sense provokes, the account of the exclusion. In the same way, the account of the exclusion produces and fulfils the account of the inclusion. It is in the midst of the mechanism of expulsion, and while he is suffering it, that the former blind man comes to have a real clarity with respect to what has been going on, and who Jesus is.

Now, Jesus' final phrases about blindness and sight come to be a commentary about exactly this double account of inclusion and exclusion. In the first place Jesus says that he has come to the world to open a trial, or judgement, or discernment. Any of these words will do. This trial, or judgement, which is not realised until his death, constitutes the subversion from within of what the world understands by sin, and goodness and justice.[2] Thus, beginning from his death, these realities will be understood from the viewpoint of the excluded one, and not from that of the expellers. It is the innocent victim who is constituted judge, precisely as victim. Those who remain under judgement are those who thought that they were judging. The story of the man born blind thus has a role as a prophetic commentary on what is to happen to Jesus, and how what happens to Jesus is going to function. It is going to function as an element which makes it impossible for the righteous, the good, those who think that they see, to maintain for long their goodness by the exclusion of people considered evil,

2. Cf. John 16:8–11.

sinful, or blind. We're talking about the same mechanism as has made it impossible for the Argentine or Chilean military to keep a tranquil conscience about what they did during their dictatorships, however many amnesties and indults they may have received. Because now, since a vague rumour about the death and resurrection of Jesus has been spread abroad, which is also the redefinition of who is just, and of God, in terms of the victim, it is not possible for them to cover up for ever their suspicion that their own victims, those whom they threw into the ocean from their aeroplanes, were innocent. In the long run nothing of the ideology of national security, nor all the arguments about the intrinsic perversity of communists, has managed to shore up their once militant belief that they were the good guys, and their victims the bad guys.[3]

All of this means that, for Jesus, the double account of the inclusion and the exclusion is not simply an instance of something interesting, but is paradigmatic of the process of the subversion from within of sin. Let us look at it once more. The one who was blind came to understand who God is, how he works, how his creative vivaciousness continues desiring the good and the growth and the life of the person. And the blind man is purely receptive: he does nothing to earn or win his sight. He just grows in the midst of the mechanism of expulsion, holding firm to a basic sense of justice: one doesn't call evil someone who has done one good, nor does one enter into solidarity with those who want to call him evil. That's all. The expellers, for their part, grow, also, but in security and conviction of their righteousness, goodness and unity, in the degree to which the mechanism of expulsion operates through them. The result is sin turned on its head. Sin ceases to be some defect which apparently excludes someone from the group of the righteous, and comes to be participation in the mechanism of expulsion.

God has not the slightest difficulty in bringing to a fullness of

---

3. Or that they were 'wheat' and their victims 'tares' in the marvellously satanic interpretation of the parable proposed to one of the officers by an Argentine military chaplain of the time.

creation the person who is in some way incomplete and recognises this. The problem is with those who think that they are complete, and that creation is, at least in their case, finished. And for this reason they think that goodness consists in the maintenance of the established order by the means we have seen: goodness is defined starting from the unity of the group, at the expense of, and by contrast with, the excluded evil one. The righteous members of the group, thinking that they see, become blind precisely by holding on to the order which they think that they have to defend. Whence we glimpse the deeper meaning of the Sabbath in John's thought. The Sabbath is the symbol of creation not yet complete. Either we grab at it, making it a criterion for division between good and evil, in which case we are resisting God who alone is capable of bringing to being even the things that are not, without rest. Or else we receive the creative goodness of God which carries us to plenitude. Sin is resistance, in the name of God, to the creative work of God which seeks to include us all.

Well, this subversion of sin seems to me to be much more important than it is normally reckoned. Please allow me to repeat its crystallised definition. *Sin ceases to be a defect which excludes, and comes to be participation in the mechanism of exclusion.* If I have taken such a long time to get to this it is because I wanted it to be evident that we aren't talking about an example of magnanimity, or liberalism, or lack of rigour, on Jesus' part, but about something much stronger. We are talking about a profound theological exercise which is, exactly as a theological exercise, the word of God. This means that we are offered something very fundamental: not a law, or a moral exhortation, but the re-forging of the meaning of sin. For humans sin is one thing, and for God it is something else, which is not simply different from the human version, but its complete subversion from within.

What we are offered is, let me remark again, not a law, nor a fixed criterion, nor an explanatory theory, but a dynamic story, the story of an inclusion and an exclusion. And it is the dynamic story which constitutes the principle of judgement for the moral activity, which is to say, the activity, of humans. Furthermore it is not something we can grasp, or learn by rote, because it is a matter of the making explicit of a mechanism of involvement. This is what is important: the story itself acts as a subversive element. If this story is the word of God, then the word of God acts in our midst as an element which is continuously subversive of our notions of order, of goodness, of clear moral understanding, and so on. And moral life, far from being a going to the trenches in defence of this or that position of incontrovertible goodness, comes to be something much more subtle. Let's do a little investigation of this subtlety.

from where do we read the story?

If you are anything like me, when you read the story of the man born blind, it is evident straight away that there is a good guy and some bad guys. That is to say, leaving Jesus to one side for the moment, there is the blind man, the good guy, and the Pharisees, the bad guys. What is normal is that all our sympathy is on the side of the former blind man, and our just despite is reserved for the Pharisees. In fact, that we should put ourselves on the side of the victim operates as something of a cultural imperative. And this cultural imperative can be very important. In fact, for those who feel themselves excluded, or treated as defective, by the reigning social and moral order, it is of incalculable importance to discover that this feeling of being excluded or defective has nothing to do with God. It is purely a social mechanism, and God rather wants to include us and carry us to a fullness of life which will probably cause scandal to the partisans of the reigning order. Well, indeed, it seems to me that this cultural imperative is extremely important, and I know nobody who is not capable, in some way or other, of feeling identified with the victim in some part of her life. The problem is that this 'being identified with the victim' can come to be used as an arm with which to club others. The victims become the group of the 'righteous just' in order to exclude the poor Pharisees, who are never in short supply as the butts of easy mockery.

Well, it seems to me that John 9 takes us beyond this inversion of roles which it apparently produces. We find it, for cultural reasons which are, thank God, unstoppable, easy to identify with the excluded one, and difficult to identify with the 'righteous just'. But for this very reason it seems to me that this chapter requires of us a great effort, which I scarcely show signs of making, to read the story with something like sympathy for the Pharisees. When all is said and done, we don't pick up even a little bit of the force of the story until we realise what a terrible shake up it administers to our received notions of good and evil. In a world where nobody understood the viewpoint of the victim, we would all be right to side with the victim. But we live in a world where almost nobody 'comes out' as a Pharisee or a hypocrite, and it seems to me that the way to moral learning proceeds in that direction.

I've underlined how the story functions as a subversion from within of the notion of sin, and this is absolutely certain, and we must never lose this intuition. Well now: the process of subversion goes a long way beyond this. This is because the excluded victim accedes, thanks to this subversion, to the possibility of speech, and of talking about himself and about God. However, in exactly that moment, he has to learn to un-pharisee his own discourse. The very moment he accedes to the word he ceases to be the excluded one, and has to begin to learn how not to be an expeller. And this is the genius of morals by story, rather than by laws or virtues. In the story there are two positions: that of the victim and that of the expellers, just as in the story of the prodigal son there is the 'bad' brother who receives forgiveness, and the 'good' brother who never wandered, and does not know of his need for forgiveness. And we don't grasp the force of the story, nor its exigency as a divine subversion of the human, if we don't identify *with the two positions at the same time*.

I don't think that there's anybody who isn't partially excluded and partially an excluder, in whom the two poles of this story don't cohabit. For, the moment we have access to the moral word (which is certainly the case at the very least for all of us who are receiving some sort of theological education) we can't grasp on to our 'goodness' as excluded ones. Instead we have to begin to question ourselves as to the complicity of our use of words, and above all our use of religious and theological words, in the creation of an expulsive goodness.

In this sense it seems to me that the key instruction of the New Testament with relation to moral discourse, and it is a doubly sacred instruction, is one of the surprisingly few places where Jesus quotes the Hebrew Scriptures with absolute approval – and he quotes it twice. The key instruction for those of us who are trying to make use of the religious word in some moral sense, and there is no moral theology that is not that, is:

> 'But go and learn what it means: I want mercy and not sacrifice.' (Matt. 9:13)[4]

Please notice that this is now no longer an instruction just for the Pharisees, but is, so to speak, the programme-guide for whoever tries to do moral theology. Being good can never do without the effort to learn, step by step, and in real circumstances of life, how to separate religious and moral words from an expelling mechanism, one which demands human sacrifice, so as to make of them words of mercy which absolve, which loose, which allow creation to be brought to completion. And this means that there is no access to goodness which does not pass through our own discovery of our complicity in hypocrisy. For it is only as we identify with the 'righteous just' of the story that we realise how 'good' their procedure was, how careful, scrupulous, law-abiding they were, and thus, how catastrophic our goodness can be, if we don't learn step by step how to get out of solidarity with the mechanism of the construction of the unity of the group by the exclusion of whoever is considered to be evil.

transforming gossip into gospel

I want to conclude with a tale which leaves me perplexed, a tale taken from the recent past and a different culture. However, it is one from which we can all suck out some nectar. I'd like to consider the story from a few years ago of the Cardinal Archbishop

---

4. See also Matt. 12:7, both quoting Hos. 6:6.

of Vienna. The distance of the tale from all of our lives allows us to consider it with a certain lack of passion. I must say, for starters, that I do not know personally any of those involved in this story, and have no more information about the truth of the matter than that offered by the mass media, which doesn't always present either the whole story or its true kernel. That is to say, I'm nothing other than the recipient of a piece of ecclesiastical gossip, part, as I imagine us all to be, of that myriad troop of slightly flapping, reddening ears. For this reason nothing of what I say can be understood as an attempt to work out the truth of what really happened, but instead is to be taken as an attempt to transform something sacrificial, the gossip, into the merciful, the Gospel. Let us see if I can pull it off; and of course this is only an exercise, and because of that is patient of any correction or development that you might like to suggest.

The details of the story are, apparently, as follows: around Eastertide 1995 a man of thirty-seven years claimed publicly to have had sexual relations on several occasions twenty years earlier with the man who became the Cardinal Archbishop of Vienna. Twenty years earlier, the denouncer was seventeen, and a minor, at least legally, though the discretion in the sexual behaviour of seventeen-year-olds is in some cases greater than the law would have us believe. Twenty years ago the Cardinal didn't occupy such an exalted position but was, if I'm not mistaken, a Benedictine superior. Well, either the accusations are true, or they are not. If the accusation is false, the moral question is pretty clear: the Cardinal is a victim of calumny. And the calumny is particularly devastating, because there is a certain prurient delight in all our societies when a piece of ecclesiastical hypocrisy is unmasked. A delight which, it must be said, is not entirely without its roots in passages of the Gospel like the one we have been studying. And it is a delight that is not to be dismissed as simply evil. That is to say, I imagine that the first reaction of a good number of people was, as mine was, and against the presumption of the civil law, to suppose the guilt of the accused. And this is because it is no secret that the monosexual clerical world tends, like the monosexual military or police worlds, if there are any left, to propitiate an

elaborately structured homosexual closet. The result of an accusation of this sort is, for that reason, particularly cruel, because it
falls in terrain where people are strongly disposed towards
believing it. That is to say, mud of this sort, once slung, almost
always sticks, whether justly or not.

In the case that the accusation be false, the moral matter is, as
I said, fairly clear. The Cardinal is a victim, and the accuser a
stone-thrower. We would have to ask why the accuser threw the
stones, whether through malice or mental disturbance. In any case,
the matter would be how to treat the accused in a merciful manner
without becoming an accomplice of his game. It may be that, when
all is brought into the light, the result is the exoneration of the
Cardinal and the trial of the accuser.

Now, let us imagine the contrary, without any attempt to know
if it be true or not. Let us imagine that the accusation is true. A
37-year-old man says that he sustained a series of sexual relations
with a man many years his senior, and in a certain position of
moral authority, twenty years previously. When he says this, the
accuser is not, as far as I know, making a particular thing of having
been traumatised in his tenderest youth by this experience, far-
reaching though its emotional consequences may have been. His
motivation, apparently (and this is all through the professional
gossip of the press) was that the Cardinal in his present position
was sending gay people to hell from the pulpit, in the time-
honoured way, by means of a pastoral letter. Against this ecclesiastical violence, the 37-year-old reacted by revealing the hypocrisy
of the discourse. Apparently four or five other men of a similar
age joined in the accusation, saying that the same thing had happened to them at the hands of the same Cardinal, at about the
same period many years ago. So, there is more than one witness,
and the belief of the public inclines strongly to the probability that
the accusations are true. Let us remember that if they are not,
then ganging up with others to give a false witness leading to the
moral lynching of someone is one of the most atrocious of crimes,
one for which, in capital cases, the Hebrew Scriptures reserve the
penalty of death by stoning. So, if the accusations turn out to be
false, we would have to exercise ourselves as to how the merciful

and non-sacrificial treatment of these proto-lynchers should be conducted. With luck, the Cardinal would lead the way, forgiving them for they knew not what they did.

However, let us imagine, as at least a part of the public has done, that the appearance of these people does not have as its end the gratuitous destruction of the Cardinal. Nor is it a question of a bust-up between former lovers, one of those nasty fights that could happen to anyone, and that are, by their nature, absolutely undecidable, and the less public their consequences, the better for everyone. Let us imagine that that is not what it's all about in the view of the accusers, but rather the desire that the Cardinal, and ecclesiastical authority in general, stop throwing stones at gay people.

Now the scene changes somewhat. Suddenly the Cardinal is not the victim. Neither are those men who, when younger, were the recipients of his favours (and who have not, as far as I know, presented themselves as 'victims', in marked contrast to some of the cases of sexual abuse in the USA where the minors involved were very much younger). Suddenly the Cardinal stands revealed as a hypocritical pharisee: that is, as someone who said one thing and did another. And here indeed, all our medium-rare, 'anonymous', Christian instincts rise up triumphant: we understand the role very well; the Cardinal's role is the same as that of the bad guys in the stories about Jesus. And there is a certain glee in the whole affair. The glee is even greater when we learn that the Cardinal, a very conservative prelate, was appointed by Rome as part of a policy of restoration of the 'hard line' in Central Europe, to counter a certain liberalism attributed to his illustrious predecessor in the Archdiocese, Cardinal König. The whole affair seems absolutely typical of those ecclesiastical attempts, which are no less ridiculous through being so frequent, to 'save' the situation by putting in some hard-liner, who turns out to be much more divisive, and leads to much worse moral consequences in the long run.

Well, here we have to interrupt with some factual details, once again derived from the press with I don't know what degree of reliability. The Cardinal kept silence for various weeks, refusing to comment on the matter. A few days later he was re-elected, by a narrow margin, as President of the Austrian Bishops' Conference (and let us remember that, under those circumstances, a failure to re-elect him would have been read as an explicit vote of no confidence on the part of his colleagues in the episcopate). The public protest was so great that, a few days later, the Cardinal published a note in which he denied the accusations formally and categorically, and resigned as President of the Bishops' Conference. A few days later a note emanated from the Austrian Government indicating that the Cardinal would no longer exercise his post as Archbishop of Vienna, but had been substituted by one of his auxiliaries, who was named Coadjutor with right of succession, and eventually became the Cardinal Archbishop himself.

However, does the matter remain there? Of course we can imagine this story within the parameters of a typical inversion of the sort: 'The one who seemed a bad guy turned out to be the good guy, and the upholder of goodness and public order was exposed as a hypocrite and a charlatan, so the story ended well.' Certainly it is possible to imagine the story in this way, and to feel very Christian while doing so, with a firm backdrop for our feeling in stories like John 9. However, let us stop and think a little . . . Suddenly the Cardinal, who knows whether justly or not, is left in the position of the excluded sinner. Suddenly he is the shame and mockery of all society. Who helps him? Who is on his side? Of course, if he is innocent of these accusations, then we are dealing with an atrocious injustice, and he has at least the consolation of a good conscience. However, let us imagine, with the public and the press, that he is not innocent. His situation is not less, but much more, atrocious. He has suddenly been marginalised by the ecclesiastical machinery that he thought himself to be serving. It is possible that in his interior he doesn't understand why these things happened to him, for, when all is said and done, he may have fallen in these ways, but has been to confession and received absolution. Why should these things now rise up and condemn him? Let us imagine also, that, as is probable in the case of a conservative churchman, he has a somewhat individualistic notion of sin: if he did those things, then they are quite simply his

24

fault, full stop. Let us imagine also that he is not capable of taking any theological distance from the incidents by means of a little sociology, and that he doesn't understand the extent to which he has acted driven by the structure of a monosexual clerical caste where repressed homosexuality is very much present. It is a world where many people take part in some very complicated games in order to maintain appearances, going so far as to commit a great deal of violence against themselves and others, precisely through an inability to talk about the question in a natural and honest manner. And this 'not being able to talk about the question in a natural and honest manner' turns out to be the 'correct' line, upheld by the highest ecclesiastical spheres. Why should the Cardinal's moments of weakness be so severely punished, while those of so many others pass by unnoticed?

Those who marginalised the Cardinal, including some of his ecclesiastical colleagues, have participated in a Christian-seeming 'inversion' of the matter: the pharisee has been transformed into the bad guy. But have they participated in an authentically Christian *subversion* of the story? Subversion goes much further than inversion, because subversion keeps alive the same mechanism even when the protagonists change. Now, the bad guy, the victim in the centre of the circle of the 'righteous just', is the Cardinal. For some people he deserves it. But are we satisfied with that? Could it be that our gossip is to be transformed only into the Gospel of 'he got his just reward'? I fear that, if we speak thus, then our justice really is no greater than that of the scribes and Pharisees (Matt. 5:20). Which of us has helped someone in such a ghastly situation as Cardinal Groër, former Archbishop of Vienna? Which of us has tried to identify with the hypocrite, trying to understand the mechanisms which tie us up in hypocrisy, so as together to cut ourselves loose from them? Which of us has spoken out publicly, yet without hate, against the violence of the 'ecclesiastical closet' which fuels a mechanism of covering up and expelling, and expelling to cover up, so strong that it is not simply a question of some vicious individuals, but of a structure which lends itself especially to this vice? And this structure means that the matter cannot be talked about in terms of this or that sinner, who can be expelled or marginalised when they are discovered. It means rather that it is an urgent requirement of a real moral theology that it stop and analyse the system which typically produces this vicious behaviour, to which far too many of its members fall victim, *whether as expelled or as expellers.*

Did anyone in Oh-so-Catholic Austria, instead of accepting the reigning terms of 'goodness' and 'badness', and rejoicing in the transformation of the 'good guy' into a 'bad guy', set about the ungrateful task of trying to dismantle the whole system of hypocrisy by which we cover up and expel? Here and now, do we recognise our complicity in mechanisms that are similar, when they are not identical, and seek to understand the violent structure of our hypocrisy so as to go about creating ways off the hook for our co-hypocrites?

conclusion

This is only a first attempt at carrying out a reading of John 9 in such a way as to allow us a sketch of an approach to moral theology that is somewhat removed from the moral discourse to which we are accustomed. I know very well that we are scarcely beginning. However, I'd like to underline this: what the Christian faith offers us in the moral sphere is not law, nor a way of shoring up the order or structure of the supposed goodness of this world, much less the demand that we sally forth on a crusade in favour of these things. It offers us something much more subtle. It offers us the dynamic of the subversion from within of all human goodness, including our own. This is the same thing as saying that the beginning of Christian moral life is a stumbling into an awareness of our own complicity in hypocrisy, and a becoming aware of quite how violent that hypocrisy is. Starting from there we can begin to stretch out our hands to our brothers and sisters, neither more nor less hypocritical than ourselves, who are on the way to being expelled from the 'synagogue' by an apparently united order, which has an excessive and militant certainty as to the evil of the other. Let us then go and learn what this means: 'I want mercy and not sacrifice.'

———◆○▶———

theology amidst the stones and dust

For surely your servants take delight in its stones, and are moved
to pity by its dust. (Psalm 102:14)

a heart-close-to-cracking

I would like to create with you something like a space in which a
heart might find permission to come close to cracking. It is a space
which I am discovering to be necessary for participation in theological discourse. This closeness-to-cracking comes upon us at a
moment when we do not know how to speak well, when we find
ourselves threatened by confusion. It is where the two principal
temptations are either to bluster our way out of the moment, by
speaking with too much security and arrogance so as to give the
impression that the confusion is not mine, but belongs somewhere
else. Or on the other hand to plunge into the shamed silence of
one who knows himself uncovered, and for that reason, deprived
of legitimate speech. This space of the heart-close-to-cracking,
poorly as it seems to promise, and difficult though it be to remain
in it once it is found and occupied, seems to me the most appropriate space from which to begin a sketch of ways forward towards
the stutter of a theology for the third millennium.

I would like to take three biblical moments to help us in the
creation of this space, three examples which point in the same
direction. The first moment is in the text, and the other two are,
rather, moments from which texts have been forged. Let us look
closely, first of all, at the prophet Elijah. The altars of Yahweh are

in ruins, Ahab's regime favours the followers of Baal. Elijah; the champion of Yahwism, undertakes to wage a valiant war against the prophets of Baal, organising a competition to see which god can burn a sacrificed bull with fire from heaven. As the prayers and litanies of the prophets of Baal pile up, Elijah mocks them, suggesting, among other things, that perhaps Baal can't put in an appearance owing to being busy with a bowel movement. When it is Elijah's turn to offer his sacrifice, first he rebuilds the altar of Yahweh, then soaks his bull completely, and boom! the lightening strikes. All present fall to the ground, crying: 'The Lord is the true God.' Elijah immediately takes advantage of this unanimity to point his finger at the four hundred and fifty prophets of Baal, ordering that they be seized and killed. His order is at once obeyed.

After this triumph, feeling somewhat depressed, Elijah goes off to the desert, where he desires death. God gives him food necessary for survival, but not even that pleases him much, and an angel has to tell him to eat up, and then to go for a forty-day and forty-night hike to Mount Horeb, like Moses to whom God had spoken at the same place. Once there, Elijah hides in a cave, where God has to come and find the disillusioned prophet. God asks him what he's doing there, and he replies:

> 'I have been very jealous for the LORD, the God of hosts; for the people of Israel have forsaken thy covenant, thrown down thy altars, and slain thy prophets with the sword; and I, even I only, am left; and they seek my life, to take it away.' (1 Kings 19:10)

God orders him to come out of the cave and to stand before the Lord, who announces that he is going to pass by. Well, you know the story: first comes a mighty wind which rends the mountains and breaks the rocks in pieces, but the Lord was not in the wind. Then comes an earthquake, but the Lord was not in the earthquake, and then comes a fire, but the Lord was not in the fire. After the fire there comes a still small voice. At this Elijah goes and stands at the entrance to the cave, and God speaks to him, asking what he's doing there, and once again, Elijah repeats:

'I have been very jealous for the LORD, the God of hosts; for the people of Israel have forsaken thy covenant, thrown down thy altars, and slain thy prophets with the sword; and I, even I only, am left; and they seek my life, to take it away.' (1 Kings 19:14)

Then, in an extraordinary anticlimax, God tells him to go to Damascus to anoint Jehu king, and to pick Elisha as his successor, adding that God will reserve for himself seven thousand men who haven't bent the knee before Baal. Elijah goes off and obeys. From then on his interventions are few until he's whisked off to heaven and Elisha's ministry begins.

So, what seems to be a story of the triumph of Yahwism is in fact presented as the story of the un-deceiving of Elijah. Elijah before his un-deceiving was a champion fighter without problems of self-esteem or self-confidence. God was a god like Baal, but bigger and tougher, and Elijah was his spokesman, the one who pointed out his victims. The contest of Mount Carmel was a splendid battle between rival shamans or witch-doctors. After the bloody interlude, which he had won, Elijah sinks into a depression, and doubts the value of all that:

'Enough, O Lord, take away my life; for I am no better than my fathers.' (1 Kings 19:4)

The sacred author presents us with something rather remarkable: not a series of praises for the Yahwist champion, but rather the story of how Elijah learnt not to identify God with all those special effects which he had known how to manipulate to such violent effect. All the commotion around Mount Horeb is presented as something rather like a de-construction of the sacred scenario associated with Moses, for the Lord was present in the still small voice, rather than in something of more imposing majesty. Furthermore, rather than taking advantage of the zeal which Elijah bleats on about, Yahweh gives the prophet some rather modest tasks – instructions for passing on command to others. Where Elijah, thinking himself something of a heroic martyr, tells God that he's the only one who has remained loyal, Yahweh tells him that he has seven thousand men up his sleeve who haven't bent the knee before Baal. One can understand what might be meant by zeal exercised on behalf of a god who appears with hurricanes, earthquakes and fires. But what on earth might it mean to be zealous in the service of a still, small voice? It is a somewhat humbled Elijah who sets off to carry out his appointed tasks.

Well, I'd like to suggest that this scene offers us a valuable witness to the theological process which is at work in the development of the Hebrew Scriptures: the theological power of the crisis of confidence which goes along with the collapse of the sacred. At the beginning we have a sacred Yahwism, which can shine alongside another sacred religion, but whose sacrifices are more efficacious, whose God is more powerful, and whose capacity to unite people for a sacred war is greater. Then we have all that undone. The still small voice says much more than it seems to: it says that God is not a rival to Baal, that God is not to be found in the appearances of sacred violence. Elijah, when he entered into rivalry with the prophets of Baal became one of them, because God is not to be found in such circuses, nor in the murders which go along with them. At the end of his un-deceiving, Elijah is more Yahwist, more atheist, less of a shaman, less of a sacrificer, because God is not like the gods, not even so as to show himself superior to them. The cave of Horeb was, for Elijah, the theological space for a cracking of heart.

Here we are face to face with the collapse of the sacred, a real demolition of personal structures and ways of speaking about God. This collapse is the crucible in which theological development is wrought. I would like to point to two key moments where just such a collapse of the sacred is combined with the boldest theological development. The first moment is the fall of Jerusalem in 587 BCE. Think what this would have meant to you if you had been a Judaean of that time. Not only had your capital been sacked and your king, court and intellectuals deported. The Temple was destroyed, there where you had thought that Yahweh would dwell for ever. The monarchy was brought to an end, where you had thought that God had promised that David's line would reign in perpetuity. Now there is no worship, no sacrifice: the priesthood is in exile. The bulwarks which gave structure to the worship of the one true God have all been knocked flying. It even seemed as though the Babylonian gods, Marduc and company, must be superior to Yahweh, since they had triumphed over him, and dragged off his followers. Let us try to imagine this from within, put ourselves in the place of these our forefathers in faith. Our books of theology imagine this as a moment of decisive rupture in the intellectual history of the development of universal mono-theism, but they absolve us from appreciating the process of that development. The process is likely to have been experienced as one of total annihilation. All the structures of group belonging, of personal, family and tribal belonging, in the dust. The whole imaginative world within which Yahweh was worshipped, torn to shreds. We gravely underestimate the force of what happened if we don't understand that the process of recovery, which gave rise to a religion of texts, and of interpretation of texts, with the Temple, the cult and the monarchy relegated to second place or, in the case of the monarchy, treated as an utopia, this process of recuperation which undertook to rescue elements from among the ruins was, in truth, little less than a new religion, the new form of community life which we call Judaism.

The process which we see is the process of an upset which forces the gradual learning of how to become unattached from everything which seemed divine and holy, the collapse of zeal for the Lord of hosts. At the same time it leads to an apprenticeship in listening to the still, small voice, and the reinvention of a new type of zeal. This means the reinvention of a new form of Yahwist life, where Yahweh is disassociated from many of the things which had seemed immutable and indispensable elements of his worship.

The third biblical moment which shares this same structure and which I wish to examine with you is the conversion of Saul. I say the same structure, because Paul himself points it out. In his letter to the Galatians, when he describes his own conversion (Gal. 1:11–17), Paul narrates it with allusions to the story of Elijah: he used to persecute with great violence, and he advanced beyond his compatriots in having a zeal (the word is key) much greater than theirs. After his experience of conversion, he didn't consult with anybody, but immediately went off to the desert, like Elijah, and from there he returned to Damascus, where Elijah had to go, after his experience with the still small voice, to anoint Jehu. So, Paul narrates his experience within the framework provided by Elijah's collapse of zeal that we have just seen. His whole life and apostolic experience afterwards is marked by the collapse of a sacred world within which he had been an especially ferocious militant, a collapse produced by the recognition that in his zeal to serve God, it had been God whom he had been persecuting. For him the still small voice was the voice of the crucified and risen victim whose breath is the Holy Spirit.

I emphasise this for a simple reason. As a backdrop for the theological discussion which I wish to begin with you, I want to bring out a very important dimension of the experience of the resurrection which normally doesn't get its due hearing. The experience of the novelty, vitality and exuberance of God which was provoked among the apostolic witnesses by the appearances of the risen Lord, and which little by little changed their whole perspective and imagination, was not only an experience of an addition to a pre-existing good. To each step of the clearer and more complete revelation of God, that is to say, to each purification of faith, there is a corresponding and simultaneous collapse of a whole series of elements which seemed to have been indispensable bulwarks of faith. For these elements turn out to be parts of an idolatrous order of things which had previously been confused with the worship of the true God. This emphasises something which I imagine to be obvious, though little mentioned in Catholic treatises on faith, which is that faith in the living God automatically introduces into the world a process of unbelieving. Someone who begins to believe in the living God automatically begins to lose faith in the inevitability of things. Things like fate, the sacredness of the social order, inevitable progress, horoscopes and so on. For, the moment our imagination and emotional and mental structures begin to absorb what is meant by the vivaciousness of the Creator God who brings into being and sustains all things, all those other elements start to be revealed as part of a dead sacred order, as attributions of divinity, and thus of fixity, to things which are human, which are structured socially, culturally and economically, and are for that reason dependent on human responsibility and potentially mutable through the exercise of that same responsibility.

There is more. The resurrection, as it was received, incarnated and understood by Paul, not only provoked a purification of the human perspective on God. That purification was shown to be absolutely inseparable from the presence of a crucified and risen human victim, whose presence inaugurates and keeps perpetually alive a process of desacralisation of the religious matrix within which the crucifixion and resurrection had occurred, and within which Saul had been a certain sort of participant. All of Paul's preaching, all of his theology, is characterised by the process of the collapse of a certain sacred structure, and by the slow discovery of the perspective given by a new focus on Yahweh, the Pauline equivalent of Elijah's still small voice. Paul's whole argument about the Law is nothing other than the attempt to make it clear that, from the moment when the resurrection makes present the crucified one as a constant hermeneutical companion in our living of the religion of Yahweh, even that which had seemed sacred and untouchable in that religion, the very Torah of God, is desacralised. It has to be understood according to whether it contributes to the sacrifice of other victims within a sacred order, or whether it is interpreted in such a way as to deconstruct the world of sacrifices and sacred orders.

I would like to suggest something else. Paul understood very well that, starting from his experience, what was wanted was not the foundation of a new religion, which might forge a new sacred order more in accordance with the new perspective on Yahweh. What was wanted rather was the preaching of the constancy in our midst of the presence of God as crucified and risen victim. The very fact of that presence opens up the possibility of living in the world by means of the continuous deconstruction of the artificial sacred in all the forms of life in which we find ourselves, contributing in this way to the construction of a new form of human social life where every apparently sacred social distinction

33

begins to be knocked down, leading to an as yet unimagined fraternity.

So this experience, the experience of the collapse of the sacred which we saw in the case of Elijah and in the Jewish exile, is not a moment of the past, but a constant part of the process of the faith which is being brought into being. We cannot understand the preaching of the resurrection if it is understood as a miraculous moment which founds a new religion. If it is taken thus, we are in fact denying the force and efficacy of the resurrection. For the resurrection brings about the definitive installation in our midst, as a constructive hermeneutical principle, of the cult of Yahweh who knows not death, and who is worshipped in a continuous apprenticeship in participating in and not being scandalised by the collapse of the sacred. A sacred whose secret is always the victims which it hides, and on whose sacrifice it depends.

This, then, is what I understand by making space for a heart-close-to-cracking: the space where we learn to forge a way of talking about God in the midst of the ruins of the forms of the sacred which are in full collapse. A space where we recognise our own complicity in the sacred forms of the past, with all their violence and their victims. A space where we are coming to understand that God has nothing to do with all that, but also a space where we learn, precisely in the midst of the deconstruction of all that, new ways of speaking words of God so as to participate in the new creation. That is to say, it is the eucharistic space par excellence, where Christ is present as the crucified one, and we as penitents learning to step out of solidarity with our multiple and varied modes of complicity in crucifixion; but where Christ is present as crucified and risen Lord, so not as accusation of our participation, but as fount of, and power for, a new, unimagined, and unending reconstruction.

If I've taken my time to get to this point, which is perhaps far too obvious, it is because it seems to me that we find ourselves in the midst of just such ruins. At the turn of the millennium, and at thirty-something years from the end of Vatican II, we find our-selves in the midst of a shouting match between two sorts of sacred, two types of sacred zeal. On the one hand the restoring trumpet blasts of a Catholicism nostalgic for a sacred and stable past, upholder of purity of doctrine and of customs, of sacred differences and sacrificial techniques for the maintenance of order and unity. On the other hand, a no less sacred trumpet blast, that of those who adopt the position of victims, who make of positions of authentic marginalisation sure platforms for protest, for the revindication of innocence and of sacred status. Both these sacred blasts have their priesthoods capable of pointing the finger at those who do not conform, demanding the sacrifice of those who do not participate in the unanimity of the group. In one case as in the other, the question which gives away the sacrificial mentality underlying group belonging is the same: are you for us, or are you one of them? It is the question which reveals the impossibility of a cracking of heart, and thus the impossibility of Eucharist. What I would like to suggest is that both trumpet blasts are phantoms, the noise of those who do not accept the reality of being in the midst of ruins, who don't accept that Jerusalem has been razed to the ground, and who neither know how to take delight in its stones, nor are capable of being moved by pity for its dust, so as, with these unpromising remains, to take part in the building up of the new Jerusalem.

receiving a perspective

One of the things which is clear from the stories of Elijah, of the returning exiles, and of Paul, is that they had nowhere to start except from where they found themselves to be. There was no universal principle, all-embracing idea, or pre-formed discourse which they could simply adopt. They couldn't be converted to something pre-existent, learning how to adapt themselves to its rules and ways of structuring self and belonging. The only perspective which was available to them, and starting from which they might make sense of the stones and the dust, was their own. And, please note, their perspective in each case was not that of someone who has just arrived at the scene, innocent, with a tabula rasa for a personality, someone who starts everything anew, a heroic founder. That would be a grabbed perspective, heroic, but incapable of a cracking of heart. No, in each case, the perspective from which they had to begin was a perspective received by the process of finding themselves to have been involved in something which had been knocked to the ground. Without that knocking down, there would have been no such perspective. In each case their perspective was received by the force of the circumstances within which they had participated, and within which their participation had been, in one way or another, shaken to the core.

I would like to suggest that if there is to be Catholic theology in the third millennium, a similar process awaits us all. The space which allows us close to a cracking of heart is the space where we learn to receive our perspective, so as from there to be able to learn to speak well of, and to imitate, God. The perspective will be, in the case of each one of us, rather different. For catholicity doesn't mean a unity of perspective from which we start, but the discovery and construction of a real and surprising fraternity which begins with overcoming the tendency to forge from our own perspective a sacred which excludes. It is in this context, then, that I offer elements of the perspective within which I am finding myself, as a resource which may perhaps be useful in your own construction of catholicity. I am very conscious that I am from a culture, race, language background, and history that is strange to most of you, and for that reason I am far from imagining that what I have to say will reach you all in the same way. However, I hope that, however foreign to your experience the elements of this story may be, you will find something in it capable of arousing an echo in your own.

Some years ago, in a Latin-American republic which I will not name, I found myself in a strange situation. I had arrived to take up a new job as a teacher of theology. After three days, my boss called me in and said: 'Bad news, James. I've received a phone call from fourteen religious superiors who are meeting in another country to tell me that if I don't sack you immediately on the grounds that you are a militant homosexual, then those superiors will not send any pupils to our course.' This threat implied the non-arrival of the money necessary for the course to function. Now please note this: the superiors made no allegation of a homosexual practice on my part, and at no time in the investigation which followed did they raise that as a question. The accusation was one of, let us say, a political or ideological militancy. My boss, an honest heterosexual, who found it difficult to understand the force of the violence unleashed by the gay question in the ecclesiastical milieu, absolutely refused to sack me, offering to resign his post rather than to accept such blackmail. A higher superior intervened, suggesting to the fourteen superiors that they had acted without the proper procedure, and that each one should put into writing and sign any accusation that he might have against me, so that the accused could answer his accusers. That is, the superior insisted on due process. However, no written charge was made. When an informal enquiry wondered whether there might be some accusation that one of them might like to mention, but not write down, again there was no accusation. One or two apparently said 'Of course, I don't know the guy personally, but I have it from a very good source that . . .'

Well, this is the story of a fairly unpleasant piece of violence, and I could embellish it in such a way as to win your sympathy, presenting myself as a victim. In that case the very act of telling the story would be something like a denunciation, and there would be goodies and baddies in the story. If that were the case, I would have learnt nothing from the incident. I would have adopted one of the perspectives which our culture offers us, that of the sacred victim. And I would have adopted that perspective as a weapon with which to attack one of the stereotypical 'baddies' with which our culture also supplies us, the obscurantist and violent group of ecclesiastics. Thank God, much though I would have liked to present things in this way, God did not indulge me. Some weeks later, still devastated by what had happened, I went off to make a Jesuit retreat, and in the midst of that retreat something totally unexpected reached me: a perspective which I had perhaps understood intellectually, but which had never got through to my gut. It was the absolute separation of God from all that violence. I understood something new: that God had nothing to do with what had happened, and that it was simply a mechanism of human violence, nothing more. What enabled me to reach this, and here I am talking, of course, of the human means, was the realisation that, since of this group of fourteen I had only ever met three, all that violence (and apparently they had worked themselves up over this for a couple of days, finding it difficult to get round to the agenda of their meeting) could not be taken personally. Rather it was a mechanism within which the participants had got themselves caught up in such a way that they couldn't perceive what they were doing. The moment I realised that I was dealing with a mechanism whose participants were its prisoners, at that same moment I was able to take distance from what had happened, and forgiveness started to become possible.

However that perception was not all. For, when I understood that God had nothing to do with all that violence, I began to understand something much more painful: the degree of my own participation in the mechanism of violence, not as its victim, but as a manipulator. For the charge that I was an 'internationally known homosexual militant' did not fall like lightning from a clear sky. Rather this incident was the third time that my behaviour and attitudes in different countries had provoked a similar rejection. In fact, even though I have been 'out' since I was eighteen, I had always denied being a militant. I had answered those who had been enraged by my attempts to open the possibility of honest and open speech, that they should indicate to me a correct and non-militant way of speaking with honesty about a matter which affects so many people in the ecclesiastical milieu, and which leads to gossip, accusations and frequent injustice. Of course, within the ecclesiastical milieu, there is, as yet, no such correct way. The very fact of suggesting that there is, in this field, something real in which we are involved, and about which we must try to speak if we are to have a modicum of transparency and honesty as Catholic Christians, the very suggestion is only perceived, and can only be perceived, as a threat. Where denial, mendacity and cover up are forces which structure a reality, the search for honest conversation is, of itself, the worst form of militancy.

Well, my reply, while formally correct, allowed me to hide from myself something which my various accusers had perceived perfectly clearly: that I was myself on a sort of crusade, that I had a zeal, and that this zeal was of a prodigiously violent force, powered by a deep resentment. In fact, I was wanting to create for myself, taking advantage of the ecclesiastical structures which sustained me, a space of security and peace, of survival. Thus I hoped to avoid what I had seen happen to gay people in country after country: social marginalisation, destruction of life projects, emotional and spiritual annihilation. That is to say, my brave discourse was a mask which hid from me my absolute cowardice of soul, for I was not prepared to identify myself fully with that reality, which I knew to be mine, with all its consequences. At root, I myself believed that God was on the side of ecclesiastical violence directed at gay people, and couldn't believe that God loves us just as we are. The profound 'do not *be*' which the social and ecclesiastical voice speaks to us, and which forms the soul of so many gay people, was profoundly rooted in my own being, so that, *au fond* I felt myself damned. In my violent zeal I was fighting so that the ecclesiastical structure might speak to me a 'Yes', a 'Flourish, son', precisely because I feared that, should I stand alone before God, God himself would be part of the 'do not *be*'. Thus I was absolutely dependent on the same mechanism against which I was fighting. Hiding from myself the fact of having despaired of God, I wanted to manipulate the ecclesiastical structure so that it might give me a 'self', that it might speak to me a 'Yes' at a level of profundity of which the ecclesiastical structure, like any human structure, is incapable. For the 'Yes' which creates and recreates the 'self' of a son, only God can pronounce. In this I discovered myself to be an idolater. I had been wanting to negotiate my survival in the midst of violent structures, and negotiation in the midst of violent structures can only be done by violence. The non-violent, the blessed of the gospels, simply suffer violence and perish, either physically or morally.

I am attempting to describe for you the form taken in my life by the irruption of the extraordinary grace which I received during my Jesuit retreat. Of course, I am describing schematically something which was a non-schematic whole, and which I have taken several years to begin to understand. First there was the perception of the absolute non-involvement of God in all that violence, then the perception of my non-innocence, and of my idolatrous and violent manner of having been caught up in all that. And then, at root, what began this whole process of beginning to untie myself from the idols I had so assiduously cultivated, what I had never dared to imagine, the profound 'Yes' of God, the 'Yes' spoken to the little gay boy who had despaired of ever hearing it. And there, indeed, I found myself absolutely caught, because this 'Yes' does not take the form of a pretty consolation for a spoiled child. Rather, from the moment it reached me, the whole psychological and mental structure by which I had built myself up over all the previous years began to enter into a complete collapse. For the whole structure was based on the presupposition of a 'No' at the centre of my being, and because of that, of the need to wage a violent war so as to cover up a fathomless hole. The 'I', the 'self' of the child of God, is born in the midst of the ruins of repented idolatry.

A further point in this narrative, if you can bear it. In the months following this incident, I had to give a course of theology. I called the course: 'Fix your minds on the things that are above', taken from Paul's letter to the Colossians. Ironically, I managed to give the whole course, which has even been published in book form,[1] without tumbling to the significance of the verse which follows the one I had chosen:

> for you have died, and your life is hidden with Christ in God. (Col. 3:1–3)

But it was exactly this that, at last, I was learning. The whole of my previous life had been marked by an absolute refusal to die. The absolute refusal to take on my baptismal commitment. Of course, because I was unable to imagine that my 'self', the 'I' who will live for ever, is hidden with Christ in God. And that was why I had to fight all those battles. The 'I' who was present in all

---

1. *Raising Abel* (New York, Crossroad, 1996). The same book was published in 1998 in the UK by SPCK who changed the title to *Living in the End Times*.

those battles was the old Adam, or Cain, a 'self' incapable of understanding that it is not necessary to seek to shore up for itself a place on this earth, to found a safe space, to protect itself violently against violence. The 'I' of the risen one only becomes present when, at last, the old 'I' is put to death. And, thank God, this was exactly what the fourteen superiors had managed to set up for me. With the force of what Paul calls the Law, that is, the mechanism of violent exclusion dressed up as the word of God, they had at last managed to kill that resentful old man. In its place, being something rather like a still small voice, something which I can in no way possess, nor grasp, is the 'I' from which I now start to live. The 'I' that is hidden with Christ in God, little by little, and somewhat tentatively, begins to build a new life story in the midst of the ruins of the previous collapse.

Well, all of that was so as to illustrate what I have wanted to call the process of reception of a perspective from which to help forge Catholic theological discourse. I will now step outside the highly risky zone of the autobiographical so as to share with you some of the hints which I am learning since I have had to start to understand theology anew, rather as someone who has had a stroke has to learn to talk again. I want to look at some themes of what used to be called fundamental moral theology. That is, rather than trying to look at a specific moral issue, I want to examine the very possibility of moral discourse starting from that theological non-place in which I am surprised and grateful to find myself, the place of the much-loved queer.

dead man talking

One of the richest and most sophisticated texts of the New Testament is the passage at the end of Luke's gospel where two demoralised disciples are walking to Emmaus. They don't recognise the traveller who joins them, nevertheless it is he who explains to them the meaning of what has just happened in Jerusalem, and he does so making use of the whole Torah and the Prophets, starting with Moses. That is to say, he makes available a new and unheard of interpretation of Scripture so that they might

find a new meaning in their lives and be empowered by this interpretation, until the moment when they recognise their companion
in the breaking of the bread, and he vanishes. Well, you all know
the story. We all know that it is a basic text for the understanding
of the Eucharist: the presence of the Lord who interprets Scripture, making it possible for the hearers to restructure their own
imagination, and, duly fired up, go out to reconstruct the world.

Well, I'd like to draw attention to one element of this story, a
story which offers not so much a key to reading Scripture as an
ongoing hermeneutical principle which we do not control, and
which is alive independently of us and transforms us. This element
is indispensable for those of us who are trying to imagine the
Catholic faith in the third millennium. It is the fact, little commented, that what is odd about the Emmaus story is that it is a
dead man who is talking. I think it very important that we don't
make the separation which we are accustomed to when talking
about the risen Jesus, imagining that he is alive, and for that
reason, not dead. No, what is fascinating about the doctrine of the
resurrection is that it is the whole human life of Jesus, including
his death, which is risen. The life of God, since it is totally outside
the order of human life and human death, doesn't cancel death,
as if it were a sickness which is to be cured, but takes it up,
assumes it. Luke offers us a vision of a risen Jesus who has not
ceased to be a dead man, and who, starting from his living-out-
being-a-crucified-man, teaches and empowers his disciples by his
presence.

Please indulge me as I try to suck out some juice from this
apparently absurd scenario. Let us imagine a prisoner in the Louisiana state penitentiary (which, curiously enough, is called Angola),
someone sentenced to die, just as in the film which many of you
will have seen, *Dead Man Walking*. Well, the prisoner is led to
the execution chamber, and, at the very same instant in which the
doctors pronounce him dead, he becomes entirely free of the law,
and of the social and police structures of the State of Louisiana, as
indeed of the Federal Government of the United States. Now,
follow me with your imagination. The moment he is free, not
only of the law, but of social structures, life commitments like

marriage, and so on, he is also absolutely free of resentment. If we imagine him a guy who had been completely opposed to the process which led him to his death, one who protested his innocence, and who considered the use of the death penalty to be an atrocity, then, up till the moment of his death he imagined himself as a victim of all that. His presence was characterised by a tremendous struggle to prevent them taking him to his death, a struggle which was, of course, ineffectual in the face of the strength and weapons of the forces of public order of the State of Louisiana.

Now, the moment he dies, he's completely free of that whole game of power and victimisation of which he was part, no longer is he struggling with those powers: he doesn't have to, for they have no dominion over him, they no longer affect him in any way at all. The resentment disappears completely, because resentment only has its place within that game. Let's stretch the fantasy a little more: since the powers of the law, of social custom, and so on, no longer affect him, our dead man can begin completely to restructure his imagination with respect to his previous experience of life in the State of Louisiana. For the first time he begins to see it from the perspective of one who is no longer resentful and pushed around by it. Perhaps he's not much interested by his former life, and heads off elsewhere, no longer weighed down by what he lived. But let us imagine that he does take an interest in Louisiana, in such a way that, now that he sees things with a certain clarity, he wants to help build a better, more just, State. So he becomes present to other people, people totally caught up, as we all are, in the reigning social, political and economic structures, in order to help them understand what they are really doing in their way of leading their lives and their social belonging. Thus, little by little, they will be enabled to undo all that is sacrificial and resentful at every level, economic, social, military, religious, and begin to be able to live with the same freedom which he now enjoys.

Well, of course, the example is at least as misleading as it is useful, and that's why I've called it a fantasy. However it's a fantasy in the service of something which is not a fantasy, but a rather important theological point. When we speak of the risen

Jesus speaking to the disciples on the road to Emmaus, we are talking about a dead man, totally free from resentment. For this reason he is not present as an accusation, seeking to avenge himself on his executioners. He is present as one who begins to make of the story of his life and death a way of opening the imagination of his disciples, offering a new interpretation of texts which they already knew, so that they, not yet dead, might begin to live from then on with the same lack of resentment, free as he is from being bound in by laws and sacrificial customs, aiming for the construction of a human way of being together not marked by the powers of death.

Now, please notice a word which I have used a great deal in this explanation: it is the word resentment. Resentment, which is typically incarnate in our world as a seeking to protect oneself against death, and, because of that, in considering oneself a victim, is exactly the opposite of grace. A resentful presence is exactly the reverse of a gratuitous presence. A gratuitous presence isn't trying to protect itself against anything, isn't insisting on anything for itself, nor is there as part of the give and take of resentful reciprocity. It is not seeking to establish itself, because it does not fear disappearing, ending, or being destroyed. Well, what I'd like to do now is to suggest some hints of an imagination of a Catholic moral theology which starts from this place of the one who, as a dead man, has no need to establish himself. One capable of offering a non-sacrificial, eucharistic, constructive critique which aims at the bringing about of a fraternity not marked by death. This we can do if we attend to the Pauline verse which I quoted to you before: 'Fix your minds on the things that are above . . . because you have died and your life is hid with Christ in God.'

towards an eucharistic morality

Let us return to the place from which I told you that I'd like to begin my approach to Catholic moral theology, that of the much-loved queer. Those many of you who are not gay will discover, I hope, by means of a small imaginative leap, changing some details, that this place is not entirely alien either to your interests or your experience. The experience of many gay people is that the Church in some way or other, kills us. Typically in official discourse we are a 'they', dangerous people whose most notable characteristic is not a shared humanity, but a tendency to commit acts considered to be gravely objectively disordered. Typically our inclusion within the structures of church life comes at a very high price: that of agreeing not to speak honestly, of disguising our experience with a series of euphemisms, of having to maintain, through a coded language shared with other 'insiders' within the system, a double life. The message is: you're fine just so long as you don't rock the boat through talking frankly, which is the same as saying: 'You're protected while you play the game our way, but the moment that something "comes to light", you're out. The moment you say something which causes scandal, watch out!' And please notice that the scandal in question is not a scandal for a great part of the heterosexual population, who tend to be indifferent to all this, when not mildly amused by what they always suspected. It is a scandal for the group which fears the consequences for itself of the revelation of truths about its group composition.

In this the non-explicit message of the ecclesiastical mechanism is exactly the reverse of the explicit message of the Church. The explicit message is: God loves you just as you are, and it is from where you are that you are invited to prepare with us the banquet of the kingdom. The latent message is: God loves you just so long as you hide what you are and deny yourself the search for the integrity and transparency of life and of virtues which it is your task to teach to others. Here I am speaking, of course, not only of the clerical and religious world, whether masculine or feminine, but of any instance sponsored by the Church – teachers in Catholic schools, doctors and nurses in Catholic hospitals, young people in Catholic youth groups, journalists in Catholic newspapers, and so on.

It seems to me that in the face of all this, there have been two typical reactions: that of pathological loyalty, and that of pathological rejection. Pathological loyalty, we all know it: the inability, or the unwillingness, to distinguish between the violent sacred of the ecclesiastical institution and the revelation of the love of God, and the consequent suppression of the latter in favour of the former. That is to say, participation in the Church is founded on an act of sacrifice of the 'other' who causes perplexity, even when that 'other' includes a large part, and maybe the best part, of the 'I' of many of its loyal members. All this is, no doubt, tremendously obvious. More interesting is the other reaction, that of pathological rejection. This is the entirely comprehensible reaction of those who are so scandalised by ecclesiastical violence that they either abandon the faith completely, at least in an ecclesially recognisable form, or seek to form groups of resistance. Typically the aim is the building up of the soul and the recovery of the psychological well-being of people who have been seriously traumatised, at deep levels of their being, by their experience with the moral and pastoral voice of the Church. And not only of the Church, but the voice of society mediated by parents, schools and mass media. In the United States a great part of the voice which has been raised, demanding an attitude that is at least minimally Christian on the part of the ecclesiastical authorities, comes from people, or groups of people of this sort. Typically this protest lays hold of the sciences of the individual, brandishing the truths of psychology against ecclesiastical barbarism and ignorance.

Well, here we are faced with a dead end. The tendency of the ecclesiastical institution is to privilege the social group with its expulsive mechanisms saying: the 'we' must prevail, and the dangerous 'I' must either be lost, or expelled. The tendency of the group which identifies itself by its victim status is to privilege the 'I', expelling or seeking to expel the 'we', considering it as a hostile and dangerous element, transforming it into a 'they', an implacable enemy. Well, where the 'we' transforms a possible 'I' into a 'one of them', and when the 'I' sees a possible 'we' only as a dangerous and perverse 'they', then we are faced with a symmetry of enemy twins which is without possible rescue. We are back with those deaf trumpetings which characterise the moral struggle in the world of so-called postmodernity. We are without the possibility of a cracking of heart, and without the possibility of Eucharist.

However there is another possibility, not so much a theoretical possibility, as one of praxis. And it is the occupation by much-loved queers of the space of the heart-close-to-cracking. In the midst of this space the dead and risen Christ offers us the means for the edification of a victimless sacred. A sacred where the 'we' creates and recreates the 'I' and where the 'I' receives its identity as a child of God from a 'we' to which it contributes without resentment, learning to stretch out the hand to other victims, yet to be identified. Now this is, I am quite sure, immensely difficult, emotionally, intellectually and spiritually. But the Gospel itself, considered as a programme for reconstruction in the midst of the ruins, which means, read eucharistically, offers us many elements for the task.

Consider quite how extraordinary is this verse from St Matthew:

> 'And call no man your father on earth, for you have one Father, who is in heaven.' (Matt. 23:9)

This verse, read from amongst the ruins, suggests a rather remarkable perspective: that Jesus taught that there is on earth no analogue for divine paternity, and that divine paternity can only come to be known by means of learning fraternity with him. This would be the meaning of Jesus' reply to Philip in John's gospel when Philip asks him:

> 'Lord, show us the Father and we shall be satisfied.' (John 14:8)

Jesus replies:

> 'He who has seen me has seen the Father.' (John 14:9)

Indeed, if there is no earthly paternity capable of reflecting God, and we only accede to the paternity of God by means of learning fraternity with Jesus, who is at exactly the same level as us, that is, who is a human being, then we can begin to understand that the apparent fatherhood of this world is not fatherhood in the divine sense, but fratricidal fraternity dressed up as fatherhood. This is exactly what Jesus says to a group of his interlocutors who were denying his teaching that his Father cannot be identified with the group paternity to which they subscribed, calling themselves sons of Abraham:

> 'You are of your father the devil, and your will is to do your father's desires. He was a murderer from the beginning, and has nothing to do with the truth, because there is no truth in him.' (John 8:44)

Let me insist a little on the extraordinary anthropological rupture which this phrase produces. When we grasp on to any form of earthly paternity, seeking to establish our identity from this paternity, then we are ignoring the fact that the principle of earthly paternity, that is, the element which has structured it from within since the beginning, was the primeval murder, that of Abel by Cain. All human paternity comes internally structured by fratricide and, *as paternity*, is incapable of truth, because it will always be protecting itself against the 'other'.

Just in case you think I'm making this up, let's go back to Matthew, to the verse before the one I quoted to you:

> 'But you are not to be called rabbi, for you have one teacher and you are all brethren.' (Matt. 23:8)

That is to say, in Matthew, Jesus inverts the order which would be natural to us. We typically imagine that biology is prior to culture, and so that first should come the phrase about paternity: 'One alone is your Father who is in heaven, and you are all brethren. And don't let anyone call you rabbi, because one alone is your Master.' However, in fact Jesus doesn't share our mentality. For him, here, as in John, it is culture which comes before biology. Fraternity is the matrix of our cultural formation, and because of that we have to attend to our absolute equality in the matter of learning about things divine, so as to avoid false attributions of divinity to non-fraternal ways of presenting the divine truth. Within this matrix of the apprenticeship of fraternity we also have to learn to deconstruct the false paternity of this world, for even biological paternity is nothing other than intergenerational fraternity, and thus capable of being exercised constructively or destructively.

Well, if all human paternity comes internally structured by fratricide, this opens up for us some extraordinary possibilities for the eucharistic construction of fraternity. For example, I suspect that I'm not the only person to have imagined and received the whole force of the social, cultural and ecclesiastical hatred of gay people as if it were a paternal force. A crushing paternal force which demanded that I either buckle under or die, or both at the same time. And of course, against paternal force there is no right of reply, since none of us is at the same level as the paternal. And for that reason, the relation, being between unequal parties, can never truly be one of love. For love depends on equality. Nor, in the case of being crushed, can there truly be forgiveness, for forgiveness also can only really take place between equals – in fact it is what is creative of equality.

Now if, as Jesus teaches, this imagination of the paternal as a crushing and murderous force is not real, but mythical, for the paternal is only fratricidal fraternity dressed up as paternity, then, yes indeed, one can forgive, really and constructively. If the eucharistic presence of the crucified and risen Christ is the fraternal presence which returns not as accusation but as forgiveness, and as a presence which opens up the imagination so that we recognise our complicities and begin to construct forgiveness, then indeed the place of the much-loved queer is a place from which one can begin to reimagine the Church fraternally. We can begin to look at the whole institutional structure not as a paternal and devastating 'they', but begin to imagine it as an occasionally fratricidal 'we'. The moment we begin to perceive that what seemed to be something paternal is only a bad fraternity, which exercises itself fratricidally, then we can begin to rethink every instance of how it works, how it teaches, how it treats people. And we do so not from the perspective of one who accuses it while on the way to being victimised by it, but from that of one who always forgives, and is, even if rejected and killed, on the way to offering new possibilities of life.[2]

---

2. A fuller account of the shift from the paternal to the fraternal, working through the passages from John and Matthew which I have touched on here, is to be found in the next chapter.

Let us try an example. If the teaching of the Church is, and can only be, at the fraternal level, then we have not only the right, but the duty to undertake the task of reimagining it in such a way that what it says, and how it says it, reflects the voice of Christ. He only imagines himself as our brother, and never as our father. Here I'm not introducing a new criterion for theological discernment, but applying a distinction which Jesus himself taught:

> 'The scribes and the Pharisees sit on Moses' seat; so practise and observe whatever they tell you, but not what they do; for they say, but do not do.' (Matt. 23:2–3)

Since it is Very God of Very God, of one being with the Father, who introduces this distinction, we would do well to imitate him. Let us notice something: the instruction to 'practise and observe whatever they tell you' is an unstable instruction. For, the moment Jesus introduces the distinction between 'what they say and what they do', he opens up the possibility of the recognition that even 'what they say' reaches us in a way that is distorted by 'what they do'. That is to say, the suspicion that their practice forms the framework for their teaching. Ideological suspicion is not something alien to the Gospel, but is rather close to the heart of the project of the removing of idols which characterises Jesus' presence. However, ideological suspicion is not for the purpose of attacking, but for self-critical reconstruction. That is to say, the moment we recognise that these people are but brothers entrapped by forces which they do not understand, the same forces which tend to destroy us all, and before whose gods we have all, on many occasions, bent the knee; the moment we understand that their voice tends to reproduce at least as much the violence of those forces as it does the truth of God, then we can begin to examine the violent mechanism, bringing it into the light, because the violent mechanism is only a perversion of fraternity, and as such is capable of human analysis, and of being redirected towards a fraternity that tends to build up others.

Discourse from the position of the crushed, victimised queer can only be a voice of accusation, demanding approval. It looks at the ecclesiastical 'closet' as something incurably hypocritical and violent, and so can only protest against it, rejecting the possibility that something evangelical, something emancipatory, something truthful, might come out of it. I'm suggesting that there is another possibility: the ecclesiastical 'closet', since it is a reality which works at the fraternal, and not at the paternal level, is available to rational discussion. For example, the Vatican published in 1992, during the election campaign which was won by Bill Clinton, a document directed to the US bishops. The document was an attempt to discourage Catholic voters from electing candidates who were in favour of introducing legislation to protect the rights of employment, and other rights, of gay people. It says so quite explicitly. Well, this document was not well received. A number of bishops, and the conference of religious superiors-general, emphatically rejected not only the abusive electoral practice (evidently inspired by some republican-leaning bishops), but also the content of the document. They rejected the idea that it can be just to fight in favour of legislation which discriminates against part of the population.

Leaving this aside, some phrases in the document were very revealing of the perspective of those writing:

> As a rule, the majority of homosexually oriented persons who seek to lead chaste lives do not publicize their sexual orientation. Hence the problem of discrimination in terms of employment, housing, etc., does not usually arise. Homosexual persons who assert their homosexuality tend to be precisely those who judge homosexual behavior or lifestyle to be 'either completely harmless, if not an entirely good thing', and hence worthy of public approval.[3]

So, with a certain clarity at last, the Vatican is not talking about particular sexual acts, but about strategies for survival in a recognisedly violent world. The person who remains silent within the

---

3. 'Responding to Legislative Proposals on Discrimination Against Homosexuals' para 14, taken from *Origins* vol. 22, no. 10 (6 August 1992). The quote is from the CDF's 1986 letter concerning 'The Pastoral Care of Homosexual Persons'.

'closet' will have no problems; the one who is 'out' deserves the problems that will befall him, and no legislation should protect him.

Well, rather than treating the authors as monsters, let us question them as brothers. You are affirming something which is independent of acts committed or avoided, for it is not simply self-evident that the closeted gay man is either more or less inclined to acts held to be sinful than the one who is 'out'. That is, you are affirming, as part of a fraternal church teaching, that the 'closet' is the most appropriate place for the human and Christian well-being and flourishing of people with a homosexual orientation. The one who 'comes out', and runs the risks which may befall him, puts himself into a less propitious place for human and Christian well-being and flourishing. This is what you are affirming. We can ask: but is this true? We might ask whether, for example, chastity, a virtue which it behoves every Christian, including the married, to learn and exercise, can better be learnt and exercised within the process of learning to relate honestly to a whole network of friends, and even close friends and maybe a partner, where the centre of emotional and erotic gravity of those involved can be talked about. Or whether, on the contrary, chastity is best learnt by detaching oneself from language, and preferring a mode of presence that is anonymous and reticent even with those closest at work, at play, in the family, and so on. The answer is not self-evident, which is why it has to be discussed.

We might ask also whether the psychological effects of remaining in the closet are more or less propitious for the process of discovering oneself a son or daughter of God than the psychological effects of 'coming out' and beginning to find out what it might mean to be a child of God in the much riskier terrain of a social world where people speak quite openly about these things. We might ask: How do you reconcile the maintenance of the 'closet' with the explicit teaching of the gospel about the fact that everything hidden will be uncovered, and what is said in secret will be preached from the rooftops (Luke 12:3)? Perhaps there is a way of reconciling it, but you haven't made the case for the Christianity of your position, and it would be important that we understand what that position is, so as to see whether it is in continuity with Christ's teaching or not.

We might note that the entirely correct affirmation that the person of homosexual orientation has, as have all Christians, to carry his cross every day, is capable of two interpretations. The interpretation of the closet suggests that the sacrifice demanded by God is that of the 'I' understood as something which seeks its flourishing in a necessarily disordered manner. This would be the application to the person of same-sex orientation of the phrase:

> 'If any one would come after me, let him deny himself and take up his cross daily and follow me.' (Luke 9:23)

However, there exists another interpretation, that of those who declare themselves. Here the denial of self and the taking up of the cross correspond, among other things, to an insistence on living in a worthy and honest way in a social milieu which tends to count those gay people who strive for honesty, as it counts all people who seek to live with a certain integrity, among the transgressors, and for this reason to despise, calumniate and crucify them. It is not evident that the interpretation which calls for a search for the private holocaust of the 'self' is necessarily a more Christian interpretation than the one where, in order to create a more fraternal life for self and for others, a person every day runs the risk of various forms of public violence. About this we can dialogue.

The moment it becomes clear that we are not dealing with a monstrous sacred block, but of strategies for survival each of which have implications about how human well-being and flourishing are understood, then the closet becomes something about which we can dialogue. Of course, we may indeed find brothers and sisters who do not want to dialogue about this. Perhaps for such people the question of the well-being of their brothers and sisters is less important than the maintenance of doctrine, and the recommendation against 'coming out' is only a manner of avoiding the further discussion of the matter. If there are people who really do think that man is made for the Sabbath rather than the Sabbath for man, then it would be very difficult to proceed. However, in fact, there will always be brethren, even in very high ecclesiastical positions, who understand that it is their task to help interpret doctrines in such a way that they don't become idols which demand sacrifice and go against the well-being of their brothers and sisters. With such people one can indeed dialogue about ways of conceiving human well-being.

However, here we tread on a very difficult terrain. For, in a dialogue, who will represent the 'closet'? Cannot this only be done by someone who isn't in it? For the moment someone undertakes to represent the closet in a dialogue, either it is a 'straight' person who has to recognise a limited capacity to represent adequately people of whose state of life he has deep knowledge only with difficulty; or it is someone who, by the very fact of speaking, 'comes out'. An accusatory mentality would rejoice at this evident difficulty. But the forgiving mentality, which tries to understand the expulsive mechanism as, at root, a phenomenon at the fraternal level, rather takes it as a sign that we must proceed with extreme delicacy and gentleness towards brothers who are unable to speak for themselves. And I say 'unable' not only in the formal sense, because speaking out would be coming out, but in the deeper sense: perhaps they are unable to start from a viable 'self' capable of creating fraternity through the medium of language. Maybe their conscience is so deeply bound by the supposed paternity which is in fact a form of fratricide that they are incapable of imagining themselves as much-loved children, except by rejecting themselves completely. For such reasons many people have killed themselves, whether physically or morally, and there we do indeed need to remember the still, small voice:

> A bruised reed he will not break, and a dimly burning wick he will not quench; he will faithfully bring forth justice. (Isa. 42:3)

Well, if we reach this point, this space close to a cracking of heart, we have creatively to imagine into existence something much more glorious, much more merciful. In the face of those who have no voice, we must, above all, avoid being strong with the weak (cf. 1 Cor. 10:23–30). Rather we have to rework Catholic moral theology in such a way as to make it capable of unbinding the consciences of people who fear, at a very deep level, receiving the conscience of a child of God. We have to offer, in a non-threatening way, the possibility of being introduced into the dynamic movement which I have tried to sketch out, of becoming detached from idols so as to receive divine sonship. We have to learn how to present in a much clearer way something which I have only begun very superficially to sketch out: the lovingkindness and audacity of God who invites us just as we are to create fraternity by means of the crucified and risen brother who opens up our minds to imagine the new Jerusalem in the midst of the ruins of all our idolatries, all our acts of cowardice. No small task for the third millennium.

CHAPTER THREE

Jesus' fraternal relocation of God

introduction

John 8:31–59 is often read as a particularly striking example of an anti-Semitic tendency which is to be found in all the gospels but especially in John's. Jesus indicates to his interlocutors, ominously called 'the Jews', that their father is the devil who was a murderer from the beginning, while he is the Son of the Father. This is taken to be an example of community rivalry, a piece of one-upmanship, 'we're better than you are', what I will refer to as tit for tat, and is read straight back into the construction of the text. Thus, according to this reading, the so-called 'Johannine community' was involved in a tit-for-tat spat either with Judaism as such or with a troublesome local synagogue. Its members read their situation of strife back into their understanding of Jesus, and so tell a story of Jesus which fits in with their concerns. It is the story of Jesus as the definitive one-up man, meaning God is also a one-up God, not so much God as a 'Gott mit uns'. The trouble with this reading is that it uses a sociology of community which leaves God wholly within the framework of human violence and rivalry. God is entirely wedded to strife and the construction of community 'over against' another group. But this is the essence of nihilism. There is nothing but strife: violence is all, only conflict is creative. The implication of this reading of John 8 is that there is nothing of divine revelation in this text, or that if there is, then all that it reveals is that God is at root tit for tat, which is to say the same thing.

Now I'd like to suggest something different. I'd like to suggest that this passage works in a quite different way. I'd like to suggest that John's Jesus is not taking sides in a particular instance of interreligious strife. Rather he is making available a coherent anthropological vision which is, even today, beyond the bounds of our customary perception, and is part of divine revelation just as an anthropological vision. In other words, the apparent tit for tat in the text is not something which governs the text as would be the case if the author were imprisoned in a tit-for-tat mentality and unable to see beyond it. On the contrary, the text is specifically about overcoming tit for tat by showing where it comes from and how it need not be the last word.

One of the constants of John's gospel is the gradual re-centring of the concept of God as Father onto Jesus. I mean, that it is only through Jesus that we have access to the Father.[1] Everything that had been associated with the Father – with God alone – comes to be associated with Jesus. So, all judgement has been entrusted to Jesus,[2] it is Jesus' commandment that resumes and fulfils God's commandments,[3] it is by honouring Jesus that we honour the Father[4] and so on.

Well, let's just suppose that this is not Jesus being a self-important prig, part of the tit-for-tat model. Let us assume, rather, that by means of this sort of talk Jesus is accomplishing something of incomparably greater anthropological significance: the removing from God of any of the anthropological connotations of fatherhood, and the recasting of God entirely within the terms of reference of fraternity. Let us read this text, then, in that most Jewish of veins, as a text about overcoming idolatry.

A brief caveat before we start. You are about to embark upon a reading of some texts which rely upon a painfully masculine use of language. I hope that it will be clear by the end that one of the

---

1. John 14:6: 'I am the way, and the truth, and the life; no one comes to the Father, but by me.'
2. John 5:22: 'The Father judges no one, but has given all judgement to the Son.'
3. John 15:12: 'This is my commandment, that you love one another as I have loved you.'
4. John 5:23: 'He who does not honour the Son does not honour the Father who sent him.'

effects of these particular texts' heavily masculine language is to undo the sort of world in which masculine language and especially male forms of cultural interaction are taken to be the naturally defining basis of social life. We have reached the stage where the language itself is painful to us. I take this as a sign that the subversion from within of the cultural world which took that language for granted, a subversion which is embodied in texts like these, has had some success. Please bracket any feeling of being excluded. I hope it will become clear that what is being interpreted is a road to inclusion.

a close reading of John 8:31–59

Jesus is teaching in the treasury of the Temple. So far he has managed to avoid an objection by the Pharisees. There are a number of listeners, presumably not Pharisees, who have been hanging on to what he teaches, despite considerable incomprehension, and have in fact started to believe that he speaks with divine authority, and that the Father is in some way involved in what Jesus is teaching. Let us take up the discussion at verse 31:

> Jesus then said to the Jews who had believed in him, 'If you continue in my word, you are truly my disciples, and you will know the truth and the truth will make you free.'

Here we have Jesus trying to get a group of people who had followed his teaching so far, whom he had been able to carry along thus far, to go a step further with him in his programme of de-idolatrising God. This is a vital point: the discussion does not start with: 'You are wrong and I am right, and I'm going to tell you how wrong you are and you are going to get angry with me'. It starts with something much more like: 'We are part of the same programme of overcoming idolatry, and we've come a long way. Now let's see if you can bear to follow the next step in this programme, which will be difficult, because any overcoming of idolatry requires personal unhooking from one's idols.'

So, the 'next step' in Jesus' fleshing out of the programme is to indicate that entry into truth and freedom are linked not to deriving identity from group adhesion to some paternal law or teaching, but to a certain sort of fraternal listening. This is the sort of listening that seeks to imitate and re-enact the kind of fraternal living which Jesus is teaching. When we talk about discipleship, it is to this sort of fraternal listening and imitating that we are referring. It is through this horizontal discipleship alone that people will come to perceive who God is, and discover God's paternity. In other words, it is only by working at the horizontal that we will begin to discover the true vertical.

This, like any new step, is a provocative teaching, and Jesus' interlocutors reply:

> 'We are descendants of Abraham, and have never been in bondage to any one. How is it that you say "You will be made free"?' (8:33)

Now, please note the word they use: 'descendants' – literally 'seed' – the Greek word is *sperma*. We will see soon why this word is important. So far they are pointing out something to which no one could take exception, that they are descended from Abraham, who of course set out on his wanderings precisely so as to get beyond and away from idols. He was in fact the initiator of the anti-idolatry programme which is under discussion. Thus their observation about bondage is an observation that they have never been subject to idols. They are not referring to their time in Egypt, as must be clear from no less a source than the first commandment. The interlocutors knew that 'I am the LORD thy God, who brought thee out of the land of Egypt, out of the house of bondage' (Exod. 20:2). That this would have been familiar to any early reader of John's text suggests that the bondage in which 'we have never been' is not the political slavery of Egypt. It is rather the bondage to error which would have been incurred if they had gone after other gods, abandoning the God of Abraham. So their reply is a properly theological one and is a response to Jesus' suggestion that there is something more to God that they don't already know about by virtue of being the seed of Abraham, that there is a freedom yet to be gained.[5]

Jesus replies to them:

> 'Truly, truly, I say to you, every one who commits sin is a slave [to sin]. The slave does not continue in the house for ever; the son continues for ever. So, if the Son sets you free, you will be free indeed.'

Now, you will notice that I have bracketed the phrase 'to sin' which you find in the RSV text. It turns out that this phrase is not present in many ancient texts, and may represent a piece of editing influenced by Paul's use of 'slavery to sin', a concept we have tended to moralise into meaninglessness. Whatever the textual history, Jesus' reply is not moralistic but theological. His inter-locutors have claimed that by virtue of being seed of Abraham they are free from idolatry and thus free. Jesus claims that anyone who commits sin is in thrall to an idol, moved by an idol. The true God lives for ever, and so does anyone who is utterly moved and formed from within by God. Anyone who is enslaved to an idol, however partially, will not live for ever: they will 'die in their sins' (to go back to what Jesus had been teaching just before this exchange at 8:22). However, if the son of the house, the one who, utterly moved from within by the living God, lives for ever, chooses to set them free – which means, making them equal in the house to the son, making them, in fact, so many extra siblings of the son – then they will have the freedom of the son. Now please notice that this is simply to recapitulate what Jesus had

---

5. It may be the case that early Christian readers will have picked up the reference to bondage as a denial that the interlocutors are sons of Abraham through Hagar, the slave woman. Paul's allegory concerning 'who are the real descendants of Abraham through Sara rather than through Hagar' in Galatians 4, with its development in Romans 9, can be, and often has been read, in 'tit-for-tat' fashion. John may well have been seeking to make available the revelatory anthropology that undercuts a possible Christian tit-for-tat reading against the Jews. In other words he may have been saying 'This is not a we-are-better-than-they-issue. There is a substantive question about what it looks like *anthropologically* to overcome idolatry here.'

already said in verse 31. It is by listening to his word and being his disciple, which means learning to imitate him fraternally, and thus becoming a sister or brother at the same level with him, that they will know the truth and be made free. In fact, it combines that with what he had said earlier, 'for you will die in your sins unless you believe that I am he'.

Jesus then expands his argument, which grows in concentric circles, beginning to make explicit some of the crucial distinctions which underlie his anthropology.

> 'I know that you are *descendants* of Abraham; yet you seek to kill me, because my word finds no place in you. I speak of what I have seen with my Father, and you do what you have heard from your father.'

Jesus agrees with his interlocutors that they are the *seed* of Abraham: their biological progenitor is not in dispute. What he points out is that being a descendant of Abraham is not the same thing as being a child of the God of Abraham. The difference is shown by the fact that they are prepared to kill Jesus. Someone who is biologically descended from Abraham and yet is prepared to commit fratricide – killing a brother-in-Abraham – because what he says challenges their perception of God, clearly has a different moving principle from Abraham. So, Jesus says that he speaks to them from the moving principle which is his Father, God. Their moving principle, their father, is, by an implication which will soon be made explicit, the father of fratricide.

The interlocutors come back to Jesus with the retort:

> 'Abraham is our father.' (8:39)

Now please notice the subtle wordplay. We have just moved up a notch in the argument: up until now Abraham has only been claimed as the male progenitor, supplier of the seed. The biological continuity with Abraham has not been in dispute. But here, with the word 'father' we have a new dimension, not that of biological continuity, but of cultural motivation. The distinction which Jesus had been making between biological descent and cultural motivation has been refused. So far all that is happening is that the interlocutors are claiming that their biological origin and their cultural motivation have the same source.

Jesus tries to make his distinction even more explicit:

> 'If you were Abraham's *children* you would do what Abraham *did*, but you now seek to kill me, a man who has told you the truth which I heard from God; this is not what Abraham *did*. You do what your father did.' (8:39–41)

Jesus has brought in the word *tekna*, children, as distinct from seed, *sperma*, to reiterate his point. If they were children, rather than merely descendants, of Abraham, that is, if their motivating principle were the same as his, as opposed merely to their genes, then this could be detected in their acting out of the same motivating principle. The sort of thing Abraham *did* did not include seeking to kill one who told the truth which came from God. Abraham had quite complex reactions to the various truths he heard from God. He laughed with incredulity, despaired of the promise and so got a child by Hagar, but the most important reaction was to have believed the truth he was told *concerning his own offspring*, and to have desisted from sacrificing his son Isaac. Now Jesus is not making a simple *ad hominem*, tit-for-tat point. He is making a more fundamental anthropological point. When he says 'You do what your father did' he is not only holding up to them what they are doing, but he is enunciating an anthropological principle: *One does what one's father does*. This is actually the premise of his argument: the cultural reality of paternity is determined by what one does. Or, in other words, our fraternal practice is the only criterion for our paternity.

Jesus' interlocutors reply:

> 'We were not born of fornication; we have one Father, even God.' (8:41)

Some have read this reference to fornication as an *ad hominem* remark to Jesus, suggesting that he, both as a Nazarene and thus from a region where various imperial resettlements had severely tainted racial purity, and as a man with a dubious family history, was of questionable paternity. Others have seen in this retort a further denial that the interlocutors are children of Abraham via Hagar, where fornication flows into idolatry. Whatever the case, the important point is not the underlying reference but the dynamic of the discussion here, which is the hardening of the refusal to accept Jesus' anthropological distinction, saying: 'There's nothing idolatrous about us, nothing to distinguish about our paternity – it's all one package.'

Jesus had been making the distinction between seed and children so as to make comprehensible a teaching about the coming freedom of children, those who are to be enabled to act out of non-fratricidal cultural imperatives. His interlocutors could only hear this as a slur on the integrity of their race and of their faith which, in their minds, are indistinguishable. So they reach the logical conclusion to the development of their own response: 'We have one Father, even God.' Now please notice John's very clever use of language here. Their previous retort to Jesus was 'Abraham is our father.' Now they say 'We have one Father, even God.' The point is *not* that they are inconsistent when they say that they have one Father, God, and yet that Abraham is their father. The point is rather that in the refusal of the distinction which Jesus is trying to make, the paternity of God and the paternity of Abraham become absolutely identified. They make the final bond between theological paternity and cultural paternity towards which they have been building under the provocation of Jesus' attempt to introduce a distinction.

So Jesus now makes explicit the contrasting visions of theo-logical paternity out of which he has been operating:

> 'If God were your Father, you would love me, for I proceeded and came forth from God; I came not of my own accord, but he sent me. Why do you not understand what I say? It is because you cannot bear to hear my word.' (8:42–3)

In other words, if the motivating force behind their cultural unity really were God, then they would be open to fraternity with Jesus. This is because Jesus opens up the real access to God by intro-ducing a discipleship which is the creation of real fraternity, and he does so in direct imitation of God. The creation of fraternity,

and the proceeding from and imitating and obeying God, are all
the same thing. Why do they not understand this? They do not
understand it because they cannot bear Jesus' word. They cannot
bear it because Jesus' word collapses the sort of group belonging
produced by the linking of cultural and biological paternity, a
group belonging which leads to exclusion and fratricide. Jesus'
word collapses this and introduces instead a fraternity which leads
to the discovery of a Paternity which is quite outside biology and
culture. None of us can bear that sort of word: it suggests that
our god, our social belonging, our sense of security, are all idolatrous. There is nothing harder than to be told that what we hold
sacred is an idol. Remember these were people who had believed
in Jesus, that is people who were, in principle, ready to move on
to the next step in Jesus' programme of the de-idolatrisation of
God. The phrase 'You cannot bear . . .' points to people on the
cusp of moving on to the discovery of a new and less idolatrous
fraternity, who nevertheless find themselves retreating into a
stronger and more exclusive affirmation of a previous paternity.

Jesus continues:

> 'You are of your father the devil, and your will is to do your
> father's desires. He was a murderer from the beginning, and
> has nothing to do with the truth, because there is no truth in
> him. When he lies he speaks according to his own nature, for
> he is a liar and the father of lies.' (8:44)

Now we are in a position to read this not simply as the mother
of all insults, which is how it is read in the tit-for-tat school of
exegesis, but as the logical summation of the anthropological distinctions which Jesus has been trying to make all along. Jesus is
saying that there are two paternities: that of his Father which
is accessible in and through the imitative creation of an inclusive
fraternity following Jesus, or its alternative, the cultural reality
proper to all humanity, one which is no respecter of anyone's
biological origin. Human culture has its origin in a fratricidal
murder, that of Abel by Cain, and all humans are by virtue of that
origin radically distorted both in our willing and our knowing.
The structure of our desire, which precedes our consciousness, is

murderous. That desire ensures that our cultural constructs, our language and our knowledge are radically inflected by the lie which fails to recognise this, fails to see God in humans who are 'other', or ourselves in our victims, which is to say the same thing.

This statement contains a piece of radical anthropology, a claim concerning cultural paternity: any earthly paternity is ultimately a reflection of the murderous distortion of fraternity into fratricide. Human paternity as we know it flows from fratricidal sibling relations. Notice what this means: in Jesus' view the cultural reality of being human fratricides, being a member of the species *homo necans*, is a structuring reality which is prior to, and structures the biological reality of, paternity. In other words: it is our being bad brothers and sisters that leads us to be bad fathers and mothers, not our having bad fathers and mothers that has made us bad brothers and sisters. Let me say this again, for it sounds so strange for those of us who have become accustomed to suckling at a Freudian breast: fraternity is the matrix (now *there's* a slip), and paternity the symptom, not the other way around. If you get two fratricides, one of whom happens to be the progenitor of the other, then it is easy to imagine, as Freud did, that the lethal violence each may have towards the other is something to do with being a progenitor or being an offspring. So we talk about the filial desire for parricide, or the paternal annihilation of a son's being. Wrong, says Jesus: this is nothing to do with fathers or sons, mothers or daughters, this is simply what fratricide looks like when it is intergenerational.

The logical extension of this perception is quite simple: there is no such thing as an earthly father, and it is vital to our task of overcoming idolatry to come to perceive this. We know from another source that Jesus, never one to buck the logical conclusions of his own anthropological insights, taught exactly this:

> 'And call no man your father on earth, for you have one Father who is in heaven.' (Matt. 23:9)

As if this phrase were not remarkable enough on its own terms, please let me point out that the words 'for you are all brothers' does not belong with the verse about fathers, as would seem natural to us. It belongs with the *previous* verse:

> 'But you are not to be called rabbi, for you have one teacher, and you are all brethren.' (Matt. 23:8)

The verse about cultural paternity and fraternity *precedes* the verse about biological fraternity. It could not be clearer: it is not biological paternity which is the model from which a distorted cultural paternity flows, but a distorted cultural fraternity which inflects biological paternity, and makes it un-fraternal. The unlearning of this pattern of desire works the same way: by attending to what should be fraternal on the cultural level, properly fraternal relationships between progenitors and their seed can develop as well.

Enough of this for the moment, and back to John 8. Now that Jesus has laid the ground by explaining the cultural paternity of all people in fratricide, with its accompanying lie that fratricidal sacrifice is necessary to keep society together, he is able to continue:

> 'But, because I tell the truth, you do not believe me. Which of you convicts me of sin? If I tell the truth, why do you not believe me? He who is of God hears the words of God; the reason why you do not hear them is that you are not of God.'
> (8:45–7)

Again, let us continue to read this as logical argument, not as *ad hominem* diatribe. For people whose cultural paternity is based on a murderous lie, to hear the truth about our cultural paternity is well nigh impossible, whereas we can hear and believe any number of flattering mystifications. So Jesus says that it is *because* he is telling them the truth about their origins in fratricidal murder that they do not believe him. This of course raises the question of 'where he's coming from'. If he were of the same cultural paternity as they, then of course what he said would be just another variant of the lie. But have any of them ever found anything in his behaviour which would lead them to think that he was part of that cultural paternity? Do any of them attribute sin to him? No. So he does not speak from out of the murderous lie, but from the truth. But if he tells the truth and their moving principle were God rather than the murderous lie, they would believe him, because they too would recognise the truth. And Jesus makes this clear by enunciating a further general principle: people who are of God hear the truth of God wherever it comes from. The fact that his interlocutors don't hear Jesus' word is what enables it to be deduced that their moving principle is not God.

Back to the interlocutors: faced with the very puzzling intrusion of an exposition of an anthropological reality that would seriously destabilise their belonging and their social unity, they have gradually regrouped ever further under the aura of their sacred paternity. What had started with the unexceptionable statement that they were seed of Abraham developed to their claim that Abraham was their father, their prime cultural mover, and then that God alone was their Father. Thus they made completely and sacredly watertight their cultural and group belonging, simultaneously making that belonging independent of their behaviour. The next step in this progression is, of course, the redefinition of someone who threatens that unity: he ceases to be what he has been until now, a discomfiting insider, 'a sonofabitch, but our sonofabitch', someone who was provocative, but ultimately 'one of us'. Jesus is now redefined simultaneously in cultural and in theological terms as 'not one of us':

> 'Are we not right in saying that you are a Samaritan and have a demon?' (8:48)

Now, please notice that this is not simply an insult, and it is not yet simply an exclusion from being one of Abraham's children. Samaritans, being descendants of Jacob, were children of Abraham. In the circumstances the interlocutors are making an *excuse* for Jesus. To say 'you are a Samaritan' is to say 'you're not really one of us, despite your pretensions to worshipping the same God as we.' But it is also to assimilate Jesus to a known class of people who are 'not quite like us' – 'oh well, no wonder he sings a bit off key, he's one of *them*.'

Furthermore, when *we* 'demonise' someone, for instance calling them 'the great Satan' or 'intrinsically perverse' it is simply a way of declaring them evil, and utterly cast out from us; but this was not how the much more socially courteous demonology of Jesus' interlocutors worked. When they said that Jesus 'had a demon', this was their way of saying that he was not really responsible for what he was saying, and should not be held accountable for it. Such a person could not properly blaspheme or be held accountable for blasphemy any more than a foreigner, a drunkard or a minor can be held accountable for infractions of the rigorous etiquette which marks proper belonging to, for instance, Japanese adult society. To be declared a Samaritan and with a demon is partially the sort of expulsion to which they have been building up by linking their cultural and racial paternity directly with their divine paternity. But it is also a brake on that expulsion, a put-down as much as a putting-out: 'he couldn't know better.'

A little observation here: Jesus uses the word 'devil' about his interlocutors' paternity and his interlocutors use 'demon' to get back at Jesus. Doesn't this sound like tit for tat? I would suggest that even here the choice of words is instructive: the word *diabolos* in John always refers to the founding principle of fratricidal order, and is a revelation of a principle that is to be overcome, not an accusation of 'bad people'. The word 'demon' – *daimonion* – is the accusatory word from within the fratricidally structured cultural order, the way one indicates someone as not 'one of us'. Jesus' word *diabolos* reveals the murderous structure of human desire; the interlocutors' word *daimonion* is a function of that desire. Its use is an acting out of expulsive desire by those who don't know what they're doing.

In any case, Jesus refuses to accept the implication that he's not really responsible for what he's saying, not a serious interlocutor:

> 'I have not a demon; but I honour my Father, and you dis-
> honour me. Yet I do not seek my own glory; there is One who
> seeks it and he will be the judge.' (8:49–50)

In fact, Jesus is insisting on carrying on with the teaching he's been trying to get through to them all along. He is acting respon-
sibly and he is giving proper reverence to God, and their

disqualification of him from serious dialogue, however exculpatory
its intent, is in fact a failure to attribute to him the honour which
should be attributed to one who is speaking well of God. Not that
he's personally diminished in any way by their treating him as
incompetent. His self-esteem doesn't depend on people taking him
seriously and giving him a sense of worth. God himself will honour
him by establishing his worth and truthfulness, and of course God's
discernment is quite outside the sort of judgements produced by
cultural group dynamics such as we have here.

So Jesus, dismissing his interlocutors' increasingly forceful
assertion of a paternally based access to an exclusive fraternity, is
insisting on carrying on his teaching about the bringing about of
the new sort of fraternity. This fraternity is the same as being
adopted as a son by God: the fraternally based access to an
inclusive paternity which has been the burden of his teaching:

> 'Truly, truly, I say to you, if any one keeps my word, he will
> never see death.' (8:51)

Jesus emphasises again what he has been teaching throughout
chapter 8: his word is about overcoming idolatry by learning to
produce that flexible imitation of himself which is called discipleship. The one who stays in that programme is entering into a filial
relationship with the ever-living God who knows not death. Such
a one will never die.

Jesus' interlocutors reaffirm the demon, as if to suggest that
Jesus is mad – preferable to his being a blasphemer.

> 'Now we know that you have a demon.' (8:52)

And please look at John's irony. The interlocutors now repeat
very exactly what Jesus had been saying all along, but as if it were
mad.

> 'Abraham died, as did the prophets; and you say, "If anyone
> keeps my word, he will never taste death." Are you greater
> than our father Abraham, who died? And the prophets died!
> Who do you claim to be?' (8:52–3)

Abraham died. The prophets died. But this is exactly what Jesus had been saying. The fact that they were slaves to sin, still not entirely free from idolatry, is shown by the fact that they died. It is only the Son who can give life. The interlocutors even repeat and lay stress on the fact that these characters died. The first time they say 'Abraham', the second time 'our father Abraham', thus linking their much-vaunted paternity with death – again, exactly what Jesus had been saying. The phrase which is translated as 'Who do you claim to be?' reads more exactly 'Whom do you make yourself?' which we might render 'Who is it that you have the pretension to make yourself out to be?'

Now Jesus gets explicit:

> 'If I glorify myself, my glory is nothing; it is my Father who glorifies me, of whom you say that he is your God.' (8:54)

There is a textual problem here: the majority of Greek texts for the last part of the sentence read literally 'of whom you say that he is *our* God'. Not only the majority, but the oldest and least polished, meaning the most likely to be original. The translation we have here not only translates but interprets this 'our' as meaning: 'You say "he is *our* God."' The translators thus read '*our* God' as an act of exclusion (i.e. 'ours not yours'), so that in reported speech it reads 'You say that he is *your* God.' But that is to introduce the tit-for-tat interpretation even into the choice of Greek text and the translation, and is absolutely not the only, or even, I suggest, the most likely, interpretation. It could be that the 'our God' should be read inclusively, with Jesus counting himself in with the 'our': 'of whom you (also) say that he is our God'. The ambiguity is probably quite deliberate: it is in such a place that the tit-for-tat or fratricidal reading and the gratuitous or inclusive reading rub shoulders.

In the light of the reading I am trying to uncover, this sentence now reads like this: the interlocutors ask Jesus who he's making himself out to be, and he replies 'If I were making myself out to be someone out of pretension, then I really would be worth nothing. As it is, it is my Father, the very same whom you also claim as God, who shows forth who I really am.' Jesus is trying to make God's paternity inclusive by showing up the fratricidal nature of the idolatrous appropriation of God, and he will make the same move with Abraham at the end of his argument.

He continues:

> 'But you have not known him. I know him. If I said, I do not know him, I should be a liar like you; but I do know him and I keep his word. Your father Abraham rejoiced that he was to see my day; he saw it and was glad.' (8:55–6)

Let me paraphrase this as follows: 'By being in fratricidal, exclusive mode, you show that you do not truly know God. I do know God, the witness that I bear to God, how I talk about God, is the true programme of purification from idols, and to pretend otherwise would be to bear false witness to God, which is what you are doing. I bear true witness to him, and truly enter into the dynamic of God's word which brings down idols. For this reason, the one whom you just referred to in an exclusive way as your father Abraham, the one who was first caught up in this project of breaking free from idols, he was delighted to think that the day would come when the process of becoming free from idols would be accomplished. This is what I am about. In fact this culmination of his project in me was what he was looking forward to. The project was the one by which slaves learned to become daughters and sons. This means that Abraham is really the name not of an earthly and deathbound paternity under which one huddles for security over against some other, which is to reduce his project to the very fratricidal idolatry he was called to overcome. Abraham is the name of a project of fraternity which overcomes that, and which leads to people becoming sons and daughters and sharing in God's life for ever.'

Now please notice Jesus' strategy: he constantly refuses the terms of the argument set within a tit for tat, for that is part of the fruit of idolatry, a dialectic based on violence. Instead he tries to show a way out of that, revealing it for what it is. Is Abraham's project to be interpreted and lived out within the terms of the 'strife is all' paternity, in which case it is reduced to that paternity, going round and round in violent circles for ever? Or is Abraham's project to be interpreted as a response to God's call from outside that paternity, a gratuitous irruption that is an invitation to move beyond idolatry and construct a fraternity? Is Abraham the name of an enclosing paternity or of an open-ended fraternity? Only the latter reality has nothing to do with the tit for tat of idolatry, and yet it can only be made visible by the subversion from within of that tit-for-tat idolatry.

This is what lies behind the next, and most staggering of exchanges. Jesus' interlocutors say to him:

'You are not yet fifty years old, and have you seen Abraham?'
(8:57)

At one level this is mockery based on the obvious chronological disparity between Jesus and Abraham. At another level it is asking the question 'By what right do *you* claim to offer this definitive interpretation of Abraham?' It is this latter question which Jesus answers:

'Truly, truly, I say to you, before Abraham was, I am.' (8:58)

A little pause for breath. Now this is not an *ex abrupto* claim of divinity as a way of resolving the argument with a bigger stick, which would simply have been blasphemous, and which is how the interlocutors interpret it. It is something much richer than that: and any commentary here is, by nature, something of a stammer.

The logic behind Jesus' answer seems to me to be this: the programme of purification from idols is simultaneously the programme of setting God free from any sort of paternal image and the practical overcoming of fratricidal fraternity. It is this fratricidal fraternity which has thrown up these idolatrous images of God. For the programme to come to its fruition, a point will have to be reached where there is no image of God left except for that of a brother. And it is only from within the learning of fraternity with the brother that God, the imageless Father, can come to be seen and imagined. This is exactly what Jesus sees himself as doing: he is that brother. For the moment he is son, which is only brother-in-potential, for the other brothers-in-potential are not yet brothers, being slaves to death. But he is present to open up for them the possibility of becoming brothers of the Son and thus sons.

The giddy-making moment in this is the appreciation that at the very end of this programme of purification from idolatry there are two possible outcomes. Either this purification is simply negative, and by emptying God out of any paternal projections derived from earthly paternity, we simply empty God out, and are left with nothing. Or else the purification is positive, and is carried out by God having been putting himself forward as on the fraternal level all along. One coming into the world as brother, so that there is a real, and positive image of God, who is brother, and permits the overcoming of fratricide by making possible a real new human fraternity. But if that is the case, if God has gradually been effecting a fraternal relocation of divinity all along, been putting himself forward as brother all along, there arrives a devastating moment in the project of purification. This is the moment when we are faced with the ultimate blasphemy considered from the viewpoint of the fratricidal projection of paternity. We are faced with the self-affirming presence of the imageless God in a human contemporary who is constructing the new sort of fraternity, but is entirely vulnerable to fratricide.

Now, here is Jesus' point: he is not only the culmination of the project, but the project itself, God made brother, offering us to become siblings, but vulnerable to fratricide. And it is this, of course, which enables him to say that he envelopes Abraham, including him as only the gratuitous initiator of the project can. Furthermore, by saying 'I AM', Jesus is literally performing the revelation which he has been describing and explaining, the gratuitous revelation of divine fraternity in the midst of fratricidal nihilism. Jesus' revelation 'I AM' is the positive enactment of his own interpretation, the moment where the divine project of the overcoming of fratricidal idolatry and the fraternal teaching about it become one.

> So they took up stones to throw at him; but Jesus hid himself and went out of the temple. (8:59)

The brother reveals himself as the God of whom the Temple is supposed to be a sign, while his brothers shore up the paternal model of the Temple, by preparing to desecrate it with an act of fratricide. I do not think it an accident that almost in the same breath as God 'comes out' as brother in the Temple, John adds two little phrases which hint at key moments of the revelation of God in the Scriptures. Jesus hides himself, echoing

> Truly, thou art a God who hidest thyself, O God of Israel, the Saviour. (Isa. 45:15)

More dramatically, Ezekiel 10 and 11 tell the story of how, in disgust at idolatry, the unthinkable happened: God went out of the Temple.

the background to Jesus' anthropology

It has been my aim to show that, within a very difficult text, there is present a very exact revelatory anthropology: an understanding of who we humans are. It is an anthropological vision which assumes that all of us are bound in to a certain sort of paternity, one where our group belonging is dependent on a number of received traditions, many of which appear to have divine backing. The divinity in question backs up inherited group belonging, giving apparent authority to those who determine who is in and who is out. Fraternity is available to those who stay within the group, going along with its apparent paternity, and agreeing to exclude those who must be excluded for the group to keep its identity.

What is new is that this sort of belonging to a group defined by an inherited paternity is shown to be an idolatrous belonging, and by idolatrous, understand a belonging demanding sacrifice. Jesus appears in the midst of such a group and, by showing up its structure for what it is, provokes it into tightening its group frontiers, into acting ever more obviously according to sacrificial type. And the threatening, destabilising element in Jesus' teaching and mode of acting out is that he refuses to concede any divine element at all to inherited group belonging. It is difficult to resist the extraordinary force of Jesus' categorical statement that we are to call no man on earth our father. But not only the statement: the revelation which goes along with it is that God himself, in order to talk to us, does so as a brother, as One on the same level as us.

Now, I want to make quite clear that I am not in the first instance having a go at the papacy or the Vatican. These institutions are frequently perceived as exercising a paternal religious teaching in the minds and hearts of the faithful, and sometimes engage in thoroughly sacrificial forms of behaviour in order to shore up their teaching, even while they claim their teaching to be at the fraternal level. Sometimes, in fact, the juxtaposition of priests being called 'father' and the pope 'Holy Father' with a sacred text explicitly forbidding this behaviour is just enough to produce the sense of wry irony and proper resistance to ecclesiastical pretension which characterises Catholicism at its best. The problem is not with these baroque excrescences, but with something which can be at least as bad in those religious and non-religious spheres where people lack such ongoing reverse reminders of the truth of the evangelical text. Our Lord does not explicitly forbid us from calling *religious* leaders 'father' – though that is obviously included in the general prohibition. Much more strikingly, he forbids us from calling *anyone* 'father'. And the most evident meaning of this is: *especially our progenitors*. I have yet to meet anyone who, however critical of Catholic hierarchical usage of the word 'father', was actually prepared consistently to ditch the normal familial use of the word.

Now I don't suppose that Jesus was much interested in the grammatical feat of eliminating a common word from everyday use, reserving the word 'Father' only for God. He does appear to have been very interested indeed in making quite sure that we learn how not to attribute anything sacred to our progenitors, whether cultural or biological, *as progenitors*. For to the degree that we do that we risk holding fast to a false form of belonging and remaining blind to our involvement in apparently sacredly inspired fratricide. If we do this, we cannot discover for ourselves, by learning to create a non-fratricidal form of fraternal living, our true paternity in God.

In teaching this, Jesus was not plucking something entirely new out of a clear blue sky. He was being faithful to some of the most astonishing passages of Jewish Scripture. The fraternal overcoming of fratricidal relations locked into bad paternity is fleshed out in the story of how Rebekah's favourite, Jacob, learned fraternity with Isaac's favourite, Esau. Before he was able to be reconciled with Esau, whom he had tricked out of birthright and paternal blessing, and in order to face up to his own rivalry, which was the root of the problem, Jacob finds himself wrestling with God. Mysteriously God is manifest in clearly human form, *at the same level* (Gen. 32:22–30) as Jacob. It is in this wrestling that Jacob 'prevails with God', and realises that he has seen God *face to face*. He has overcome not God, but his own rivalry. After this mysterious struggle he was able to recognise his wrongdoing and look his brother Esau *in the face*. Thus he was able to learn to live in peace with his brother – and become Israel, a community of brethren.[6]

Even more gloriously the same dynamic is shown in the story of Joseph (Gen. 37—50). There is a clear symmetry in the story between Jacob/Israel who is shown up at the beginning as a 'bad dad', and Pharaoh, who is shown at the end as a 'good dad'. Jacob's favouritism induced rivalry among his sons – favouritism is a way in which a father lowers himself to the level of just another quarrelling brother. And in fact at first Jacob deservedly does not enjoy the love and respect of his sons. Joseph is sacrificed within the fratricidal logic of bad paternity but comes to discover himself capable of building fraternity from beyond his own annihilation at the hands of his brethren. He is able to do so from a far-off land. Not only is he able to give his brethren abundance, but does so living under the grace of an entirely new father figure, one who is in no way in rivalry or envious, and doesn't even appear with any personality traits at all. This is because, just as in Jesus' teaching about God in the gospels, he has pacifically entrusted all authority to Joseph, to be exercised fraternally. That the Hebrew Scriptures are able to imagine the Pharaoh of Egypt, by the time the story was written very definitely a symbol of 'the

---

6. I am indebted for this insight to Angel Barahona, whose article 'From Cain and Abel to Esau and Jacob' is forthcoming in *Contagion* 8 (Spring 2001).

enemy', as the 'good dad' entirely without rivalry, is simply outside any normal structure of cultural writing or understanding. It is a sign of the presence of what we appropriately call divine revelation.

The one time Pharaoh does appear personally after he has put Joseph in charge of Egypt is as someone whose immediate reaction on hearing that *his* favourite 'son' had a father and brothers was to welcome them and give them land – the very definition of lack of envy (Gen. 47:1–12). Even more overwhelming in this story is that Joseph, acting as his own man, entirely bereft of interference from an envious father figure, but entirely supported by a gratuitous one, is able step by step to nudge his brethren out of their fratricidal logic. He tests them to see if they will sacrifice Benjamin. Finally he coaxes out of Judah's mouth what is to my mind one of the really astounding passages in any culture. This is the speech where Judah recognises his previous fratricide and refuses to go down that path again by sacrificing Benjamin, offering himself instead – the sign that he has at last learned fraternity (Gen. 44:18–34). And in doing so, he has learned to treat his father gently, not out of rivalry:

> 'For how can I go back to my father if the lad is not with me?'
> (Gen. 44:34)

The anthropology of this story, and that in Jesus' teaching are the same.

towards being given a conscience

It is clear from all this that when Jesus taught about Abraham in John 8, he was not inventing something new. He was interpreting the story of the first man to be told to 'Go from your country and your kindred and your father's house to the land that I will show you' (Gen. 12:1) in the light of the deepest tradition which gave substance to the Abrahamic project.

The programme for escaping from the idolatry of earthly paternity is not only a demand that we stop treating each other from within the belonging of sacrificial groups, and learn to stretch out to those who have no belonging, a stretching out which will tend to threaten and ultimately collapse the borders of our own groups. It is that, and we must do so if we are to be siblings of the Son, and thus discover his Father as our own. But it is much more. It is also a programme for the unbinding of our conscience from any form of paternal cultural and religious teaching.

Jesus always appears in the gospels as someone who is already living the divine paternity, and thus already treats his progenitors as on the fraternal level. So, at a tender age, he tells Joseph and Mary that he must be about his Father's business (Luke 2:41–51). He is also explicit that he considers his female progenitor from within the paradigm of his fraternity towards her and many others, and refuses the assumption that the mother–son relationship is a 'special' one escaping from his teaching about fraternity. Jesus explicitly saw his female progenitor, the guardian of his infancy and childhood, as, in the first place, his sister, and only as his 'mother' in an analogous sense that he was perfectly happy for others to occupy as well.[7] He was also clear that he saw those of his contemporaries who were progenitors as people who, even though *evil*, were capable of giving good things to their children – of satisfying their desires rather than binding them up in double binds.[8] However, what appears in Jesus' case as something that was always already in place in his consciousness, is only reached by us through a massive learning upheaval. We have to learn step by arduous step how to think and act free of our 'paternal' group belonging and how instead to live and act as ones who only have siblings, including intergenerational ones who need fraternal treatment appropriate to their age and strength.

One of the key steps in this process is the realisation that any particular instance of bad paternal and/or maternal relationship

---

7. Mark 3:31–5: 'Whoever does the will of God is my brother, and sister, and mother!'

8. Matt 7:9–11: 'What man of you . . . if his son . . . asks for a fish, will give him a serpent? If you then who are evil, know how to give good gifts to your children, how much more will your Father in heaven give good things to those who ask him!' Luke throws in an egg and a scorpion as well (Luke 11:12)!

with a son or daughter is not, as, alas, Freudian discourse has suggested to us, the result of intrinsically paternal, maternal or filial conflicts deep in our respective unconsciouses. Bad paternal and maternal relationships with sons or daughters are simply part of a package of skewed fraternity. Nothing buried in the Freudian complex is anything other than sibling rivalry – intergenerational sibling rivalry. What is profoundly liberating about this realisation is that it means that there is nothing in these conflicts that cannot be worked out *in the present* by means of learning fraternity with our contemporaries – including our intergenerational contemporaries, and especially our progenitors. Bad fraternity precedes any of our parents' relationships with us, and shapes them, to a greater or lesser degree. But that means – thank heavens – that none of us has any right to see the conflicts as 'especially' our parents' fault. All of us, including our progenitors, are born within the bad fraternity which dresses itself up as cultural and familial paternity, and all of us are equally well – or badly – placed to begin working our way out of its consequences. Any profound damage or hurt which we may well have received at the hands of the guardians of our infancy and childhood are particular instances of the package of bad fraternity which precedes those guardians, and which they, just like us, have not overcome fully enough. Nothing more.

This is an enormous relief, because we can learn to forgive fratricidal fraternity that others have exercised towards us, often convinced they were doing the right and holy thing. As sons and daughters we can never forgive paternal and maternal damage held to have formed us, because *as sons and daughters* we can never be on the same level as the 'paternal' or 'maternal'. If you have the experience of having forgiven one or both of your progenitors, or your offspring, did you not find it to be a process of becoming aware of them as people on the same level as yourself, of fraternally letting go of what seemed paternal, maternal or filial? So we can either ontologise the damage as of the sort done by progenitors to offspring or vice versa, which means we stay at the level of resentful recipients. Or we can begin to realise that the distorted paternity and maternity we received are simply particular instances of the fratricidal nature of human culture. That is to say: nothing to do with our progenitors *as progenitors* or our offspring *as off-spring*. Rather it is the case that *as brothers and sisters* we are all called to take part in the overcoming of that universal cultural tendency.

So the moment we start looking at our task as beginning to undo the effects in our own and others' lives of violent fraternity, having no one to blame, we find ourselves speaking with our own, adult, fraternal voice. At that moment also we begin to 'see through' a huge amount of what appeared to be sacred, and what appeared to be 'paternal' in the lives of our families, our culture, our countries and our religion. Indeed acceding to responsible living is strictly related to our grasp of the fraternal mutability of all inherited structures. Instead of being 'victims' of the 'dead hand of the past', or nobly regretful 'champions' of unalterable divine traditions,[9] we start to be able to treat these structures as something on the fraternal level with us, and this is true of our family life, our political structures, our national heritage and our religious institutions. And it is true whether or not they accept being so treated by us, and whether or not they reciprocate by treating us fraternally, instead of fratricidally thinking that it is right to act paternally. There is no wicked and numinous paternal 'they'. There are only brothers and sisters like ourselves: fragile receivers and mete-ers out of ambivalent and often fratricidal fraternity.

Now, here is where this is leading: what has enabled us to begin to accede to this gradual realisation that the matrix of our entire social life is *fraternal and nothing else* is the fact that God himself, the Creator of the universe, has spoken to us definitively as brother. The only authentically divine voice we have ever heard or will ever hear is spoken to us not through the clouds and mystifications of some paternal schema, demanding sacrifice, laying

---

9. 'Even if I wanted to change this teaching, you must see that I can't because it doesn't depend on me, it is an unalterable divine command.' Ah, Abraham, Abraham, raise the knife to your son's throat, but don't look around you too hard, lest you see a ram caught in a thicket, and suspect that the divine command may change!

down prohibitions, or fixing the limits of our belonging. The only authentically divine voice we have ever heard taught us to move beyond all that, speaking to us uniquely and rigorously at the fraternal level. This is the point of Jesus (among many other Jewish commentators before and since) reading Abraham and Moses and the Prophets *against* sacrifice, and as brothers on the level with us. It means that *there is no paternal divine teaching*, no paternal voice to which we must pay heed independently of the fraternal voice. The only places in the gospels where the paternal voice of God appears independently of Jesus is precisely to indicate that it is to Jesus that we must listen, and that in him God is glorified.[10]

Now the phrase 'there is no paternal divine teaching' sounds so drastic that I wish to issue a caveat. This is not so as to diminish the phrase, but to protect some of its force by making it more difficult for it to be regarded as simply a piece of radical chic. I do not of course mean that there is no divine teaching in the Christian faith concerning God the Father. When all is said and done there is in fact little else! Certainly the whole point of this chapter is to make the stunning truth of God's parenthood more, not less, available. So, of course there is in the New Testament a huge amount of teaching concerning praying to the Father, imitating the Father, being rewarded by the Father and so on that is fundamental to the Christian faith. The point I want to drive home is that it is never a *paternal voice* which teaches us these things. It is rigorously a fraternal one. For if we are to accede to allowing ourselves to be loved by a Father entirely without rivalry, one who does not want sacrifice but mercy, it is by learning a new mode of fraternity that we will do so. We hope indeed to come to know ourselves loved as children of a non-rivalrous Parent, but the voice which leads us to that knowledge is entirely at the fraternal level, unbinding our sibling rivalry and fratricide. If it is a paternal voice teaching us, it will bear within it too many of the ambivalent tones of previous cultural belonging. It will limit the

---

10. Matt 17:5; Mark 9:7; John 12:28. See also Matt 3:13–17; Mark 1:9–11; Luke 3:21–2.

fraternity which is 'acceptable', and we will eventually discover that it was not the divine voice.

This teaching has very marked consequences for our understanding of the development of conscience. If the divine voice speaks to us only at the fraternal level, then we will receive the conscience, which also means consciousness, of being sons and daughters of God, only, and strictly, in the degree to which a new 'I' is called forth in each of us by our learning to listen to the fraternal voice which addresses us as 'you' and calls us into being. And only and strictly in the degree to which we learn to say 'you' and thus call forth each other's 'I', at the fraternal level. In every case, this will mean the hard work of our learning to distinguish between those voices which would address us as 'you' in a non-fraternal tone, a paternal tone, or that of a resentful child, masking fratricide, and the authentically fraternal voice calling us out of fratricide. It will also simultaneously mean the hard work of our learning to say 'you' only ever from fraternity, learning how not to pass over into someone else's 'I' the ambiguous vestiges of paternity which mask our fratricide.

To give you an example of this: one of the best fraternal critiques I have received of my own writing pointed out to me that I do not give enough space for the proper anger which annihilated gay people feel in the face of the intransigence and hypocrisy of religious authority. This criticism goes deep. For it is true that I am, for reasons of my own history, so frightened of being blown away by my own anger at my own experience of annihilation, and thus losing the possibility of engaging in the sort of constructive conversation which might make me count as a person, that I am perhaps over-desperate to deny the pain and instead rush to accede to rational and courteous discourse. I probably would never have become a theologian but for this dynamic! The result is that, out of my own denial of pain, I sometimes write in a way which makes others feel guilty for not moving as fast as I into seeking to avoid violent victimary language. I might be bullying you into short-circuiting your own process of dealing with your reaction to pain undergone. It is one thing for a theologian to attempt to point the way towards a certain sort of adulthood of faith. It is another for there to be a hidden and unpitying voice of cultural paternity (part military, part English boarding-school, part Conservative party) just beneath the surface of my own tone barking at me, and through me, at others: 'Grow up, and stop feeling sorry for yourself!' In short, I have little doubt that even in my attempt to talk fraternally I am passing over into someone else's 'I' the ambiguous vestiges of paternity which mask my own fratricidal tendency. All of us sit in a process of learning our way beyond mechanisms such as this.

Typically, we very rarely manage to imagine God's voice as speaking to us entirely at the fraternal level. We very rarely believe rigorously in the incarnate Word of God as God's definitive form of address to us. We persist in taking some of what Jesus taught, and then bolstering up our paternity by quick recourse to hastily constructed arguments derived from some independent source and attributed to God as Creator, sustainer of eternal laws, and deliverer of special prohibitions which lead to sacrificial belonging. In short, we do not test all things and hold fast to what is good (1 Thess. 5:19–22), but very quickly compromise God in the tradition of men (Mark 7:8) and protect ourselves from learning fraternity. But in doing so, we are not being more, but much less faithful to the gospel which has been entrusted to us by the first of many brothers (Rom. 8:29).

a fraternal consideration . . .

This teaching on Jesus' fraternal relocation of God and its consequences for the proper development of conscience manifestly has implications for all Christians. For instance, it suggests a self-critical route by which we can work our way out of our tradition of 'divinely' guaranteed misogyny that is somewhat different from a massive victimary investment in criticising 'patriarchy'. As our conscience becomes free, so our imagination is unbound from reaction and we become able to create new ways of being together. Nevertheless, it is as a Catholic who is gay that I have come to these things, and I think for gay Christians the teaching has particular consequences, one of which I would like, briefly, to hint at.

Do we find ourselves reacting to official teaching, to official intransigence, and to official incapacity for adult discussion in any of our churches with resentment, dismay or a desire to provoke? This, rather than with healthy anger at injustice, and sorrow at the plight of our brethren caught in a trap whose nooses of their own making they keep pulling tighter and tighter? If so, then there is a good chance that we too are still bound in our consciences into the paternal and sacrificial mode of fraternity which we so easily detect in official words and actions. It may be that we are stuck in this way out of the weakness of those who have found ourselves annihilated, and have yet to learn to live with the strengths and limitations of our own anger. In which case, I hope, for my own sake, that little blame attaches to it. But as we become stronger, more capable of words, happier in our discovery that God does indeed love us, then might it not be important that we learn to withhold the excessive tribute of our resentment from something which doesn't really exist?

The one sure way to prevent church teaching from being changed except in the direction of more closed-mindedness is to pander to the paranoia which undergirds it by playing its game. While those upholding the teaching and those attacking it are locked in the world of fratricide disguised as sacred paternity, with all its bizarre twists, then no one gets anywhere. Instead we get 'innocent children' trying to gang up on wicked 'father-figures', or a 'victim' hierarchy claiming that it has never hurt anyone, but protesting its need to speak the 'divine truth' against those who would sully and 'affront' it. This has nothing to do with the revelation of God in Christ – except as a parody of it, on both sides.[11]

The real discussion about church teaching will only really get

---

11. It would be traditional to hold that hierarchs, supposedly beneficiaries of the divine gift of faith, are far more likely on the Last Day to be held responsible for having self-importantly portrayed themselves and the Church as 'victims', thus falling straight into paranoid parody. Those who do not know that God is the self-giving victim, without self-importance,

under way when we have done the hard work of ensuring that both our listening and our speaking are only at the fraternal level – never mind who else is shouting, or refusing to talk, in either case fratricidally. It is only by attending to this development of our own fraternal listening that we'll be able to sift through the hateful rhetoric and the half-baked philosophical traps, stop living in reaction to them, and really hear whatever it is that our Lord actually does want to say to us. His voice is something which has so far successfully been drowned out by what we mistook for 'paternal divine voice'. Since it is increasingly clear that that voice is a 'paternal' double bind, and doesn't appear capable of the open-endedness and unwillingness to bind which characterises fraternal teaching and is the hallmark of the Gospel, maybe it had indeed better be relegated to the category of 'noises offstage'. But that relegation should not, I suspect, be spoken of lightly. If it is not the fruit of a process of discernment which involves moving out of reaction into fraternity, then all we will have done is scandalised those brethren whose weakness of conscience keeps them dependent on a sacrificial paternity (1 Cor. 8:12). In that case, however free we may feel, we will have done them, and thus ourselves, no favours at all.

---

who never retaliates when slighted, cannot be held to the same measure of accountability. But then again, being able to speak honestly as a gay man nowadays is such a privilege, considered in the light of what this planet has offered our predecessors in earlier generations, and what it still offers many of our contemporaries, that maybe our very process of having discovered dignity should teach us accountability when we are tempted to behave in this way . . .

spluttering up the beach
to Nineveh . . .

fleeing from the word

Jonah, if you remember, was a most unwilling prophet. The word of God came to him, telling him to go and preach against the great city of Nineveh, for its wickedness had come up before God. Jonah immediately went in the opposite direction. Rather than heading across the Fertile Crescent to Nineveh, he rushed down to Jaffa and booked passage on a ship. Scripture tells us that

> he went on board, to go with them to Tarshish away from the presence of the LORD. (Jonah 1:3)

Not only was Tarshish quite the wrong way to go, it was a serious attempt to get away from the presence of the living God. Why was Jonah so frightened? What was it about Nineveh that scared him? We get a clue later, when Jonah gets cross with Nineveh for repenting on cue. He hated Nineveh. He wanted it to be destroyed. He knew it to be wicked. Why go somewhere which should be destroyed and shout at its inhabitants to change their ways? They will probably give the messenger a rough time! Jonah did not appreciate that he was being sent to Nineveh for the good of the people there, yes, but also for his own good. At the end of the story he tells God that he hadn't wanted to go because he knew God was a loving God, and was too angry at the thought that the people of Nineveh would get off so lightly. But we're not told that at this stage.

Jonah is the son of Amittai, which is to say son of 'My Truth'.

So the whole story is set up from the beginning as one in which someone who is wedded to his own truth comes to learn God's truth the hard way. He knows what is wrong with the gentile world, but was at first able to hear only half of the word of God. He heard it as he was able to receive it: as a stern word of rebuke that he was to pass on to others. That was the state of his soul. Luckily, God had chosen someone who, invincible as he was in his righteousness, knew perfectly well that it is a terrible thing to fall into the presence of the living God, and suspected, at some level of his being that if, he, Jonah, were to obey God, God would certainly break through the carapace of ordered adhesion to true religion, and come into contact with a much more turbulent, stormy world, the world of shame and fear and hatred that is the underside of all ordered righteousness. Shame is a compulsion which heeds only one command: flee! And Jonah fled.

Thank heaven for Jonah's flight! Think how much more damage is caused by those who are not vulnerable to their own shame, who really do manage to fool themselves that their righteousness and God's are cut from the same cloth. Something in Jonah's being was vulnerable to the suspicion that the word of the living God would wreak havoc with his own carefully covered hatred and fear – the suspicion that that hatred of others and fear of himself were aspects of the same as yet unredeemed dimension of his own life. In that vulnerability was his flight, and through it, ultimately, he was reached so as to be taught how to be a bearer of God's word.

Andrew Sullivan has a line which catches this dynamic exactly: 'Shame forces you prematurely to run away from yourself; pride forces you prematurely to expose yourself. Most gay lives, I'm afraid, are full of an embarrassing abundance of both.'[1] Faced with the prospect of shouting at an uncomprehending Nineveh with the hollow pride of those who love neither themselves nor those whom they must convince, Jonah, who knew at the root of his heart that he had been given something to say, went, as many of us do, into exile. Shame forced him prematurely to run away from the presence of God. He didn't yet know that the presence of

---

1. *Love Undetectable* (London, Chatto & Windus, 1998), p. 92.

God is where he is as someone loved: in fleeing the presence of God, he was running away from himself.

Now someone who has run away from themselves is not easy company. They are not at ease with themselves, and other, less complicated, people easily pick up the vibes. If we are in violence towards ourselves, that violence is magnified and projected on to, and picked up by, others. Jonah in full flight is in the centre of a storm, yet he is asleep in the bowels of the ship. That is, he doesn't appreciate at all that there is a storm going on, even less that it has something to do with him. Like so many who are in flight, he has managed to cut himself off from the pain and violence which is his, so the violence rages around a superficially imperturbable and serene centre. Jonah's shipmates, who are after all his hosts, are not fooled. Like the good, straightforward pagans they are, unbothered by the responsibility of the command not to hide behind sacred structures but to face the living God, they react as good pagans know how to when threatened with a violence beyond their ken. They cast lots, for they have known from time immemorial that if they sacrifice the troublemaker, then peace will ensue.

Quite rightly the lot falls on Jonah. Of course: he is the outsider, not one of them. Furthermore, he has the sense of superiority of the Yahwist in gentile company. In short, he is the obvious recipient of the short straw. When the worried sailors form an unanimous circle, their fingers pointing at him, Jonah understands what's going on. He draws himself up with all the superiority of his birthright and tells them that he is a Hebrew, with true access to what is really going on. After all, it is the Hebrew God who is in charge of all that surrounds them. The shocked fingers both signal the unique excellence of the victim-to-be – from his point of view he is much better than they – and the unique awfulness of his transgression, about which the sailors need no explanation: the violence which has engulfed them is clear indication that something terrible is afoot.

Let us imagine Jonah, waking from his sleep, but wakened only at one level of his being. The shouts of the panicking sailors summon up in him at least the 'pride' part of his being – the knowledge of his faith and his privilege in having been addressed by God. A good Jewish prophet knows how to react to violent interaction with pagans: you stand up for your uniqueness and get yourself lynched. Isn't that what it's all about? He hasn't yet allowed the word of God to get to the deeper part of him, his shame, where he might be loved, and so stop causing all this chaos. At that level he is still running away. He is not yet aware of the real source of the turbulence, and so can't act out of the calm of one who is loved.

So Jonah himself suggests to them that they cast him overboard, and all will be at peace. In flight from bearing the word of the living God to its appointed destination, he knows at least the surface story of what must happen to a good Hebrew prophet: he gets lynched, and that's how he gets to be canonised as the good guy. His hosts, however, are savvy enough in their paganism to appreciate that one really shouldn't sacrifice someone so easily. It probably occurred to them that the self-importance of their guest was at least a contributing factor to his being so obviously a candidate for victimhood. In other words, that he was asking for it, and one shouldn't yield too easily to playing the part of the lynch-mob for the benefit of stoking someone's prophet-martyr complex.

So, with a decency not to be despised, they do their best to pay no attention to Jonah's confession, and carry on trying to get to calmer waters under their own power. To no avail – the crisis which Jonah's flight from himself and the presence of God has brought upon them is far stronger than one with which they can cope. In very truth, their lives have been thrown into tumult by something much more turbulent than a normal social life can know about, let alone negotiate peacefully – Jonah's resistance to the determination of the living God to get through to the heart of someone he loves. As the loved one flails about, trying hard to avoid that love, he unwittingly causes real chaos around about him.

Finally, the sailors give up. They recognise that the whole situation is beyond their puny mechanisms for putting things right, and agree to sing to Jonah's score. With an appropriate covering prayer, whose entire purpose is to transform what they suspect to be a Jonah-inspired murder into a divinely inspired sacrifice which will bring all the trouble to an end, they consent to cast Jonah overboard, and do so. Immediately, of course, peace and calm are re-established, and they recognise, as good pagans after a lynch sacrifice, that they have been visited by a transgressive god of extraordinary power – one who brings chaos, and then brings order out of a violent sacrifice. So they quickly do what good pagans should: they reproduce the violent lynch in a liturgical sacrifice, and show their fearful adhesion to this new order by making vows:

> Then the men feared the LORD exceedingly, and they offered a sacrifice to the LORD and made vows. (Jonah 1:16)

At this point these delightful stage extras sail off into the sunset, presumably to a barbarian island north of France and east of Ireland, where to this day their religion is alive and well, and mistakenly thought to have something to do with the living God.

Meanwhile what about Jonah? Remember where he had been before: half of him had been awakened – the pride half: just enough for him to put up a good stand on behalf of his religious heritage, orthodoxy and the true faith. His shame half, the half that had led him into flight, was still unrecognised, and so was playing its compelling role in the drama, urging the sailors on into throwing him overboard. To be killed as a martyr is, after all, a highly convenient way of sorting out the conflict of pride and shame – the pride tells you that this is what should happen to a good man and a prophet, the shame is a dishonest consent to that. It says: 'I hate myself and cannot live with myself, but on the other hand, I know that it is wrong to kill myself. What if I manage to set it up so that I get killed "in the course of duty"? Then of course, the only story that people will read will be the unambiguous one, the story of the prophet and martyr. Who need know of the suicidal shame that was, in truth, driving my story with its violent and unreachable compulsions? Who need know that I was worse than a pagan, for I was co-opting them into my terrible drama, while allowing them to be blamed for it, when all I really wanted to do was to kill myself?'

Such, we may imagine, were the conflicting facets of Jonah's soul as he pitched over the side of the vessel, and into death.

Jonah, of course, did not have the advantage of having read the book of Jonah, and so knew nothing of what is, for us, the most memorable element of the story:

> And the LORD appointed a great fish to swallow up Jonah; and Jonah was in the belly of the fish three days and three nights.
>
> (Jonah 1:17)

Jonah had thought he was plunging into death. There must have been something of relief in his descent. At last it was all over. But it was not. Unknown to him, while he thought he had engineered his death, setting it up so as to avoid finding himself in the presence of the Lord, God had a different idea. His plan was to tag along while Jonah would not allow himself to be reached, and then, when he had plunged into the deep, to hold him in being while he was devoured by all that tumultuous fear, hatred, and darkness which had glowered beneath the surface of his faith. The great fish is nothing other than God holding Jonah in being in the midst of the darkness and fear. It is as if, in the midst of a suicidal depression, there where even a person of faith can find no foothold, where there is no remedy, where the person's very being is disintegrating and there is no light, nor even a tunnel at the end of which a light might be, just a downward sucking whirlpool which drags you out of being, even yet you are held in being by a force which is not your own. I imagine the great fish to have been transparent, so that Jonah was not aware for a good part of those three days and nights that he was anything other than being lost, utterly swept away by forces whose swirling he had always dreaded. He could see and feel the darkness, and yet not be aware that, in the midst of that, he was being stitched together, reached, held at a depth which he had been unable to imagine.

Yet, as the storm of destruction went on, Jonah eventually found that he *had* been reached, that, in the midst of all that, there was, after all, a real 'he' that could be reached, that could be held in being, that could be put together. So, as the three days and nights went by — maybe years in which the suicidal depression had left him flailing without being or belonging — for the first time he finds himself able to do something utterly new:

> Then Jonah prayed to the Lord his God from the belly of the
> fish. (Jonah 2:1)

Earlier God had addressed his word to Jonah, but the word of
God was not heard as a word is heard by a person, it was heard
as a goad which produced the Pavlovian response of flight. Jonah
hadn't been up to complaining of God raping him, like Jeremiah,
had not even tried to excuse himself on the ground that he was a
man of unclean lips, like Isaiah, before getting on with his task.
He had just bolted. Now, in the depths, where he has been
reached, and an 'I' put together that is capable of dialogue, he
prays to one who is no longer described as just 'Lord', or 'God',
but, for the first time, 'the Lord *his* God'. And he comes out with
one of those psalms of gratitude for deliverance from the depths
of distress, with all the usual imagery: the pit, the flood, weeds
wrapped around his head, definitively cast out and so forth. When
he gets to the end of his psalm he says something which is both a
bit of a surprise, and yet what it is all about. The RSV translates
it:

> 'Those who pay regard to vain idols forsake their true loyalty.
> But I with the voice of thanksgiving will sacrifice to thee; what
> I have vowed I will pay. Deliverance belongs to the Lord!'
> (Jonah 2:8–9)

However, that's not quite what it means: that still sounds like a
self-righteous Yahwist being one-up on the gentiles. It would be
a little closer to the Hebrew to translate the passage:

> 'Those who hold fast to what is vain apostasise from their own
> lovingkindness, but I will sacrifice unto *thee* with the voice of
> thanksgiving; I will pay what I have vowed.'

These are the words of someone who has been reached, and has
realised that he had been holding on to vanity, and so had apost-
asised from his own being where alone he might be loved, but
now is turning towards the source of that being with the voice of
thanksgiving. When Jonah announces that deliverance is of the
Lord,

the LORD spoke to the fish and it vomited out Jonah upon the dry land. (Jonah 2:10)

It would not be impious to observe that the very moment that Jonah was able to speak as one who had ceased to apostasise from his very own being, in that moment the fish had served its purpose, and Jonah had made it to dry land.

on the beach

In the rest of the story, Jonah gets to Nineveh, and scarcely opens his mouth when the whole city goes into an over-the-top repentance routine. Even the cattle get decked out in sackcloth in what must be one of the campest scenes in Scripture. Jonah is furious – in fact the whole thing is an elaborate Jewish joke in which God camps Nineveh up completely just to get through to the anger of his humourless prophet. Finally God does break through to the point where Jonah is able to confess his desire to die, the real nihilist in comparison with whom the sinners of Nineveh are guileless. Then God is able to plant in this soul of a wounded prophet, in the form of the unanswered question with which the book ends, a hint of the depth and breadth and tenderness of his love.

> 'and should not I pity Nineveh, that great city, in which there are more than a hundred and twenty thousand persons who do not know their right hand from their left, and also much cattle?'
> (Jonah 4:11)

But it is no purpose of mine to do a reading of the entire book – which, let it be said, is to this day the appointed reading for Yom Kippur, the bleakest penitential day of the Jewish year. I want to stop on the beach, since that is where I find myself, and ask you to join me there as I bounce off you some of my splutterings, as we gather ourselves and head for Nineveh.

Jonah's story is exactly the classic story of death and rebirth – so much so that Jesus is on record as having used it as the only

sign which would be given to his interlocutors.[2] I bring it to you
here because I have found myself inscribing my own story into it
and am sure that I am not alone. My own story has been one in
which I knew at some level, since the wrenching experience of
falling in love with a school colleague when I was nine years old,
that the word of God was one of love. But as I grew I was unable
to allow myself to hear it in the depths of my being. Those depths
were utterly prisoner to the voices of hatred which form us as gay
people, the lynch shout of the school playground, magnified into
adult tales of horror at the sort of people we are becoming, and
canonised by an ecclesiastical voice which has been so tied up in
all this that it has been incapable of discerning between the voice
of the world and the voice of God. So it says: love, and do not
love; be, and do not be. The voice of God has been presented as
a double bind, which is actually far more dangerous than a simple
message of hate, since it destabilises being into annihilation, and
thinks that annihilation to be a good thing.

And of course, the true horror is not that there is a 'they' out
there, doing this to a pure and innocent 'us', but that we are all
deeply personally involved in the 'they', finding it both necessary
and apparently righteous to hold on to vanities and apostasise from
the source of lovingkindness. Even when, deep down, we may
suspect, and then repress, the utterly destabilising possibility that
whoever God may be, he cannot be involved in all this. The result
is that at some time our 'I's are likely to have been fully consenting
participants in the hatred and fear. Often it is those of us whose
conscience is worst who are most drawn to, most defensive of,
and most likely completely to identify with, the sternest and most
watertight expressions of religiously or politically orthodox hatred,
hoping to whitewash all our ambivalence by turning ourselves into
crusading martyrs for the cause of some righteousness which we
know, deep down, will never be ours.

In my own case, the exile into which so many gay men, at
least, send ourselves, as our battle between pride and shame wags
our lives like some unremitting tail on a hapless dog, was a real

2. Matt. 12:39–41; 16:4; Luke 11:29–32.

geographical one, acted out a whole ocean away over many, many years. Like Jonah, I managed to set myself up to be thrown overboard in a storm which was at least in part my own, and like Jonah, I found that just where I thought that I had at last managed to get myself thrown completely away, I found myself caught and held through the depths in which the utterly terrifying and yet completely gentle, unambiguous 'yes' of God started to suggest into being the consciousness of a son, to bring forth the terrifying novelty of an unbound conscience.

I find myself having been vomited up on the shore, and wondering where on earth is Nineveh, and what on earth to say to it. As I stumble up the shore, spitting out remnants of salt water, astounded to be alive, let alone to be a human being, there's so much to be worked out, and I come to you for help, to ask you to join me in my splutterings.

elements of the birth of a catholic conscience

I'd like to stop and think a little about the novelty I described, that of the consciousness of a son or daughter, the unbound conscience. This is really quite extraordinary. For normally we think of conscience as to do with morally informed decisions or dilemmas, and consciousness as to do with awareness of being, even though the two are the same word in most Latin languages. Here I am talking about a being-held-in-being that is not over against anything at all, a state of being that is simply not frightened of not being. And rather than being worried about whether or not certain things are right or wrong, is excitedly curious about what I am being given, as part of a becoming whose parameters I can neither measure nor imagine. And not being able to measure or imagine this means that I'm spluttering about, not really quite sure what life project I am to build, because not really sure what story constructively to tell.

The old story was easy to tell, because it was always a story over against others, with goodies and baddies, the taking of positions, and the desire to be a hero or a victim, or both at the same time. The new story has no clear script, though it does have a short preface: the preface is one of being killed, and finding oneself held in a life that can no longer be destroyed.

Another part of this birth of the consciousness of a son, is that it is simultaneously the birth of the consciousness of a brother. For me at least, part of my exile was never being able to say 'we', never belonging or feeling quite part of anything through childhood, school, university, religious life. In 1995 I had the extraordinary good fortune to find myself in Chicago, attending the gay parish mass organised by AGLO, with its regular attendance of between three and four hundred men and women. Not only was this the first time in my life that I had ever been to church because I wanted to, rather than out of some mysterious obedience (and this after seven years of priesthood). It was the first time I had ever been to a liturgy in which I was an invited guest at the party, rather than a tolerated spectator at someone else's party. A principal effect of this was that I found myself able for the first time ever to say 'we' and actually mean it, relax into it, relish it, and roll around in it.

Shortly after this experience I read a Holocaust survivor's description of the lengths to which the captors went to destroy any possible sense of 'we' among the inmates. Where people could be reduced to individuals, they were stripped of their humanity. Where people managed a 'we', their humanity was indomitable even when their lives were so easily destroyed. Yet the ecclesiastical package of doctrine and practice, classifying us as defective heterosexuals, recommending and institutionalising the closet, and refusing any suggestion that we be treated as a class, and therefore with a respect according to who we are rather than what it is feared that we might do, has had as its effect, wittingly or unwittingly, this constant reduction of our humanity. How much more extraordinary, then, is the fact that the discovery of the conscience of son and brother for a gay man should be the discovery of the most profoundly Catholic sense of conscience. For this is not the heroic romantic conscience, an 'I' all alone against a wicked church or world. This indestructible conscience of a 'we' beyond being killed is the very possibility of Church as sign of an as-yet-unimagined Kingdom.

A friend has suggested to me that what I experienced in this birth of a hitherto unsuspected 'we' was merely the solidarity of the suffering group. I can imagine such a solidarity, but that is not what I was feeling, for there was in it no sense of group limits, of a group over against other groups, even of a group over against ecclesiastical structures. It was part of the birth of a Catholic conscience: that 'I' is only possible as part of a potentially limitless, and hence universal 'we' and that 'we' are being called into a playful, exciting, responsible construction of a new creation.

I bring this up, because, as I stagger up the beach I find myself becoming aware of, and coming into contact with other tentative shore-treaders, cast-ups from analogous storms, vomitees of similar whales. Are we huddling together for comfort, sharing the solidarity of the survivor, with the temptation to wallow in what has happened, so that what we share is a mutually comforting self-pity? I suspect that this is not what it's about at all. If we have come through death and find ourselves born again and held in being at a level which we never imagined, this is of itself a forward-looking thing. For the amazement is not that we have survived: in one sense we haven't. We've been killed, lost a being, and find ourselves being given a new one. No, the amazement is that it is our experience of being killed which both empowers and obliges us to learn to tell a new story at a depth and in a way which actually makes it good news for others. Remember, we have not been asked to preach resentfully to the sailors on the boat, but to Nineveh. *And God adores Nineveh so much that he would not have us talk to it until we're able to imagine it as utterly lovable*, so that we find ourselves thrilled with all the transformations in that great city, which God, who sends us as a few labourers into a huge harvest which is doing pretty well without us, is bringing about before we even open our mouths.

hints of a new creation

As part of my splutterings, I would like to give a tentative example of this dynamic: among the forces which we have found contributing to our death has been a particular sort of understanding and use of the doctrine of creation. You all know what I'm talking about: creation has been presented as part of a moral story which goes something like this: God created everything good, and in particular God created male and female as complementary to each other. Original sin happened, so the order of creation, with its natural laws of flourishing as we grow towards the Creator, has been severely corrupted. Luckily, Jesus was sent along, and by paying the infinite price of agreeing to die so as to cancel out the infinite debt which humanity had amassed against God by perverting his creation, he saved us. This means that our lives now consist in being empowered to recover and live out the original order of creation, a task which is arduous but possible. Since in the original order of creation, male and female were made complementary to each other and told to multiply, it is manifest that any other form of coupling is intrinsically disordered and must of its nature be a partaker of the order of original sin, not of the order of renewed creation. Therefore, while many of us may be weak as regards avoiding particular incidents of inappropriate coupling, these can be forgiven so long as they are not justified. However, any attempt to justify any other form of coupling must be resisted as a serious offence against the objective truth of the order of creation, and ultimately one which could exclude us from heaven.

Now, this is a pretty watertight argument, and the moment an argument is watertight, a responsible intellect has to wonder whether this can really be a theological argument at all. Curiously, I don't want to go down the path of arguing with it, since I suspect that to do so is to stand on the beach shaking a fist at the sailors on board the long-departed ship. That is to say it is likely to be an argument born from resentment, not from grace. It is furthermore the case that there is no point arguing with a watertight argument, since those who produce such arguments are, by definition, the sort of people whose first reaction when challenged by something different is to see it as a threat, and to circle the wagons. It is only when the Indians ride on by without paying them any attention that they may be drawn out of their circle and nudged by a timorous curiosity into the free flow of grace. And if they don't come out, judging an invitation to play to be a threat to their goodness, well, that's God's problem, not ours, and they are well in his hands.

No, I'd rather look at it as we find ourselves and each other on the beach, wondering at how our experience at the hand of this story of creation-as-moral-package leaves us in an extraordinarily good situation to prepare our words for Nineveh. I suspect I am not alone in understanding that this moral package, which seems an expression of Christian orthodoxy, is very much at work in what has killed us. However many caveats are put into it concerning the distinction between acts and orientation, this package grinds down on us and says: 'as you are, you are not really part of creation. While it is true that for heterosexual people their longings, desiring, seeking after flourishing and sense of what is natural really do correspond to the order of creation, however much they may need pruning and refining on their path of salvation, this is not true for you. Your longings, desiring, seeking after flourishing and sense of what is natural, however they be pruned and refined through experiences of partnership and love, have absolutely no relationship with creation. There is no analogy between them and creation. For you creation is a word whose meaning you simply cannot and do not know from experience. Since everything most heartfelt that you take to be natural is intrinsically disordered, it is only by a complete rejection of your very hearts that you may come to know something of what is meant by creation. Until such a time as this happens, limp along, holding fast with your minds to the objective truth about a creation which can have no subjective resonance for you, and when you are dead, you will enter into the Creator's glory.'

I suspect that all of us have, to some extent or other, allowed this package to bear down on us, have interiorised it, and have allowed it to chew deep down into our souls. It is part of the theological double bind: love, but do not love; be, but do not be, which I mentioned earlier. This is a profoundly destabilising force, since over time it means that our lives are not real lives, our loves are not real loves, our attempts to build stable and ordered relationships have no real worth, our minds and hearts can only produce sick fruit, not worth listening to or countenancing, let alone receiving or blessing. We are not children in a garden, we are living blasphemies, and since with every footfall we tread illicitly on a sacred lawn, it would be better not to tread at all, let alone walk confidently and make something of our stay. Many of us experience this as having killed us.

But here's the part which interests me: those who are killed are free from their killer, and can stand back and wonder what it was all about, not with a view to pointing out what was wrong with the story, but with a view to rescuing and revivifying what is right. Let me say this more strongly: where we have found ourselves killed by forces which include a blasphemous and sacrificial understanding of creation, as we come to find ourselves held by God in a being which is immune from death, so we are in a quite extraordinary position to begin to provide something new to offer Nineveh, its people and its cattle: an emerging understanding of creation that is tied in with the sense of an utterly gratuitous being-held-in-being over against nothing at all. For this understanding, the particularly privileged starting point is that of those whom the apparent order of creation has reduced to nothing at all. I think St Paul was onto this when he told the Corinthian community:

> For consider your call, brethren; not many of you were wise according to worldly standards, not many were powerful, not many were of noble birth; but God chose what is foolish in the world to shame the wise, God chose what is weak in the world to shame the strong, God chose what is low and despised in the world, *even things that are not*, to bring to nothing things that are, so that no human being might boast in the presence of God. (1 Cor. 1:26–9)

We are in fact set free to begin to reimagine creation starting from our position as ones who, though a thing that is not, have found ourselves held in being by a force of invincible gratuity depending on nothing at all, part of no argument, simply giving life out of nothing. And this, let it be clear, is not only a permission to jump up and play, but is also an invitation to rescue a part of the Good News that has fallen prisoner to Babylon.

There are few more important dimensions of the Good News than the access which it gives us to our Creator as our Father, and to the sense of creation as of a given and undeserved participation in an extraordinary and constructive adventure out of nothing, the shape and fulfilment of which becoming and flourishing is as yet very difficult to sense, the rules and natural laws of which are discovered by its participants as they develop. And, wonder of wonders, we who were treated as 'not-part-of his creation' are beginning to discover ourselves as 'delighted-in co-workers in my creation' (cf. Isa. 62:3–5).

Again, what is extraordinary about this is not that it is a secret gift to us poor downtrodden queers. But rather that God is using his unspeakable creative vitality to make out of what seemed like an excrescence on the face of creation what it really has been all along: a delighted-in, precious and valuable part of his creation which is able to offer to others a quickening of their awareness of what an adventure it is to be a child created from nothing! You have heard it said, 'The stone which the builders rejected has become the head of the corner' (Ps. 118:22). But I say to you, 'Unless we find ourselves sharing in the being rejected, we have no sense of the coming into being of the head of the corner.' And if that sounds blasphemous, then perhaps it is because God who was 'counted among the transgressors' (Mark 15:28) makes a habit of waving blasphemy like a red cape before the horns of the theological wisdom of the world.

The Christian understanding of creation has been in crisis for several hundred years, a crisis provoked almost entirely by the obstinacy with which the order of creation and the order of this world, which includes its human social structures, violence and prejudices, have been yoked together. The doctrine has found itself press-ganged into service as a raped handmaiden of those for whom the status quo is sacred, and has been wielded as a weapon justifying every conceivable resistance to change. Think of arguments about the naturalness of slavery, about a pyramidal monarchical form of government being the structure most analogous to God's ordering of the world; think of the huge problems surrounding the discovery that the earth goes round the sun. Here I'm not only thinking of the row between the Roman Curia and Galileo, but also the shifts in ordinary people's imaginative vision and social relationships which the fallout from the discovery has tended to produce. Think of the battle lines drawn up as the birth of the understanding of evolution crossed those whose literalistic reading of Genesis was part of their maintenance of established order, values and so on.

And yet the increasing shrillness of those who have insisted on reading God's creation from established order, thus turning the Christian doctrine into a sacred taboo rather than a truth which sets free, has never successfully impeded the ongoing, vulnerable, tentative truth about God's creation from emerging, usually at the hands of those considered its enemies. I think we find ourselves at the tail end of this long, sad argument. I rather suspect that the issue of gay love and relationships, really rather unimportant and banal in itself, has become a sort of hermeneutical flashpoint because those who find the 'natural' order of the world and of their own lives gradually melting away beneath them under the pressure of an ever more obviously socially constructed world – and that means one for which we are invited to take responsibility – are flailing about trying to establish an order outside themselves. A crisis of identity needs someone else to be responsible for it so that they can be sacrificed and decent order and stability established, which of course it never really is. It is the mysterious centre of the Christian faith that the one who finds him- or herself to be that sacrificial hermeneutical flashpoint gets to be the one who tells, not as accusation but as forgiveness, the story of what was really going on, thus enabling many, many others the peaceful breaking of heart which allows them into the dizzy party. This means that we are coming into the wonderful position, having been sifted like wheat, of turning again to build up all our brothers and sisters (cf. Luke 22:31–2).

While in theory the teaching on the natural order of creation should fall even-handedly on straight and gay alike, in fact there is usually enough residual sense of being 'natural' among straight people for the teaching not to pursue them to the depths of their being as it tends to do with us. The result is that we have found ourselves forced through into being the advance guard of a serenity about nothing human being simply 'natural', but everything being part of a human social construct, to the extent where we can begin to imagine God quite removed from any justification of the present order, and yet ever palpitating beneath the vertiginous possibilities of the bringing of a divine order into being. This is likely, increasingly, to be immensely important as straight people face the fragility and directionlessness of what seemed natural, except it be received as an invitation to build something for which the rules of the game are being written as we go along. The collapse of the 'natural' is not the collapse of belief in creation, it is a part of clearing the human space of violent idolatry and it allows the persistent gentleness of the Creator and his invitation to adventurous participation to become apparent.

These are only splutterings – but I'm beginning to sense that we've been invited to recover something of immense value to our brothers and sisters in Nineveh, and that as we develop it, we will find that we offer to them not a rebuke, but a relief, and a relief that will be turned into a shared delight.

and so much more to come . . .

I have talked here about creation because a rediscovery of a Catholic sense of creation seems to me to be such a joyful possibility, inviting deep and far-reaching reflection – a possibility which, given time and leisure, I would love to explore more fully. But we could have talked about reading the Bible, and the same dynamic would have become apparent. One of the reasons why the gay issue has become so vastly over-important in Christian circles is because we belong to a generation that is finding it increasingly impossible to read, understand, and not be scandalised by, the Bible. So either we stop reading it, or we cover up our scandal by hanging on to an idolatrous literalism which is completely invulnerable to penetration by the living word of God. For those tempted to this latter course, once again, the unflinching holding to a peculiar literal reading of certain texts held to deal with gay people is the last gasp of a struggle, already several centuries old, desperately to try to get sense out of Scripture without letting go of power, and learning instead to read the texts from the only place from which they can fruitfully be read, which is in the company of the crucified and risen victim as he accompanies his disappointed disciples to Emmaus. Scripture as vulnerability to God rather than Scripture as protection from God!

Once again the mechanism is the same. Those who are ground down and killed by the idolatry of a certain reading are given the extraordinary pleasure and task of turning again and confirming our brethren, making it possible for the Scriptures to become the finely tuned instrument through which the Spirit of God plays words into all our hearts. In this task too we will find we have something to offer to Nineveh, something which we will be surprised to find being greeted with cries of relief.

I could go on – the same dynamic is true of the doctrine of revelation, of salvation, of the sacraments. However, I don't want to suggest that we must all become theologians. What I am suggesting is that as we take on board the gratuitousness of finding ourselves alive and on the beach leading to Nineveh, we will learn to respect what brought us there, and look back at our journey and our lynching without resentment. We will increasingly find a vivifying and unstoppable dynamic inviting us to create new structures of being together. This dynamic has in itself nothing to do with our being gay or lesbian. Yet it has been released because God himself is once again making a spectacular show of creative forgiveness out of a serious refusal on the part of humanity to accept part of itself as God-given – which is a refusal to accept being created. For this is the sort of show which can subvert hard carapaces and melt stony hearts into what we really want to be all along, but are too frightened to access – playful, spoiled children called by name to frolic and to be indulged at an enormous party.

There is coming upon us an invitation to be heralds announcing this party, so let us sit together upon the beach before Nineveh and ask each other like good Catholics how the hell we're going to put off doing anything about it.

moving on:
the exilic transformation of
anger into love

introduction

I would like to talk with you about love spurned. There are few emotions more powerful than that. Think of the rage, disorientation, loss, mourning and anger which emerge when someone who has desperately been holding on to something they love, something to which they feel utterly and viscerally bound, finally lets go, or more often than not, finally recognises that they have been kicked out. The depth of the anger is a terrifying testimony to the depth of the love, and the visceral tornado of the separation is a sure sign of how little of that love has been worked through.

Some of our reactions to positions taken by the Vatican in the sphere of 'homosexual persons' over the last few years seem to me to show signs of exactly this sense of spurned love. Gay men who have been holding on against all the odds to a Church and faith which we love in the hopes of better days, finally finding ourselves so utterly alienated that the desperate love tips over into hatred, rejection, criticism and accusation. Please note that I am not here talking about a superficial petulance and delight in being rejected. There are those for whom any sign of ecclesiastical hard-heartedness is positively welcome. It merely confirms me in my chosen identity of pious indignation, giving me a sense of religious belonging and righteousness which is strictly dependent on there being a bad guy (usually the Pope or Cardinal Ratzinger) by comparison with whom I feel good. No, I am talking about a depth and turbulence of resentment so complete that it could never be satisfied with shallow posturings. So powerful is it that it threatens completely to devour and annihilate the being of one swept up by it. I am talking about a certain sort of terrifying anger both whose power and whose impotence hints at a headlong rush into death.

What I would like to suggest is that, far from our anger being simply bad, we have in this apparently nihilistic whirlwind something of the raw material from within which the God of Israel delights in bringing into being something new. And that means something utterly non-reactive, something of the new creation whose birth in our midst we are so good at holding back.

a christian problem

In the Acts of the Apostles, there are a number of moments when the apostle Paul seems to be inscribed within just the sort of dynamic of resentment which I have described. I don't think that the man himself was like that, and we have his own writings by means of which to assess his gradual working through of various forms of resentful approach to God towards an understanding of the new creation which knows of no resentful dualisms. Nevertheless, in the Acts of the Apostles Luke gives us a number of phrases that bear witness to moments in a process which, taken by themselves, suggest a being stuck in resentful dualism. After a violent set-to in Antioch of Pisidia where Paul and Barnabas have been reviled by leading lights in the local synagogue, they speak out boldly, saying:

> 'It was necessary that the word of God should be spoken first to you. Since you thrust it from you, and judge yourselves unworthy of eternal life, behold, we turn to the Gentiles. For so the Lord has commanded us, saying, "I have set you to be a light for the Gentiles, that you may bring salvation to the uttermost parts of the earth."'

And when the Gentiles heard this, they were glad and glorified the word of God; and as many as were ordained to eternal life believed. (Acts 13:46–8)

Now that phrase 'behold, we turn to the Gentiles' is very striking. It seems redolent of just the sort of petulance that I have been describing. We can easily imagine it as a piece of resentful childishness: 'If you're going to be like that, well then, I'm off to the other side.' Behind it is the suggestion of someone who deeply, deeply loved the Jewish faith. Far from being a natural rebel or someone who took the faith lightly, he has seen something which is of the essence of that faith, and is trying to make available a profoundly conservative insight into what that faith is all about. Yet this person finds that the standard-bearers of that faith are in no way willing to recognise the authentic nature of the insight, and are scandalised by it to such an extent that they close ranks violently against him. In reaction to this, we might well expect love spurned to come up with something of the tone of 'behold, we turn to the gentiles'. I don't suppose that I'm alone in having experienced this phrase as a temptation to self-justification when faced with the sort of violent obduracy which has been the mask of ecclesiastical paralysis when it comes to re-imagining the gay question. Others will have been tempted to just this sort of petulance by other circumstances of life, but the emotion is common enough. The emotion could be reduced to this: 'If you're going to be like that, then I'm moving on.'

At the very end of the Acts of the Apostles we get something apparently rather similar. Paul gathers round him the Jewish elders in Rome, and explains how he comes to be there as a prisoner. They receive him with considerable courtesy, having heard nothing of him from other Jews, let alone evil reports, and ask him to tell them of his views. Paul expounds to them his understanding of the Kingdom of God, explaining who Jesus was in the light of Moses and the prophets. The result is a division of opinions, with some being convinced and others not. There is no suggestion of a violent disagreement of the sort we had in Antioch of Pisidia, or any attempt to whip up public opinion against Paul. Before the elders leave, Paul makes what must seem like a provocative statement:

> 'The Holy Spirit was right in saying to your fathers through Isaiah the prophet: "Go to this people, and say, You shall indeed hear but never understand, and you shall indeed see but never perceive. For this people's heart has grown dull, and their ears are heavy of hearing, and their eyes they have closed; lest they should perceive with their eyes, and hear with their ears, and understand with their heart, and turn for me to heal them." Let it be known to you then that this salvation of God has been sent to the Gentiles; they will listen.' And he lived there two whole years at his own expense, and welcomed all who came to him, preaching the kingdom of God and teaching about the Lord Jesus Christ quite openly and unhindered. (Acts 28:25–31)

In the midst of a much more peaceful meeting, Paul uses a Jewish text concerning Jewish incomprehension of God's ways to make a point not far removed from 'behold we turn to the Gentiles'. Here the key phrase is 'Let it be known to you that this salvation of God has been sent to the Gentiles; they will listen.' Again there seems to be something of petulance in the phrase '*they* will listen' – that emphasis is present in the Greek text as well: *autoi kai akousontai*. But there is also a greater serenity in the exposition – no lynch mobs, no obvious rejection, no personal reaction to rejection, merely a statement of something Paul takes to be central to the Jewish faith, which is likely to produce an inevitable division of opinions among his synagogue audience. Thereafter Paul is left in peace, and the Acts of the Apostles leaves him teaching in Rome unhindered. We know of course that he will eventually be murdered there. However, this will be the result not of Jewish intrigue, but of the frenzy of a thoroughly gentile persecution.

What I would like to suggest is that in these passages we have two phrases which are signs of slightly different moments in a process which has not yet been completed. The first is the petulant reaction to spurned love. The immensely conservative, loyal

Pharisee gradually being forced into detachment from his previous love and loyalty as he discovers that the insight he has been given makes it impossible for him to dwell within the recognisable boundaries of what he knows and loves as his home. Along with that process of detachment, an anger and a reactive quality which causes him in part at least to set up the storm which will cast him out and cause him to 'move on' in anger. The second moment is the more serene realisation that it is in the very nature of the insight he has been given that it will provoke a division. Furthermore the sort of moving on that is provoked is not the personal and resentful fruit of rejection, but a terribly painful part of the dynamic of the message itself, the fruit of a divine command.

Linked to these two moments, there is another key phrase in the Acts of the Apostles. This phrase serves as a kind of mysterious and overarching command within which our man of spurned love must work out his path from resentment to catholicity, the only way in which he can actually be faithful to the insight he has received. There is a rough session in Jerusalem (Acts 23:1–10). During this it becomes clear that Paul cannot simply be seen as having turned angrily against his former loyalty. His development beyond resentment is shown by his respect for the High Priest and by his refusing to lump his audience together as one mass of hard-hearted rebels against God. He discovers that there are already within his audience some who are close to his position, and he appeals to them, the Pharisees, who, like him, believe in the resurrection of the dead, against the Sadducees who do not hold such a belief. The result is that a violent disturbance breaks out between the two parties from which Paul must be rescued by Roman soldiers.

Now this may look at first sight simply like a clever trick – divide your enemies against each other and then escape while they fight it out. However, I wonder whether it doesn't show that Paul, far from having simply turned his back on the Jews, was not rather appealing to something close to the essence of the Jewish faith. He was fully aware that bearing witness to it could only lead to violent dissension because the consequences of it were so destabilising for any sort of group belonging. Yet he had to proclaim this message, even though he knew that to do so might prove fatal for him.

Then comes the key phrase to which this builds up:

> The following night the Lord stood by him and said, 'Take courage, for as you have testified about me at Jerusalem, so you must bear witness also at Rome.' (Acts 23:11)

Now, previously we have heard Paul quoting Scripture; here we have the fraternal voice of God himself speaking to Paul, and immediately we are plunged into a voice much more complex, rich and puzzling. It assumes our weak, still partially resentful man who has felt buffeted and shattered by his (no doubt still partially provocative) confrontations with the representatives of his great love and loyalty. It assumes the collapse of belonging and the frailty which all that must have provoked, along with a certain shallow bravado which Paul also knew how to wield. And yet the voice doesn't tick him off for that, nor despise him for the residual petulance which must have been still there. It takes him as a whole, and builds him up: 'Take courage.' In the midst of all these rows with Jewish authorities, no doubt imperfectly, Paul had managed to give something of witness to the living God in all his destabilising and vivacious creativity. He had begun to become detached from the violence which goes along with the petulant form of moving on I have described. The voice then manages, in a non-directive, non-paternalistic way, to open out a new form of moving on: 'As you have testified about me at Jerusalem, so you must bear witness also at Rome.'

Now please notice what this voice does not say. It does not say: 'Because at Jerusalem they would not listen to you, turn your back on them, and go instead to Rome.' That would be a voice pandering to resentment. The voice doesn't offer Paul a new form of belonging over against his previous one, it doesn't even contrast Jerusalem and Rome – Jerusalem bad, Rome good. It commands instead a new form of open-ended continuity in Paul's life, one bereft of any comfortable identities on which to lean. Paul must learn the terrifying lesson of moving into the serene waters of bearing witness to the truth of the living God not over against anything at all, but in the midst of a world simply indifferent to it. He has to leave behind the painful comfort of taking part in an intra-Jewish row, and learn instead to make available the truth about God quite outside the terms of reference of that row. For that is the only way to bear witness to God among the gentiles. That, the command within which the rest of Paul's mission is inscribed, is, however imperfectly lived up to, quite frankly, a much more terrifying and humbling form of moving on than any we have seen thus far.

If I have spent time on this, it is because I think that it highlights a typically Christian problem. We short-circuit our reading of these texts by inhabiting the petulance, and turning it into doctrine. By doing this, we fail to see the moments of yet-to-be-resolved resentment as stepping stones on the way to a catholicity which, by its very definition, can admit of no resentfulness, no excluded other by whom we make ourselves good. So we side with Paul against 'the Jews', we read the gospels in a way which sets up easy oppositions between Jesus and the Pharisees, and refuse to see the persistent hints at how those oppositions are being undone by the coming into being of something entirely new. I think we'll only learn to inhabit our texts, if we allow ourselves to dwell a little in the painful story of the Yahwistic revolution which alone breathes life and gratuity into them. So, behold, I turn to the Jews . . .

jewish hints

Ezekiel is in exile in a house in Babylon. There is already something weak and fragmentary about this. An exile is someone cut off from a huge seedbed of human belonging, someone without base or root, someone whose cultural paternity has been brought to nothing and whose loyalties have been made both deeper, since one is obliged to reimagine the object of loyalty, and more tenuous, since there is no one immediately obvious to be loyal to. An exile is someone who is in the process of being obliged to let go of one self and discover another. We can imagine something of the tenor of the ambience sustained by Ezekiel and the elders of Judah with whom he dwelt by the river Chebar.

Ezekiel was a priest, one of the group of people carried off to exile with King Jehoiachin, before the destruction of Jerusalem which occurred some years later in the reign of Jehoiachin's brother, Zedekiah. So, at the time of Ezekiel's first vision, Jerusalem is still standing, and the Temple is still intact. His first vision is unclear – a strange mixture of forms and faces with wheels, whose exact purpose has not yet become apparent. Above these forms there is a throne with the glory of God in something approaching human form.

The heavenly vision immediately rings a chord with Ezekiel's anger. His mission is to go and criticise the people of the house of Israel. Ezekiel is angry, Oh, how angry is Ezekiel! His vision certainly plays to that anger. He talks of how the Spirit of God fuels his bitterness, and he utters warning after warning to people, whether they would hear or not. He is confident of his role as a critical watchman whose salvation is dependent on his uttering reproof to others. Soon his anger turns to Jerusalem, and he and God between them heap scorn on that city: 'Disaster after disaster', 'Behold the day! Behold it comes! Your doom has come' and so on, criticism after criticism for several chapters.

Allow me the suspicion that at this stage the word of God and the heat of Ezekiel's emotions are a little too closely intertwined. Are we not dealing with something not far removed from spurned love? Ezekiel has been torn away from all he holds dear, and somehow both God and Jerusalem seem to have rejected him. The first fruit of his being reached by God – and it is only the first fruit, for we will see it develop – is a huge outpouring of anger and criticism.

However, this is only the beginning, for we see Ezekiel develop and shift as the visions continue. Ezekiel has a second vision in which he is taken by a lock of his hair to Jerusalem. It is a wonderful image of the strength of the One taking and the weakness of the one taken – for what weaker link do we have than a lock of hair? It is as if you or I were to undergo a complete loss of personality, and then, after a period, begin to recover ourselves and discover that we have been given a new self, and recognise that, all along, where we had thought only in terms of loss, there had been a hidden strength holding us up and giving continuity precisely by means of what seemed most vulnerable and precarious about us. Here we are unmistakably plunged into the world of the Yahwist revolution, of the self-hiding God (Is. 45:15) – *Él Mistatér* – of astounding strength who is utterly undetectable amidst the glories and splendours of the gods except as a still small voice, a puzzling breath, or a hand holding someone by a hair.

In Jerusalem, there begins to unfold one of the great visions of the Hebrew Scriptures, one of those texts whose bizarreness shields us from its extraordinary resonances of rupture and re-creation. Ezekiel is taken to the Temple and immediately shown a series of abominations. The first part of the vision is full of the evils which the elders of Israel, those who should have known better, were doing in and around the Temple. Ezekiel finds himself launching a diatribe against his own people and the practices by which they have defiled their Holy Place.

After this critique, which is, let us face it, not unusual among the Prophets, we then get given something rather more breath-taking. In chapters 10–11, there unfolds a picture of God de-taching himself from the Temple step by step. The key places of the presence of God in the Temple, symbolised by cherubim, become something like wheels. And the cherubim wheels offer something like an extraordinary self-moving chariot which becomes the moving base for the Glory of the Lord, which little by little becomes entirely mobile. From each different segment of the Temple, the Glory of the Lord, held up by cherubim wings over wheels, moves out, leaving the Temple behind until, finally, the wheels, God become mobile, abandons the Temple and the city altogether and goes and perches on the mountain on the East side of the city.

Now I would like to point out that this is not, in fact, a different vision from what Ezekiel saw in his first vision. It is exactly the same vision, of the beasts and the wheels and the glory of God, but it has come much more into focus. It is much less angry. If the first vision, when unclear, provoked Ezekiel straight into the pavlovian response of anger, using typically prophetic types of reproach, the second vision, which is the same, but in clearer focus, sees Ezekiel having begun to move beyond his spurned love, his sense of outrage and being left out, and sees him beginning to undergo the step beyond that, the process of detachment from his hugely violent and loving loyalty.

All the imagery of cherubim and wheels underscores precisely what a difficult, indeed unimaginable, rupture is being made. It is the vehicle by which Ezekiel is able to experience something very terrible indeed: God abandoning his Temple. If Ezekiel had been basically antagonistic to the Temple, one of those prophets who railed against sacrifices, then this might not have mattered much. But this was not the case. Ezekiel was a priest, someone who loved the Temple and all it stood for. What Ezekiel was describing was part of an experience of devastating loss, a heart transplant of his own heart.

Yet the key thing about this experience was that it was not simply one of loss. Someone very conservative, someone who loved the fixed and stable world of sacrifice and worship, is describing both the loss of all that, and, at the same time, the terribly painful process of detachment by which all that was most important in it becomes separated from the forms it used to take, and becomes flexible, new, and life-giving. It is towards the end of this process of detachment and rupture that Ezekiel is able to reimagine God as tending to the exile, giving people a new heart and a new spirit (Ezek. 11:19–20) the first mention of something which Ezekiel will develop even more fully later on in his book (Ezek. 36:28). Ezekiel, the conservative Temple priest, is learning to move on.

Over the next chapters, Ezekiel's criticism of Israel and its puppet king becomes more focused, and the anger in it becomes more tinged with compassion. A further sign of the huge change that is going on in Ezekiel's perception appears in chapter 18, when Ezekiel understands God as becoming detached from endless pouring of punishment on generation after generation because of the sins of the fathers. There begins to emerge a picture not of a god of blanket condemnation, but of a more nuanced God who wants people to turn from evil and live, and judges people according to their individual responsibility. These are signs of a re-creating God emerging from what seemed to be an endless cloud of indiscriminate wrath.

More diatribes follow against not only Israel, but Tyre and Egypt as well, along with prophecies of the coming end of Jerusalem and its Temple, prophecies tinged now with sorrow and mourning rather than merely with anger. We get again the vision of Ezekiel as a watchman (Ezek. 33:1–16), the same vision we had in chapter 3. But it is less stark than before, less a message of condemnation, and it combines with elements from chapter 18 where the picture of the god of indiscriminate multigenerational punishment was modified: there are signs of the watchman's role being inscribed within an overall message of love. Out from under the huge weight of Ezekiel's wrath, as he develops in his understanding of the things of God, spurned love is being turned, slowly and with great difficulty, into real love for his people.

It is only at this stage that a fugitive brings to Ezekiel the news of the fall of Jerusalem and the destruction of the Temple, something Ezekiel had been expecting. We might imagine a rather grim pleasure in this from Ezekiel's point of view, a kind of 'told you so'. But no, the sign that he really had been moving on (indeed perhaps being prepared by God to be able to help his people deal with this crisis by undergoing it himself beforehand) is that the real love, the hard-won love which had begun to emerge from beneath the reactive spurned love, continues to develop and grow stronger. It is here that we get the strong critique of the shepherds of Israel who have scattered the sheep and fed themselves, who have not taken care of God's weak ones. But God is not simply associated with the critique. Rather God has become dissociated from yet another apparently sacred function of the leadership, so that now it is God himself who is going to search for his sheep, and feed them and care for them. As spurned love becomes capable of detachment from the object of far too terrifying a loyalty, so it becomes possible to have an imagination set free to perceive the emerging voice of Yahweh the creator and holder in being, the lover and gatherer of the weak, a voice far too quiet to be able to be heard in the midst of all that wrath of spurned love.

We continue to move back and forth between angry denunciations and hints of love, but as the book moves on, so the loving bits get longer, stronger and more focused. In chapter 36, the anger serves simply as a build-up to a newer and richer version of the same vision which Ezekiel had had in chapter 11, with God taking the people from among the nations, cleansing them from all their uncleannesses, giving them a new heart, of flesh instead of stone, and providing them abundance. Out from the ruins of Ezekiel's spurned love is emerging a re-creating God. This develops even more strongly with the vision of the dry bones, and the bringing to life of the dead. Ezekiel's perception of God has become detached even from death, so that gratuitousness is able to call into being what is not, a staggering breakthrough, since it was not at all clear at that stage of the process of revelation that God had power to hold in being the dead. God is imagined not only as bringing into being a people, but as making available a new sort of David. God has become detached from the sacred line which was brought to an end with the fall of Jerusalem, and instead is able to make available a perpetual David, who will be his people's prince for ever.

We have one more outburst, but by the end of that, Ezekiel has already begun to put things into a new perspective. The whole purpose of the destruction and the exile was so that the people might know the holiness of God: he will restore their fortunes and they shall know that he is God because he sent them into exile among the nations and then gathered them into their own land (Ezek. 39:28). This means that Ezekiel has moved on enough to put a distance between God and all that anger and destruction – now it turns out that all that was part of an ongoing plan of love and building up. I don't want to pretend that this is an acceptable way of looking at things from our point of view, two and a half millennia on. Moving us beyond a perception of divine paternal ambivalence, one in which 'divine wrath' is a necessary goad towards our understanding 'divine love', is at the heart of Jesus' proclamation of the unambivalently Good News concerning his

Father. Nevertheless I do want to point out that Ezekiel's perception is a vastly important milestone on the road to a perception of God which is not bound up with spurned love.

The remaining chapters of the book of Ezekiel are taken up with a vision of the new Temple. Where before he had been taken by a lock of hair, now he is taken much more strongly. He is taken to a mountain opposite the city, perhaps the very same hill on which the vision of wheels had perched after it left the Temple and Jerusalem. There, methodically, and bit by bit, God shows Ezekiel the new Temple that is, slowly, deliberately, massively, strongly displayed before him. A massive exercise in re-creation of holiness, but not for Israel alone, for out from the threshold flows water which makes all things alive, and the water flows from all sides. And on all sides and to unimaginable distances, the water flows bringing life.

How Ezekiel has moved on! He has moved from being a man of spurned love, to one who, from within the whirlwind of that anger, has begun to see glimpses of a hard-won love, the breakthrough into his heart of the breath of Yahweh. Little by little it has been this love that has turned out to be what the breath of Yahweh was all about, until slowly, oh so slowly, there has emerged the tone of a strong but gentle voice which builds up, bringing into life, loving people, re-creating, and tending towards catholicity. Ezekiel's journey brings into focus a number of milestones in the much huger journey that is the Yahwist revolution. His life is a magnificent example of the dislocation and recreation of being which began when Abram left behind the city of Ur, the city of his father and his idols.

The point that I have wanted to drive home is that it seems fair to inscribe Ezekiel's journey within the three stages of (1) spurned love, pierced by a vision of God which it is as yet unable fully to take on board. This is followed by (2) a long process of working through the spurned love, and beginning to glimpse what I have called hard-won love, a non-reactive love which tends to bring together. This yields finally to (3) the relaxing into a gratuitous upbuilding, creative love which empowers the imagination to project and work towards building a huge catholicity of life: the discovery of God as creator and lover of all humanity with a project of bringing people into a mutual rejoicing.

the dynamic of eucharist

Now I'd like to try to see whether we can't begin to find ourselves within this process of the Yahwistic revolution, and I'd like to suggest that we can if we allow ourselves to discover what I call the eucharistic dynamic of Catholic faith. Let us imagine ourselves within a well-structured group, with clear insiders and outsiders (which is what a well-structured group tends to mean). Let us call this Church, and let us imagine its central act of worship called Eucharist. If this is the act of worship of a well-structured group, then the act of worship is also well structured. It tells the story of, and makes present, the saving moment which brought the group into being and holds it together. Part of what enables this group to function is that there are a very definite, if nebulous and somewhat mythical, bunch of people who are 'not us', the bad guys, differentiation from whom has made us good. These people are sometimes known as Egyptians, sometimes nations, sometimes gentiles, sometimes Pharisees, sometimes Jews, and they are necessary, for without them there would be no story by which we might be good. Our central act of worship is a glorious sacrifice by which payment is made for our sins, and we are reconciled to God by the efficaciousness of the act. Wonderful theories are developed to explain how it is that, within the holding together of the group, the sacrifice is efficacious, transferring grace and merits, restoring order and balancing creation. It is thus that we can hold on to our belief that, just so long as we carry on performing the sacrifice, God will be in his heaven, and the order which he ordained will be restored on earth, and we will be part of it. We are in a world in which love, loyalty, obedience and belonging are so close in meaning that the very idea that there might be an irony in loyalty being considered so close to love would be incomprehensible.

This is the world of innocent idolatry. Here we are in the world of Ezekiel before he was carried off to Babylon, of Paul before he had ever heard of Christ and his Way, let alone felt it as threatening enough to be worth persecuting. We are in a world in which many of us have been at different stages of our life with relation to our own group belonging. But such worlds do not last for ever!

Next, let us imagine something wrenching: we find ourselves, owing to some strange dynamic beyond our control, unable to inhabit this ordered house of worship which was our own. Either we have been taken militarily into exile, like Ezekiel, or like Saul find ourselves thrown from within by a discovery about the deeper roots of our belonging and our loyalty. For many of those of us who discover ourselves to be gay, this strange dynamic beyond our control takes the form of being ambushed into finding that we are part of the 'they' whose 'evil' made 'us' 'good', and this throws all belonging, loyalty, love and bearings into chaos. This is the seedbed of spurned love, the feeling of rejection, loyalty despised and made worthless, the helplessness and indignity of being borne away by a rushing power beyond control.

But worship carries on in the midst of this turbulence, violent worship to be sure, but worship nonetheless. At first we cannot really distinguish between God and the anger of spurned love and we get something rather like Ezekiel the outcast pouring forth wrath against the house of Israel and the Temple. A form of this which is common enough among us gay people is holding on to the Jesus of the gospels as a protest gesture against the religious household, the Pharisees, our former dwelling place. This is the moment when we have the beginnings of vision, albeit utterly girded about with violence. So we begin to be able to read and understand 'Jesus against the Pharisees' from within, identifying with Jesus, and blasting the hypocrisy and mendacity of all the dwellers in the ecclesiastical closet. We know exactly what is meant when Jesus tells the Pharisees that they bind up heavy burdens to put on people's backs and do not lift a finger to help them. We understand exactly the point of Jesus when he tells the scribes 'for the sake of your tradition you have made void the word of God.' And of course, we are right to hold on to this beginning of insight, clothed about and distorted with anger as it is: it is the beginning of learning to read about the things of God from the point of view of the victim. It is also the beginning of a detachment of the texts of our faith from their mythical referent outsider, and the use of the same texts to talk about our contemporaries, and thus to start to re-create the biblical world in our midst.

However, this is a romantic moment, a moment of protest, the moment of the confrontational word still bound within a certain angry self-righteousness. It is a dialectical moment, when what was good becomes bad and what was bad becomes good. The danger of this moment is that we can get stuck in it. If we do so, we have acceded only to a rather cheap sort of 'moving on', a shaking of the dust from our feet. We still remain much more bound to what we imagine we are rejecting than we like to think. In this moment we have not yet acceded to Eucharist. Jesus is a powerful word, but something of a cardboard cut-out figure. There is as yet no real hint of the dynamic behind the word. However, and this is not to be despised, spurned love has found the wherewithal to shout.

If we are lucky enough to be able to avoid the temptation of getting stuck at this level, we begin to find ourselves moving on into Ezekiel's second phase, the painful detachment of love from loyalty, and the beginnings of the discovery of a gratuitous love. In my own experience, this is a terribly painful time of growth. It is very painful to work through the anger and righteousness of the protest against the hypocrites, cowards and false shepherds who have abandoned their sheep. To let go of distorted anger is also to let go of the structure and the shelter which the anger provides. But this period is the beginning of the accession to Eucharist. If the first step was a positive group identity reading Jesus as the True Shepherd and the Jewish scribes and Pharisees as false shepherds who have now simply been superseded, the second step with an inverted or negative group identity was simply to make a fundamentalist identification of what before had been mythical outsiders (Jewish priests, scribes and Pharisees) with certain living contemporaries (cardinals, bishops, preachers, televangelists) who can be read as exercising exactly the same role now as their forebears in hypocrisy. With both of these steps, there is a 'we' and a 'they'.

The third step, which is the beginning of accession to Eucharist, is the beginning of the collapse of the difference between 'we' and 'they' and the reading of those texts as part of an ongoing dynamic. We begin to discover Jesus not as a cardboard bearer of a confrontational word, but as the crucified and risen Lord on the road to Emmaus. His presence, known in the breaking of the bread, becomes dynamic. He is constantly making himself available as a living interpreter of the texts so that we are able to find ourselves not stuck in either a positive or a negative group identity, but constantly enabled to move on.

I'm not sure that this step can be acceded to without a certain form of death. It is only when we accept that we have been thrown out of whatever our first loyalty and love was, and painfully discover the pointlessness even of being in reaction to it, that there begins to become available to us a perception of the gratuity of Jesus' being alive beyond death. This is the same as the gradual emergence of a love which is not bound by, or in reaction to, all that whirlwind of anger and spurned love. I am, I think, only making the perfectly traditional point that the one real access to Eucharist is Baptism. This is when resentment finally packs it in, and we begin to be able to love beyond reaction.

I suspect that the symptom that this has begun to happen is when we no longer identify the scribes and Pharisees and hypocrites with any real people, past or present, but begin to see that the whole purpose of those texts is to enable us to inhabit a 'we'. This we do not by detecting others' errors and hypocrisy, but by becoming aware of what I might call a mechanism of bad religion in which we all tend to be involved. A mechanism which is made available and comprehensible to us so as to enable us to move beyond it. I found this happening when I started to discover myself, somewhat to my surprise, pitying and loving the people I had previously seen as hypocrites, cowards and place-holders, for the hypocrisy, the cowardice and the place-holding are merely signs of a fear that has not yet been reached by the devastating love which brings into being. And that is exactly where I was, someone who had not yet been reached by the devastating love which brings into being. The word 'pity' sounds patronising, but I'm grasping after something slightly different, a form of freshly discovered equal-heartedness, the equal-heartedness of the visceral love which the gospel writers detected in Jesus. It is *we* who are being nudged into being.

Once we start to learn to see such people not as caricatures but as brothers, then maybe we can begin to read in quite a different way the texts, like those of the 'woes to the Pharisees', which before served to keep the caricature alive. The texts themselves become a gift which both shows us what an idolatrous building of our home looks like, and how to move beyond it in charity. Rather than a confrontational word creating a 'we' and a 'they', they become gratuitous words helping us to detect our own involvement in a world of 'we's and 'they's and enabling us to begin to imagine what it might look like to live together without such a barrier.

This is, I think, the real beginnings of access to Eucharist. It involves the terribly painful process of detachment from the Temple which we saw with Ezekiel – and in our case that means detachment from both the innocent idolatry of our original loyalty, and the turbulent reactive worship of our loyalty made confrontational. The Eucharist gets detached from either form of group belonging, and we begin to discover, beyond any ludicrous theories of sacrifice, the real presence of the re-creating heart of love which makes available to us a dynamic of detecting and moving beyond the mechanisms of violence that we set up for ourselves and inhabit so doggedly, such is our fear of death and of falling into the hands of our Creator.

I'm not talking about anything magic here. Just the slow drip, drip, drip, of regular participation at Sunday Mass mysteriously yielding the real, non-resentful presence of the risen Lord who interprets words of Scripture at the fraternal level and thus keeps alive the dynamic of enabling us to find ourselves within a catholic story. And this is regardless of the excellence or stupidity of the sermon, of the human transparency or sacral mendacity of the priest, the informality or the pomp of the liturgy. The eucharistic dynamic works *ex opere operato* because it is the gentle obstinacy of God in refusing to be spurned.

This is, I think, what I might call the beginnings of a Catholic moment in the process which I have described. The moment when Jesus moves from being cardboard confrontational word to becoming living real interpretative presence collapsing group boundaries. It corresponds to the gradual emergence of a love which is beyond reaction and beyond death, and which enables us to become aware of the presence of the crucified and risen Lord as making available a dynamic utterly without resentment. However, and here I am treading on very difficult ground, I would like to suggest that it is not yet really and fully a Catholic moment. It does not yet really and fully make available the eucharistic dynamic, if it is not also discovered as inhabiting the breath of the Yahwistic revolution.

Here I want to say that I think there is a moment beyond the freedom from resentment, and the beginnings of the re-imagining of a fraternity, of a sort which is only made possible by having undergone a certain sort of death. This is the discovery not just of the eucharistic dynamic, but of what lies behind that, of the Creator's giving of Eucharist. This means something like the discovery that Yahweh, the self-hiding God of Israel, is made manifest as the hidden voice of the self-giving presence of Christ in the Eucharist.

What lies behind the eucharistic dynamic is the invitation out of idolatry and into being. And the Eucharist is the continuous self-giving of the still small voice as a continuous undoing of the whole world of sacrificial violence which we inhabit. The undoing works by providing us continuously with the interpretative and linguistic tools to enable us to discover ourselves, beyond all our own violence and all our own cowardice, as being called into being so as to become co-participators in an unimagined creation. This really is the dynamic of moving on, as the fledgling thrown from the nest gradually finds that she has been given wings, that they work, and they really do bear her up and beyond.

What I want to say is that as we sink into the eucharistic dynamic, and as we find ourselves held in being, we can also discover something much deeper, richer and more extraordinary: the divinity of Christ, the human nature and word of Yahweh spoken as a silent interpretative breath which brings to life. This bringing to life is not something different from the creation of all things. What amazes me, as I stumble and stutter around this, is the realisation that this creative project of Eucharist, which is nothing other than Ezekiel's creative reimagination of the Temple, is not in reaction to anything at all.

Indeed, what has begun to become apparent to me, is that the Yahwistic project of making us participants in creation through involving us eucharistically in the life of Christ presupposes someone loving us so much that he could anticipate and be aware of all that spurned love, all that anger and hatred and violence, and be so little upset by it that he could project to bring us through it and call us into being. I am talking about beginning to sense a creative project of love which is not really beyond resentment at all. It is so much prior to resentment that it has to hide a vast, playful laugh at bringing us into being, lest we misinterpret such playfulness and such joy from within our resentment and shrink back, refusing to believe that all that tenderly suppressed mirth is not 'at' us but 'for' us.

clothed and in his right mind

the gerasene demoniac

Jesus has left Jewish territory. He has come to the land of the Gerasenes.[1] There, among the tombs, he comes across someone described as with an evil spirit. The townspeople do not know what to do with this man. They have put him out into the place of shades, and have fettered him to a rock. In his troubled state he is so strong that he continually breaks free. Finally they have given up shackling him and just let him be among their dead. Yet even abandoned to his own devices among their tombs, he carries on acting out what they have done to him, continually bruising and punishing himself.

The man, or the spirit, recognises Jesus from afar. He runs and worships him, and adjures him by God not to torture him, for Jesus has told the spirit to leave him. Jesus asks the spirit to name itself, and it names itself Legion 'for we are many'. It begs not to be sent out of the country. Not surprising, for Legion is entirely part of the economy of that place: it is the interrelationship of compulsions and driving forces that keep that people together by enabling them to agree on having someone who represents what is not them, all that is dangerous, unsavoury and evil. Out of that country, removed from the relationship between town and demoniac, Legion could have no existence. Its whole structure and *raison d'être* would collapse.

Jesus is completely removed even from feeling threatened by

---

1. My reading of this passage is entirely indebted to René Girard's 'The Demons of Gerasa', Ch. 13 of *The Scapegoat* (London, Athlone, 1986).

the spirit of Legion. He doesn't bark at it, or order it, or command it where to go. Instead, with courtesy, he allows Legion to do what it wants: to enter into some nearby swine. Jesus doesn't need to send Legion out of the country. Legion's identity as self-destruction will reveal itself anyhow the moment it gets outside the purely human game of setting careful boundaries and structures for negotiating group survival at the expense of a scapegoat. The pigs will become a perfect representation of what Legion was all about. They do not have the defining human capacity for building something constructive out of the forces of self-destruction, of forming a social group by expelling someone. The pigs, being a herd, are merely very good at imitating each other: either all are at peace, or all are expelled. So they tear off down the escarpment and into the sea.

The herdsmen go and report what has happened to the townspeople, decent folk who no doubt were convinced that the demoniac was an evil figure. Heretofore they had no idea of how dependent they were on him for their own stability.

> And they came to Jesus, and saw the demoniac sitting there, clothed and in his right mind, the man who had had the legion; and they were afraid. (Mark 5:15)

What made them afraid? They hadn't been afraid when the guy was running around bruising himself, breaking chains and so forth. That was pretty much business as usual. What was shocking was seeing him *sitting*, the position of the peaceful, *clothed*, where they were used to his familiar bizarreness, rent garments, gashed body and so forth, and, even more perplexing, *in his right mind*. Their being afraid is only odd if we don't understand the dynamic of the story at all. Before, *they* had been 'in their right minds'. Indeed, one of the things that had kept them in their right minds was the comforting knowledge of one of their own who was not in his right mind. If the demoniac were not part of their fragile economy of group survival, they would of course have been pleased to have him returned to useful life among them. But it is as a demoniac that he was part of their economy, and they sense it.

The townspeople probably have very little idea why they are

afraid. What holds them together, including their relationship with their demoniac, is at the level of what forms their consciousness, not something of which they are conscious. It is that way of being held together that has suddenly been challenged. Whatever strange force it be that has taken their demoniac quite outside the rules of the game by which they survive, it is, they sense, terribly threatening. So they beg Jesus to leave.

Jesus doesn't want to overwhelm this gentile town with what he knows to be a power that would completely destabilise them. The commandment to worship the living God and live without idols was difficult enough for the sons and daughters of Israel who had the benefit of the Law and the Prophets. For a gentile village, the living God is too much, too soon. So Jesus leaves. But not without planting a seed. The former demoniac wants to come and be with him, but Jesus will not allow this. Exactly the reverse of his usual instruction throughout the gospels: 'Come, follow me.' Does this sound cruel? I suspect not. I suspect that the reason is this: throughout the demoniac's life he has been bound in to a crazy game of belonging and not belonging. For him to leave his people now is too close to his being expelled, which was what had been going on all along.

Jesus instead gives him what is perhaps a much harder task:

> 'Go home to your friends, and tell them how much the Lord has done for you, and how he has had mercy on you.' (Mark 5:19)

The hard task is not the act of telling how much the Lord has done for him: that he will do naturally in order to explain himself at all. The hard task is the vertiginously domestic instruction: 'Go home to your friends.' Home! Friends! Realities as strange and new to our former demoniac as a missionary journey to some exotic land for one of the apostles. The man's witness to the living God will be most powerfully given by *sitting, clothed and in his right mind, at home, among friends*. The fully unsettling nature of the Gospel, the strangeness and exuberant vivacity of God, will be shown in all its force simply by being a former scapegoat in a gentile society which must learn to live without the benefit of this necessary crutch.

One of the first things the demoniac had done on recognising Jesus was to adjure him by the Most High not to torture him. This sounds so strange, for what could be more of a torture than being the living whipping-block of his society, where they tortured him, and he agreed to torture himself to play their game? Yet the whole drift of Jesus' action is in fact exactly the inverse of torture. To someone for whom the torture of 'business as usual' has all the comfort of familiarity, the arrival of the living God looks like torture. Yet the form actually taken by that arrival is nothing less than the humanising and domestication of the man in question, even at the expense of the stability of the social group of which he has been such an important part. This is not the logic of 'it is better that one man should be cast out than that the whole nation should be disturbed'. This is the logic of 'it is good that one man should be made human and that the whole nation should learn to live differently', the logic which prefers the one lost sheep to the ninety-nine which never strayed; the logic which knows the cost to the one of the ninety-nine keeping their righteousness.

Now, it is with some caution that I retell the story of the Gerasene demoniac. For many of us, any talk at all about evil spirits and possession brings up extremely painful memories. Many of you have, as I have, been treated by different Christian groups as though with an evil spirit. Whether this has taken the form of exorcisms, to cast out the 'spirit of homosexuality', or the various 'reparative' prayer ministries designed to turn us into 'ex-gays', many of us have known what it is to be supine to the annihilation of being which the whole language of the demonic has produced for us. I am aware that by rekindling those memories I am inviting all of us into dangerous territory.

Yet there is a clarity in the gospel text which can begin to help us find ourselves on the sort of solid ground that the language of the demonic is not normally thought to offer. First there is a logic in which 'god' and 'being' are linked to the social group and to belonging. This is the logic which says to us: 'We can allow you to belong, in fact we can give you the real being which comes from our god, if you go along with us in annihilating the part of your being which is over-against our group belonging. What you think is part of your being is not really any such thing, it is an evil spirit, or a spiritual sickness which can be cured, or at least neutralised. Allow us to treat it as such, and you can be part of us.'

In this logic, god, the gift of being and the gift of belonging are entirely dependent on the group of the 'good', who know what is right and invite us to trust them. The results of this cannot be less than catastrophic, for we are invited to make our being dependent on a group's need for unified righteousness. So we agree to cast out part of ourselves in exchange for the precious belonging and being which are offered. But when we cast out part of ourselves, it wanders around in the outer places of our group's social imagination, quite out of control, utterly dehumanised, reduced to a vagrant spirit, acting out the role of evil which it has been given by the group. And many of us have gone along with this, for how long, and at what cost!

The very fact of the evil acting-out reinforces our adherence to the belief structure offered by the group: the group can explain it, make it seem tolerable, even forgive it on occasion, because it actually contributes to making what they claim to be good appear to be, in fact, good. If you only know being gay as a series of sordid, furtive, highly-sexualised sorties from 'normal life', where you are constantly ambushed by guilt, then you will consent to the group definition, and agree with them that since this is what being gay is all about, the group's portrayal of it as the dark side of normal life is right. A bit of will-power and all will be OK. Perhaps this is why so many closeted gay people in religious organisations are so prone to persecuting other gay people, because their goodness, and hence their belonging, depend on their having agreed to displace, and expel as evil, part of their being, an expulsion which needs constant reinforcement, a sacrifice which needs constant repetition.

Many of us have participated actively in groups whose idea of religious conversion is that we should become like them, for whom the standard of righteousness and soundness is being 'like us', behaving like them, sharing their world-view, their politics, their bad guys. And often enough, to buy into their package, to consent to a blackmail of our being, has been for us the nearest thing to a port in a storm. A shelter, however precarious, is better than none at all.

So we understand well enough the position of the demoniac. No longer do we need to be tied up and fettered to a rock to prevent us acting out. Our consenting to be agitated by the spirit of the group teaches us to act out harmlessly to them, and harmfully only to us. We agree to this modus vivendi as if it were from God.

Yet this is not the logic of the Gospel. In the logic of the Gospel, the language of the demonic and of exorcism has a quite different function: it points to the Creator peacefully calling to life those whose being has been trapped by the violence of cultural belonging. At first view what could be more terrifying than the suggestion that we do not need to play the belonging game? It suggests that we do not need to have our being formed on those terms. The living God gives being and belonging quite outside the rules of the game of human group formation, and this is a terrifying wrench, of the sort that causes us, when we become aware of it, to cry out and adjure it not to torture us. The adjuring is made even stronger because in our case, after two thousand years of Christianity, the living God is spoken in the same words as the god of group belonging. The Gerasenes at least had the advantage of a different religion for each of the two realities. We have to learn to discern between the logic of grace and the logic of expulsion dressed in the very same words.

Yet the living God, who is courteous and gentle to our familiar demons as only one who is entirely outside their logic can be, will not be stopped. He begins the huge but hidden process of freeing us from the pagan shelter. Where group belonging seems to give being and forges an understanding of creation which is entirely dependent on group order, one which demands sacrifice to keep it going, the living God who calls all things into being is in no way dependent on group belonging. Being is given, terrifyingly for us, in the crack of unbelonging where we can be weaned from our passionate loyalty and pathological belonging into a resting in the gratuitousness of one who calls into being – one who rejoices in nothing so much as someone made human, sitting, clothed and in his right mind, at home, among friends, sharing the story of how he came to be in this strange new place.

This is the real dynamic behind the story of the Gerasene demoniac. It is the story of what it looks like when the living God, the utterly vivacious Creator out of nothing, draws near to the ersatz god of group being and belonging, and by gently taking the weakest member of the group, begins to collapse the group's belonging, humanising the 'bad guy' and thus initiating the possibility of a quite different sort of social formation. It is only in this utterly Jewish perspective that we can begin to have access to the dynamic at work. God is the Creator God, quite outside the world of the gods, and it is the presence of the Creator in the person of Jesus, confessed as Very God of Very God in our Creed, who brings this dynamic to bear in Gerasa. Any attempt to understand the things of God which does not reach back into the astounding Jewish perception of the Creator, entirely without rivalry, who has a loving plan for humanisation which involves the collapse of our idolatry, does not accede to the Gospel. The god of group-given being and belonging is only yet another form of practical atheism, whatever the language with which it is dressed up.

betting on the breath of God

Now it is obvious that I am offering you a story on which to feed, one I hope may spark off resonances in stories of your own. Nevertheless there is something odd about this story being able to be told at all, and I want to bring that strangeness out before I move on.

Imagine that you are in the world of the Gerasenes before Jesus comes along, whether as one of the townspeople or as a demoniac. You are not stupid, or primitive – whatever that means. You are just used to the daily run of your culture. You are used to negotiating living day in and day out within the strengths and limitations of your group. You share both adherence to, and scepticism about its gods, its taboos, its sacred barriers. Like most people in most societies you both go along with and yet relativise, approve of and yet resent, the structures which give meaning to your life.

Yet there is one thing you cannot do: whether you are a towns-person or the demoniac, you cannot imagine the innocence of the demoniac. The structure which holds everything together is relatively tolerant, as is the case in most human groups. It is fairly ready to turn a blind eye to a whole lot of failings, indeed has mechanisms for reincorporating those who fail. Yet there is one point where this apparently easygoing form of life is implacably totalitarian, where there is a definition of good and evil which cannot be overturned. It never crosses your mind to question it, and indeed it cannot really be talked about, since it is what allows other things to be talked about and given value. This immutable fact which the group's imagination cannot conceive in any other way is the definition of the demoniac as demoniac. Before the arrival of Jesus, whether you are a townsperson or the demoniac, you are all fundamentally yet tacitly agreed on what holds the whole of your order together. You are a participant in a closed system. And of course participants in a closed system do not know that they are in a closed system. It is only the vantage point of a system that does not depend on a hidden but secretly structuring scapegoat which enables us to detect other systems as closed. Before the arrival of Jesus on the shores of Gerasa, such a vantage point was not available to you.

If someone had come along and said 'Well, of course, your demoniac is really innocent, and all he's doing is acting out what all of you are dumping on him', you would resist this violently. It would be inconceivable to you that such a person was anything other than a troublemaker, someone who wanted to disturb order and subvert morality. The key word here is 'inconceivable'. The notion is not one you could imagine, let alone tolerate. You would read the claim entirely from within your own group structure, and would reject it as impossible. So impossible that it could not really be talked about at all. In fact, you wouldn't need to talk about it. All you would need to do is point to the indisputable evidence of the evil and craziness of your demoniac. Something there is clearly wrong.

Now the reason I ask you imaginatively to inhabit the world of the Gerasenes before Jesus' arrival is that it highlights the vulnerability of my own story, the one I have been telling you. I have been telling you, as a gay man talking to a group of gay people, a story which relativises an implacably totalitarian structure. My point is that unless we understand a little that what I am doing is, from the point of view of our fellow Gerasenes, impossible, we won't sink into and inhabit the depth of the impossibility of the story which we are being empowered to tell, and we won't have access to the novelty of God, nor understand the potency which palpitates in the naming of God as one for whom nothing is impossible.

Jesus did not come and give the Gerasenes a lecture on the structure of their society. He didn't argue with them about definitions. He didn't propose an alternative form of legislation. He did something much more three-dimensional. He empowered the demoniac to become a human being, sitting, clothed and in his right mind, going home to his friends.

My claim is that it is only possible for a gay man to talk to other gay people, reasonably and quietly, if we have already begun to be overtaken by the power of the Creator, who is already beginning to humanise us, give us right minds, and enable us to be at home with our friends. In other words, the very fact of our being able to talk like this, here, as you read this, is entirely dependent on something huge, quiet and unimaginable already happening. Very God of Very God is already, even as we speak, 'doing something new', speaking to us in tones and at a depth which our former belonging could never reach, and in a way which our former groups can find nothing other than inconceivable and scandalous: calling us into peaceful and gratuitous human being.

Now this is a very vulnerable starting point. For I cannot prove my position. I cannot argue to it. I am aware in advance that the claim that God is doing something new and that we are part of it, cannot but sound like pernicious rubbish to the Gerasenes. From a Gerasene perspective, this sort of talk must be interpreted from within their system. It has to be seen as a form of special pleading. I am sure that I am not alone among you in having seen people describe our attempts to talk the language of the Gospel as the fruit of minds so utterly darkened by our perversion that we have become incapable of seeing, let alone talking about, the truth inscribed in the created order. Indeed, they say we are obsessed, or possessed, by a spirit which has taken us out of our right minds and left us flailing about in self-induced darkness.

There are a couple of moments in the New Testament when the vulnerability of a position like ours becomes apparent. On one occasion Jesus tells the Pharisees who have accused him of casting out demons by Beelzebul:

' . . . if I cast out demons by Beelzebul, by whom do your sons cast them out? Therefore they shall be your judges. But if it is by the finger of God that I cast out demons, then the kingdom of God has come upon you.' (Luke 11:19–20)

And on another occasion, in the Acts of the Apostles, the Rabbi Gamaliel warns the assembled council concerning the apostles:

' . . . keep away from these men and let them alone; for if this plan or this undertaking is of men, it will fail; but if it is of God, you will not be able to overthrow them. You might even be found opposing God!' (Acts 5:38–9)

Both speakers have perceived that there are two logics at work: a logic which analyses from within a closed system, and a logic undetectable from within that system. In terms of argument, the matter is undecidable, and Jesus and Gamaliel can only say 'if this, then this, but if that, then that'. In both cases the vulnerability of truth is made clear by two 'ifs'. Jesus and Gamaliel both point towards something which cannot be proven, but only bet upon: the coming into being of something new which flows from the One who makes all things new.

I say all this, since when a gay man talks to a group of gay people about the things of God, inviting us to inscribe ourselves into, and inhabit the story of the Gerasene demoniac, we cannot do so from a position of strong argument. Rather than talking as ones borne along on a wave of certitude, we trust instead that we are surfing home on drops of condensation from the breath of God. Nothing can be more vulnerable, but could anything be stronger?

inhabiting the process

In the gospel story, the humanisation of the demoniac happens so fast, and with so little detail that, even though it is the very reverse of magic, we are tempted to imagine the change as though it were without process. What I would like to do with you is explore the process of divine humanisation that is at work here, the normal anthropological change which is undergone, and to which, I believe, we are no strangers.

I would love to be able to give you a serene account of this process, the sort of account which the former demoniac was able to give when, in his right mind, he was seated at home among his friends. Yet, it is too early, I think, for us to talk with serenity. I think that I would be short-circuiting the process if I were to try and lay hold of an objectivity which is not yet mine. Part of that gingerly surfing home which I described is that it is not yet serene, but is often panic-stricken amidst the birth contractions of the new creation. A serenity grasped too soon may well prevent us being given the deeper serenity of loved children. Too quick an objectivity may turn out to be an enemy of the faith that allows us the space to flail and splutter with pain as we are called into our rightful being. So please bear with me as I try to talk without anaesthesis.

One of the first things I experienced as the living God came ashore – and before, of course, I understood how different the living God is from my Gerasene gods, was a terrible shriek: 'It doesn't have to be like this.' Yet this is, itself, a huge crack in the system. It is already an astounding statement of faith, because it is exactly opposed to what faith in the system says. Gerasene faith says: 'This is what it's like, and has to be like, and there is no way outside it.' It is why faith in destiny, in fate, in nature, in created order and so forth are always threatened by the arrival of faith in the living God. To be able to believe that 'it doesn't have to be like this' is already a quite extraordinary and disturbing irruption of faith in the living God in the midst of the fixity and impossibilities of idolatrous faith.

There was for me something narrow and hysterical about this shriek which comes along with faith, for it seemed to rest on nothing but a crack in the system, a pained gasp as the system begins to come apart. It didn't yet seem to rest on anything as solid as the emerging breath of the living God. Yet to be reached by this crack, by the certainty that 'it doesn't have to be like this', despite the implacability of those who claim to speak for an immutable divine order, is already the beginning of the discovery of a way of being human that is quite outside what could be understood from within the system.

A further moment in my process, as perhaps something of the foundedness of being held by the living God began to emerge, is the perception that this is not simply another crazy shock, of the sort to which I was used while being tortured within the system (and how else can any of us interpret anything new, except starting from within an understanding formed by the old?). Rather I became able to say something like: 'If God is true, then this cannot be true.' In other words, to relativise what had held us in being before, a capacity which can only grow as we find that we are gently held in a way which loosens the compulsions which kept us in their thrall.

As the process of being reached grew, I was able to say something like 'God has nothing to do with all this violence.' This is a sign that a new person is indeed emerging: the discovery of a surety of being which owes nothing to all to the violence in which I was previously bound up as both victimiser and victim. The new person begins to be able to perceive the utter and unfathomable difference between the logic of grace and the logic of expulsion with their respective forms of being. This is a staggering breakthrough, an extraordinary possession by living faith, and along with it there comes into being a rational capacity to distinguish between God and the gods, between grace and violence; a capacity actually to begin to be able to analyse and point out what before had bound us in such a way that we couldn't perceive it, much less talk about it. Here we have the beginning of the sort of peaceful reason which only faith makes available, the first stutterings of someone who is coming into their right mind.

Something immensely painful accompanies this process: the realisation of how much I have been bound in by lies. I don't think that we gay people can accede to truthful talk except by undergoing the utterly disorienting discovery that we have been lied to from the beginning, and we have bought into and been driven by these lies. This is not the incidental discovery that the government, or a bishop, or a relative has been lying to us. It is the much thicker and more complete discovery that what we had been breathing for years was in fact not oxygen but some noxious and corrosive gas that sought our death. It is not so much that someone told us a lie, as that our very being was formed by and enveloped in accusatory mendacity.

There is a famous gay pride banner which reads 'We are the people our parents warned us against.' How much pain there is behind those glib and clever words, how hurtful the lie we were told about ourselves! From our tenderest youth we have been fed lies about who we are, about what we are becoming. Before we were even told 'it's only a phase', we had already started to learn to negotiate the rules of surviving the threat of the playground lynch mob. We had already started to take our cues from the ambiguous messages given off by schoolteachers who were themselves negotiating survival by living a lie; from the hints of acceptance emitted by admired clergy who could not themselves share a self-acceptance which they didn't have, and couldn't lay hold of at the same time as keeping their jobs; from apparently friendly employers who let us know that 'of course it's OK just so long as you don't say anything'. 'Don't ask, don't tell' is the merciful-seeming motto of systemic mendacity. Yet mendacity is never merciful in the long run. It is merely the decent cover beneath which arbitrary violence and expulsion flourish, as even the Pentagon has belatedly begun to acknowledge. And the Pentagon is way ahead of our churches, which are prodigal with their expulsions in a way no accountable body could ever be, and bereft, as the Pentagon is not, of rational ways of exploring their own mendacity.

Of course the thing about all those lies is not merely that we are told them, but we ourselves buy into them, and tell them, to our deepest selves and to others. We become those guilty bystanders at the playground lynch, we become those parents, those teachers, those clergy, those employers, and find ourselves reproducing the lie so as to survive.

And of all the lies, none is more terrible and more utterly destructive of being than the one which tells us that we cannot love. That our love is sick, perverted, and can only bring harm and degradation to those to whom we would reach out. The lie is always told about a mysterious 'they' to whom it is applied, and yet is always read by us as being told to a 'you', and ingested by us into an 'I'. This 'I' knows itself to be promiscuous, not capable of emotional stability, handicapped as regards commitment, unable to take responsibility for the well-being of another, in short, definitively prohibited from incarnation. What you prohibit from incarnation you condemn to the lifestyle of a demon. This is one of the strongest forces in the Gerasene construction of the gay demoniac into which so many of us have bought.

Yet, as we emerge, spluttering and groaning from being nearly strangled by so much mendacity dragging us into the mud, we find that the very fact of having come to perceive the depth of the abuse of being to which our cultural paternity has treated us is already the beginning of the birth of a right mind. Being able to feel the pain, the anger, the rage, is itself, I'm afraid, a sign that we are letting go of its causes; while we played the game, we rarely dared to feel the pain.

What should be absolutely impossible, if the Gerasene religion is right, is peaceful, constructive loving of each other. Heterosexuals are taught by a thousand films and novels to distinguish between good love and bad love. They learn to discern when love is love for another person, and when it is self-love using the other as a mirror. They can come to tell the difference between love and jealousy, between possessiveness and a passion for the growth and well-being of another. They can learn the difference between demanding that the other, whether partner or child, conform to their own fragile 'I', and on the other hand creating the space which protects the growth of another's 'I' as it becomes strong. They can learn to tell the difference between sexual relations which are a form of rape or self-gratification using the other, and those which are constructive ways of building each other up. Well, that's the theory!

Now if the Gerasene religion, which has been far too deeply ours, is true, then we can make no such distinctions. There can be no good same-sex love, no distinction for us between love which builds and possessiveness which belittles and destroys, no difference between the gang rape and murder of the myth of Sodom and the mutual electrification of playful partners or the reciprocal edification of respectful friends. Yet little by little, as we emerge from the devastation of a lie which always accused us, and could only find our love a sham, we find that we are able to make these distinctions, really, for ourselves, in real relationships with real people. We discover, not that we are condemned to flail about in irredeemable perversity, but, most wonderful of human-ising discoveries, that we are capable of sin – which means that we can distinguish between getting it wrong, and gradually learning how to get it right, how not to settle for less than we are worth.

It is one of the ironies of church teaching that, unlike the Good News of the living God, it renders us incapable of sin, since only those for whom there is a right way of being can fall short of their created potential. To be able to get something wrong, and learn from that something of what we can aspire to is, itself, a huge step on the divine road to the humanisation of the demoniac.

The very fact of discovering that we can distinguish for our-selves between good love and bad love, good sex and bad sex is, I want to insist, a quite extraordinary rupture of the Gerasene religion. Since if we are able to do that, if our love is not intrinsi-cally, but, like that of the rest of humanity, only accidentally, perverse, then of course everything else follows: there can be good gay partnerships and bad gay partnerships, good gay parents and bad gay parents, good gay clergy and bad gay clergy, and what is good and what is bad can be worked out, what to strive for and what to avoid, by talking. But this means that our being has become available to language, and we are already halfway to being in our right minds, among friends, at home.

a process of the heart

I am aware that I tend to describe the process of the emerging human child of God in negative language – and that is how I have felt it, at least initially. I have found it much easier to detect and feel the collapse of the old, the stripping away of the comforting shelters of Gerasene belonging, than to perceive the emergence of the new. This has been accompanied by a seemingly endless sense of mourning and of loss, without any apparent welcoming presence of something new coming into being. And yet I am aware that only the very hugeness and gentleness of the living God, coming up the shore of Gerasa, could cause my false selves to collapse and shrivel up. I suspect also that, as with many gay people, particularly gay people brought up in religious households, the sense of non-being, of annihilation, is so strong, the lack of self-esteem so sacred-seeming, that it is part of the courtesy of God that he doesn't patronise us with too quick and easy a new being, but prefers to unfurl his humanising divinity in such a way that we will be late to notice it, lest we reject it, still tied to our Gerasene self-flagellation.

Nevertheless, even I am aware that we are not simply rubbing up against an archaic force, but are being called into being this-rejoiced-in-by-God-person. That words like 'chosen' and 'personal' are not simply the clichés of sectarian code, and that part of discovering oneself being called into being is a growing awareness that being chosen, and becoming a person, are only descriptions of what it is to discover ourselves as loved. Even words like 'plan' or 'project' start to make sense as little concrete things we manage to do in the world cease to be the tired and random scatterings of those who just have to get through with it, and come to be discovered as the givenness of stories which can be shaped and shared. Little achievements conceived as the unseen preparation for not-yet-noticed building blocks of stories still to be told.

Part of what I have begun to learn, as the painful idols and compulsions of Gerasene belonging are stripped away, and a new sense of being given to be someone I could never have dared to invent comes upon me, is a glimpse of what Paul meant when he told us that if we are children, then we are heirs (Rom. 8:17). For children may be loved, but they play irresponsibly. As we discover ourselves heirs, then there is born in us an awareness that we are in on the deepest meaning of the project of creation, able to take an active part in what it's all about. I can imagine the Gerasene demoniac, on his way home, beginning to see that all the craziness of the group-belonging which had so driven him looks futile and fragile as he begins to discover himself part of a much huger, quieter, more serene adventure, the open-ended adventure of human sharing in creation. There can be no more powerful, and yet less tangible form of belonging than the entirely given, and never grasped form of belonging that is coming upon the heirs.

One of the signs that this is coming upon us is that we are released from the rivalry of having to try to belong. There is a stage in our gradual release from annihilation of being when we are overwhelmed with a huge anger and bitterness at what we have lost, at what has been done to us. Often this takes the form of violent protest against those we perceive as our torturers, and we are ready to name the people, bishops, preachers, politicians, who have so easily joined in the torture thinking that in so doing they were serving God (John 16:1–4).

Yet part of the discovery of being a child and an heir is the gradual being able to let go of the need for their approval, the need to put them right, the need to belong to their world. Having dropped through a hole in the bottom of their world gives us the extraordinary freedom of not having to grasp at belonging at all.

So our anger can begin to collapse, real righteous anger, really felt, and instead of the cruel insights which allowed us the clever – and truthful – detection of bigotry, there begins to emerge the heart that has no rivalry because it knows itself a child and an heir.

Now I'm aware of the temptation for me of skating over this

process of the heart. That is, itself, a sign of how difficult and painful it has been, and is, for me to work my way through all this, rather than grab at some convenient vantage point from which to speak, or shout. In fact, at every stage of being possessed by anger, and mourning, and resentment, it has been quite extraordinarily difficult to begin to glimpse the next stage in the process of the heart. It was already a triumph to begin to name the evil, and understand the mechanism of victimisation, and to brandish it as if that alone would make things better. But that was not enough. The hard part is allowing myself to cease being fixated on pastors and politicians, named individuals who either silently or vociferously wage a war against us, determined that it is God's honour that is at stake, an honour to be defended by whatever means, however great the cost.

When we can cease to be fixated even on these, along with all the sterile excitement of belonging to a political and social struggle with good guys and bad guys, forces of progress and forces of atavism and taboo, then something mysterious comes into focus:

> For we are not contending against flesh and blood, but against the principalities, against the powers, against the world rulers of this present darkness, against the spiritual hosts of wickedness in the heavenly places. (Eph. 6:12)

Now this is not a piece of pious piffle. Naming and attacking particular people, campaigners, bishops, politicians, is to be stuck contending against flesh and blood. But the truth is that the named individuals are stuck, as our church structures are stuck, in a world in which there are still 'spiritual hosts of wickedness in the heavenly places'. This doesn't mean nasty demons in heaven. This means voices of accusation and expulsion dressed up in the language of grace so that what seems to be heavenly is in fact part of the order of social belonging dictated by the logic of expulsion. You can imagine our former demoniac gradually becoming aware that the leaders who seemed strongest in defining him as demonised were themselves, for all their fine language, just as trapped as he had been by the principalities and powers, locked in, as he had been, to the logic of expulsion apparently ordered by God.

Curiously, I think that part of what must have come upon the Gerasene demoniac as he began to sit and talk to his friends at home was a deep and gentle pity. I want to be careful here, since the word 'pity' is so tied up for us with a sense of superiority, a comparison which masks a certain contempt. I'm struggling here, but I think there is another quality of pity. It is quite without comparison, quite without rivalry or contempt, and it goes along with a certain sort of longing, creatively imagining the possibility and glory of joining with others in being unbound. As the anger, the grasping at belonging, the comparison which reinforces self-approval, begins to collapse, so this very mysterious longing pity takes its place. This pity, for all its quietness and seeming vulnerability, is no volatile emotion. This pity reaches right back into the heart of the Creator, present in the man striding up the Gerasene shore. It enables us to intuit something of the visceral movement of love which led God to come among us as one of us at all.

The violence of the group knows only how to shout defensively, how awkwardly to bury the unspeakable in convenient silences. The violent heart dictates the tone and tenor even of fine-seeming words. Being in a right mind means coming, tentatively, through a process of the heart, into a place where speech rests on a quizzical imagination, unperturbed by the apparent impossibility of a new sort of gathering. It is confident that the truth can be spoken peacefully, and it is quietly immune to strength.

If the Gerasene demoniac was able to come into his right mind, if, as I sense to be the case, we gay people are, despite all the odds, on the threshold of being able to talk among friends, at home, in our right minds, this is because the demoniac has indeed, and at last genuinely, been possessed. Possessed by the Spirit that was within the man who walked up the shore of Gerasa. What had been outside the demoniac as one who talked to him is now within him as the heart of the Creator who longs with a passionate and visceral longing for us to be free, and rejoices in nothing so much as our quiet, gentle contamination of each other with the first hints of that longing, translated into the first stutters of a right mind.

PART TWO

attempting a voice

on learning to say 'Jesus is Lord': a 'girardian' confession

a tale of two spirits

Now concerning spiritual gifts, brethren, I do not want you to be uninformed. You know that when you were heathen, you were led astray to dumb idols, however you may have been moved. Therefore I want you to understand that no one speaking by the Spirit of God ever says 'Jesus be cursed!' and no one can say 'Jesus is Lord' except by the Holy Spirit.

(1 Cor. 12:1–3)

The whole of what I want to say is in this passage. Many of us are used to a cheap reading of these words. All we need to do is avoid saying 'Jesus is cursed', which it wouldn't occur to most of us to want to say anyhow, and instead to say, or to sing, repetitively and maybe obsessively, 'Jesus is Lord'. This would be a way of proving to ourselves that we have the Holy Spirit, and are on the right side.

Now of course, this is nonsense. The devil can quote Scripture, and Paul is proposing for us something much more dense than a merely verbal test of our orthodoxy. This passage suggests that there are two forms of cultural life at work. In one of these, people are moved by spirits which incline us to dumb idols, and which issue forth in someone being cursed. This is the cultural world in which social belonging and religion lead people to maintain their group unity by fixing on someone or some group who can be thrown out, anathematised, cursed. The semi-conscious group dynamic of ganging up against someone – the 'however you may have been moved', with Paul's implication that there are evil spirits at work here – leads to a sense of unity. And the unity needs 'the cursed one' to be able to maintain itself.

Paul is suggesting that there are some people who have been trapped into understanding Christ's death and resurrection from within that cultural mentality, making of Jesus the 'cursed one' which the group needs to maintain its unity and its sense of goodness.

The other form of cultural life, which moves beyond being trapped, knows that no form of social and cultic belonging can survive the perception that our victim was in fact God himself, present in Jesus.

When our expulsion of him was revealed for what it was, at the resurrection, far from our being given a superior crutch by which to keep our world of moral and social order intact, what we received turned out to be the explosion of our cultural order, a major question mark over any of our attempts to shore up social unity, and the beginning of an entirely new way of human being-together, gradually constructed without the need for a sacrificial victim.

Now it would be easy enough to demonstrate that for far too long, Christianity in both its Protestant and Catholic 'orthodoxies' has relied on an explanation of salvation which does in fact fall straight back into saying, with many a polite circumlocution: 'Jesus is cursed'. All the bastardised Anselmian substitution theories which tend to underlie seemingly attractive presentations of the Christian faith in fact turn on God cursing Jesus so that we can be 'saved'. Jesus as cursed comes to be the necessary bit of the formula which allows the sleight of hand by which salvation is proclaimed without making any real difference to the social and moral enclosure within which we live. Cursed Jesus is simply the guarantor of an independent and pre-understood definition of good and evil into which we are required to fit as best we may.

I mention this en passant, rather than trying to argue with it. It is one of those things which cannot really be argued against. For those who hold it, it has a dangerously sacred status. For those who have moved beyond it, it needs no arguing against.

What I am interested in is something different. I am interested in sharing with you what I hope you will agree to call an experience of the Spirit. The Holy Spirit which allows the words 'Jesus is Lord' to become not a slogan, but a gasp at the three-dimensional wonder of Yahweh in our midst as one of us, with all the mystery of the Lord's vulnerable revelatory power intact.

'can this be the Christ?'

In early 1985 I found myself picking up a thick French paperback as I snivelled my way through one of those five-day bouts of English spring flu. I had no idea of where it would lead me. The book, which has since been translated as *Things Hidden from the Foundation of the World*,[1] had come into my febrile paws because a couple of stray references to the thought of René Girard pointed me in the direction of an interesting new theory which might have something to say about Christology . . .

The stray references gave me no hint that I was about to be ambushed by what I understand to have been an experience of the Spirit, the one which allows us to say 'Jesus is Lord', such that fifteen years later I'm still trying to work out what it was all about. Instead of reading that book, I found myself being read by it. I came away certain that I had met someone who had told me everything that I had ever done – an experience of being exposed to a massive amount of truth about the world I live in and about myself in particular. Glimpses of course, no immediate capacity to give a coherent account of myself; but glimpses which pointed to a coherence in the voice telling the truth. And, along with those glimpses and that coherence, the knowledge of being pulled out of myself to know more and more about a truth which might be very challenging, but would never frighten me or bind me up in traps and double binds. There came upon me an uncharacteristically fresh-breezed rush of which I had heard tell, but never

---

1. Stanford, Stanford University Press, 1987.

imagined for myself. That of the man who found a treasure in a field and, going and selling everything, he bought it. And I am aware that someone so delighted by something that he is prepared to dispossess himself of everything in order to obtain it will never possess the object of his delight. He will be possessed by it. So it had better be the right Spirit!

Even then, I knew exactly where I had heard of this experience of being told the truth before. The woman at the well of Samaria reported just such a sensation. After a conversation with Jesus she returned to the city and addressed her compatriots:

> 'Come and see a man who told me all that I ever did. Can this be the Christ?' (John 4:29)

No one needed to tell me that it was not Girard who was speaking to me all that truth. Little in Girard's works points to René Girard. I sense it to be a sign of the presence of the Spirit when what is taught points the pupil outwards, beyond the teacher and towards a discipleship richer than any clinging imitation could begin to yield. No one who knows Girard's thought or has enjoyed his company could imagine that *he* thinks that he is the Messiah he has come, ever more explicitly, to announce. The truth was coming from the source to whom he points, the one he recognises as having made possible what he has to say, the same source who had given the experience of truth to the woman at the well.

Since I embarked upon the adventure of following that voice, of allowing myself to suspect that this could indeed be the Christ, indeed could be no one else, I have had a crazy life, lost countries of residence, culture, home, security of belonging, reputation, possibilities of professional advancement, indeed what anyone might describe as 'my senses'. Yet not even when in clinical depression have I had cause to wonder whether I mightn't have embarked upon an entirely mistaken journey. The journey, one of uncertain faithfulness on my part, is one in which the one thing that matters is the merciful honesty of that voice.

If, in the chapters preceding this one, you have had no inkling of a sense of being told the truth by someone other than the author of those pages, then I have, quite simply, failed you as a theologian, failed to be a conduit for the Spirit of God to speak words into your heart. If, however, you have found that you are able in some measure to discover yourself within the stories I have told, if you found yourself being spoken into being with words of truth which opened up new vistas of the sort 'Oh, so that's what I've been doing all along', then this is not because James Alison is a natural storyteller. It is because James Alison would be being seriously unfaithful to what he has received if he were not at least to try to make available to you something of the 'well of Samaria' experience, which he takes to be 'what it's all about'. I would also be being unfaithful to what I have learned if I were not to indicate that the process of living with Girard's thought has provided very exact and specific tools. It is these tools that have given people like me the chance to have a go at reproducing for others the possibility of dwelling in a particular experience of being told the truth.

So in this chapter I am going to do what I normally have serious reservations about doing. Rather than simply attempting to put Girard's thought to work in the service of the Gospel, my normal modus operandi, I am going to talk about that thought. I fight shy of anything which sounds like academics discussing other academics, and find myself unable to stick rigorously to theoretical analysis. So, instead, I have tried to set forth something like a hymn to the Spirit – an account of how prayer-peppered living with Girard's thought over the last fifteen years has turned the freshness and embryonic coherence of the 'well of Samaria' experience I described to you, into a sustained attempt to confess the Christ.

the density of God in Christ

As I have sought to understand and practise the Christian faith in the light of Girard's thought, gradually there has grown in me a quietly elusive, yet extraordinarily solid faith perception of Jesus as God. It is as if a set of words has gradually been replaced by something like a pillar of personal presence, which I particularly associate with the Eucharist. What I am interested in sharing with you is some hints of the process by which this has happened. In other words, I'm coming up from the coalface after a long time down there to ask you to help me determine whether I really am still mining the right stuff, or have missed the seam and am churning out mud.

This three-dimensional presence, which is of Jesus who is not me at all, and is quite outside me, and not linked to any formal belonging to any group, did not come suddenly. Rather, I associate this presence, this perception, with a gradual collapse of a whole series of elements that stand in the way of what I am coming to see is meant to be a very normal part of Christian life.

My first appreciation of Girard's thought, then, is that it gives the elements which allow the collapse to happen peacefully. Anyone can deconstruct any set of texts or religious practices in a destructive way, leaving nothing at the end. It is a quite different order of genius which posits that the deconstructive element is present not as part of a furious tearing at fake substance, but is instead itself the quiet breath which remains behind as all the idols come tumbling down.

In this sense, Girard's first contribution to our theological endeavour – by which I mean our Christian living in its speakable form – is christological. He gives us an anthropological phenom-enon detectable in ancient texts and, *mutatis mutandis*, in modern life: a gathering together of all at the expense of a randomly selected one. The act of expulsion of the one itself creates the unanimity of peaceful coexistence which is then attributed to the ambivalent one, first hated on its way to expulsion, then revered as the beneficent effects of its expulsion dawn on the group.

What Girard sets out is the way in which this, sadly unremark-able, feature of the life of *homo sapiens*, or *necans*, is turned on its head by the Gospel. Jesus in the gospels shows perfectly well by word and by action that he understands this mechanism, under-stands the religious and political structures which depend on it and shore it up, and lures it into behaving according to its usual pattern. But he does so in order to reveal that it is not necessary, that God is in no way involved in the mechanism, and that those who are of God are born again into a form of social gathering which is in no way dependent on this mechanism. Little by little I have come to appreciate the huge, and usually hidden, deliberateness behind the whole of Jesus' teaching and action in the gospels, a deliberateness whose sense is revealed only in the resurrection, which is the declaration of God's having been acting all along in Jesus, the definitive separation of the perception of God from any sort of social life that is tinged with the mechanisms of death, and the making available to violent humanity of the beginnings of the sort of breaking of heart which can lead us into a new form of social life.

Now this deliberateness, this solid emergent dynamic, is usually masked from us by the language of Jesus having been sent by, or of Jesus obeying, the Father. As long as our whole approach to reading the gospels takes place within the parameters of a pre-existent understanding of Christ's sacrifice, then we are condemned to understanding such language as elements of a puppet show, one in which celestial magic is worked according to a prearranged script by a puppet master and his obliging marionette. What Girard's insight enables is the collapse of any such puppet show, of any sense of different actors playing roles of 'sending' or 'obeying'. Instead we begin to be able to hear the words 'sent' and 'obey' as pointers to the solid dynamic of Jesus' human deliberateness. Far from positing a new theory of sacrifice, as some seem to think, what Girard's thought has made possible, at least for this reader, is the explosion of all and any possible theories of sacrifice. In the midst of their ruin, we are left with the entirely gratuitous way out of our being bound by such forms of thinking, a given way out which is identical with the human being Jesus of Nazareth as the culmination of a long and entirely Jewish history of non-sacrificial divine presence.

So, my first point is that Girard's understanding helps clear away the idols which prevent us from perceiving the inner dynamic of deliberate revelation present in the way Jesus lived out his life and lived into his death.

creation in Christ

My second point is similar. I have, since childhood, been alter-
nately puzzled and tortured by the ease with which religious
people speak about our having been created, as though it were
obvious. Created good, we fell into sin, and needed Jesus to be
sacrificed in order for our created goodness to be re-established.
The trouble with this was that it had for me, and has for me, no
existential bite at all. It is meant to be something like a pacific
given at the outset of any theological discussion that God created
us, and not merely all of us by setting off the process in the
beginning, but each of us individually at the moment of our con-
ception. Given this, then any subsequent discussion about Jesus
leaves the issue of the Creator entirely alone, and proceeds to deal
strictly with the subject of sin. In fact, sin becomes the controlling
factor in the discussion, and Creation a largely irrelevant matter
of the *mise-en-scène* necessary for sin to have a spectacular gravity.

One of the most frequent early theological criticisms of Girard's
writing was that he had no theology of creation. I always thought
this was silly, since it was judging someone for not having done
something that was not in any case part of his brief as a theoretician
of desire and a reader of texts. In fact, for me at least, what
Girard's understanding has done is to open up, at last, a plausible
way not only of talking about, but indeed of discovering, a sense
of God as Creator, of myself as created, and of Jesus as the human
presence of the Creator bringing creation to a possible fulfilment.

The key for me was in realising the implication of the results
of the victimary mechanism for the understanding of order. Girard
has been able to show in text after text how a group's understanding of the created order, of the cosmos, was entirely
dependent on the re-establishment of order after a bout of victimary bloodletting. Accounts of creation, of the gods setting up
an order, a nomenclature for tribes and animals, are all, always,
accounts told, *after the event*, of where things have come from.
And what they are dependent on is a victim having been sacrificed.
Of course, what was prior to the act of victimisation was not a
peaceful idyll, brutally and arbitrarily interrupted by a savage

decision to kill. What was prior to the killing was the social chaos and turmoil of a group crisis which was eventually brought to an end by a killing. This means that all accounts of created order which we have are more or less obviously dependent not on a prior peace and goodness bringing things into being out of nothing – a very late Jewish discovery, not even present as late as the re-write of Genesis during the Babylonian exile – but on a suppression of disorder. In other words, typically, accounts of creation are accounts of prior conflict being resolved – the epic of Gilgamesh is not alone in making this terribly obvious.

What Girard's insight managed, for me at least, to make clear, is that the explosion by Jesus of the victimary cycle raises suspicion about the relationship between the victim and the account of creation. If creation is narrated by the victimisers after the victimisation, the account cannot do anything other than reinforce the order that has been brought into being as a result of the party guilty of disrupting the order having been punished. Yet, if the victim was innocent, randomly chosen, then of course the account tells us nothing at all about creation, and everything about the self-justification of the persecutors, and the sacrificial nature of their order.

Now if Jesus had merely happened to be the person who revealed that the choosing of the victim was random, that itself would have been enough to cast suspicion on all accounts of creation. But if his being that person was not itself the result of happenstance, but turned out to be part of a deliberate project which preceded the violence leading to his victimisation (and I ask you to understand both 'project' and 'precede' in terms of an anteriority bereft of temporality), then we are into an entirely different field of vision. For not only do all accounts of creation in which order is linked to a sacrifice begin to collapse, but instead we start to be able to imagine an account of creation which comes directly from the victim, not in spite of the victim, but as part of the victim's prior and deliberate intention.

There are enough hints in the apostolic witness that this was how the apostolic group began to perceive this – with talk of creation in Christ, and the Lamb slaughtered before the creation of the world – for me to attempt to follow this through. The results are remarkable. If we are right in seeing a deliberateness in Jesus that was able to explode the sacrificial nature of human gathering, then that same deliberateness is in no way part of any account of created order. In fact, it is prior to any account of created order in exactly the same way as God is prior to creation. The deliberateness in Jesus was also the givenness of the Creator, making available the entirely peaceful, gratuitous nature of creation as an ongoing dynamic in which we can become involved as we learn to let go of sacrificial idols.

I think that this may be one of the most exciting directions in which the Spirit is taking us, by enabling us to understand afresh that Jesus, by exploding the victimary mechanism, *also exploded the way in which creation can be talked about*. No longer can it be talked about in the order of logic, as something which happens first, setting the field for other things to happen. Rather it can only begin to be talked about at all in the order of discovery, as the end result of the collapse of all ways of talking about order which are the products of the mechanism of the random victim.

This is a further step in the collapse of the victimary puppet show, in which there is a Father who is the Creator, and then things go wrong, so he has to send his Son to sort it out by, guess what, a sacrifice. In fact, the Father, exactly as Jesus tells Philip in John's gospel,[2] can only be seen in the deliberateness and givenness of the entirely human teaching and acting out of Jesus. As the picture of creation which is enclosed within victimary order collapses, so we begin to be able to imagine an entirely gratuitous, unbound, peaceful and genuinely creative process at work in and through a human being. Furthermore, this is something which is always discovered by us as being contemporary to us, and wherever it emerges, it tends to break down the sacralised constrictions of victim-creating order.

What could be more Christian than this picture of our discovering ourselves in the midst of a process of coming-to-be which is painfully held back by all sorts of forces claiming to represent

---

2. John 14:8–11: 'He who has seen me has seen the Father.'

an implacable 'thus it must be, for such has it been since the beginning'? For this enables us to recover the language of the birthpangs and travail, to be found scattered throughout the apostolic witness. The separation of creation from victimary order is the end result of a process of discovery in the New Testament. But once discovered, it can be read back into what Jesus was doing all along in the miracles, the healing and the allowing himself to be killed, as indeed it clearly was, especially by John in passage after passage of his gospel.

This for me is a further step in the sinking into the perception of Jesus as Lord: the gradually dawning awareness that the emergent presence of deliberateness which I have attempted to describe, is not that of a god. It is that of the Creator making contemporary and available a project conceived outside all cultural order and time, of enabling us to share in a dynamism of which we have scarcely begun to be aware, and before which all our idols melt away. As we recover this perception of Jesus, we recover also what I suspect to be most needed in our current Christian life, the utter rootedness of our faith in the entirely Jewish process of discovery of the Creator.

God who undoes 'the sacred'

The third 'moment' in which Girard's thought has cleared out some of the mental junk which I carry about, thus allowing an ever more three-dimensional and living perception of Jesus as Lord to emerge, is what I might call the moment of the ongoing institutional critique.

A two-dimensional Jesus gradually moves through the gospels performing a series of miracles to demonstrate that he is God. He manages to annoy the religious and political authorities of his homeland, and succeeds in getting himself killed, thus fulfilling Scripture and pulling off his famous all-sufficient sacrifice. His sacrifice enables those of us who appropriate it, whether by baptism or adherence to some formula of soundness of faith, to be 'in on' the inside of the new group, which like all other pagan groups, has its key sacred sacrifice, the relationship to which defines group membership. In this way the truth is the group's truth, there is an inside and an outside, mechanisms for shoring up the truth at the expense of, or by the creation of, traitors and so forth, scenarios we all know far too well.

What Girard's thought has begun to open up for me is something of the truth behind the parody. It now begins to appear that Jesus was not setting up the stage so as to be able to pull off a sacrificial coup. On the contrary, he did not have anything to do with sacrifice at all (except in the sense that the ultimate and definitive explosion of all sacrifice can, by definition, be referred to as 'the one true sacrifice' just so long as it is remembered that we are dealing with an analogous use of rhetoric here, not a literal fulfilment of a pre-established formula). By not having anything to do with sacrifice at all, Jesus was making available a perpetual and ongoing mode of presence of God as nothing-to-do-with sacrifice. This enables us to have a look at Jesus' teaching not as incidental to his sacrificial mission, which it has largely been reduced to, but as what he himself said it was, words which shall not pass away.[3]

The reason they do not pass away is simple. Jesus was not setting up a new sacrificial foundation within which, once people were on the inside, they could be taught his words of wisdom 'as well'. No, he was offering an ongoing set of words and acted-out stories which always serve as ways to detect how sacrificial mechanisms operate in any human group, how we must not accept them, and what the consequences are of refusing to accept them. Once it has been said 'the Sabbath was made for man, not man for the Sabbath' (Mark 2:27), the possibility of analogous acts of discernment being made by humans who know that in doing so they are obeying God, is literally endless. Once it has been said 'Go and learn what it means: I want mercy and not sacrifice'[4] the gloves are off – there is literally nothing that can stand in the way of the subversive force of people learning to apply this for themselves. Particular teachings about particular acts and observances will always eventually fold against the force of these much deeper utterances,

---

3. Matt. 24:35; Mark 13:31; Luke 21:33.
4. Matt. 9:13 and 12:7 quoting Hos. 6:6.

utterances which demand that we develop our own capacity to discover God for ourselves as loving of the human state and condition.

We can look again at the various occasions when Jesus faces up to the scribes and Pharisees in the gospels. Here we are not dealing with particularly clever comments by Jesus in the face of certain bad guys who were performing their role in leading up to the new and all-sufficient sacrifice. On the contrary, the point of the 'Woes to the Pharisees' and other similar remarks is that God himself is making humanly available in words the capacity rationally to analyse and understand the sacrificial tendency present in the very best religious form available at all, anywhere, the Jewish one. This was not so as to stigmatise the Jewish religion, as we have tended to do, disgracefully, but to make available the deepest, non-sacrificial truth of Jewish revelation, to all comers, everywhere, as an ongoing self-critical dynamic.

The staggering truth is that this, while painfully difficult for religious leaders to understand in practice, is perfectly obvious to ordinary people of no particular religious allegiance. It is not an unchristian thing to do to be able to detect hypocrisy in the ranks of our religious authorities. It is not an unchristian thing to question the peculiar forms of structural blindness to which religious professionals are prone when we construct ways of living and modes of discourse which set us apart from others. On the contrary, such questioning is one of the most especially Christian things we do. This means that there is an ongoing dynamic of the collapse of the sacred present in our religious life which has gradually enabled us to do something quite extraordinary: begin to develop a rational and analytic understanding of how our own and other religions work, especially with regards to their and our tendency to demand sacrifice, and also to see how pointless those demands are.[5] In other words, the false mysteries of the sacred

---

5. Typically members of those cultures strongly influenced by Christianity are far better at critiquing the sacrificial nature of religions other than our own, in strict disobedience to Jesus' teaching about not pointing out the speck in someone else's eye until we've removed the beam from our own. But it is only as self-critical that we have any right to consider ourselves recipients of divine revelation.

have begun, on a regular basis, and despite themselves, to become available to peaceful language. Far from this being some sign of a 'faithless generation', it is a sign of quite how powerful and subversive something as unique and paltry-seeming as a teaching leading to a murder two thousand years ago actually is. Our faith involves, intimately, the collapse of sacrificial faith and eventually of all the sacral forms of living-together which sacrificial faith spawns.

What differentiates this from a simple 'liberal enlightened' critique of religion? Well, in the first place, I would want to say that it is this that has made possible a liberal enlightened critique of religion at all. The trouble with such critiques is that they are usually unaware of the extent to which they are parasitic on what they criticise. Second, liberal enlightened critiques fail to understand the process by which reasoned understanding becomes available. It is not that people work out rationally what is wrong with religion and then alter their behaviour, as though everything takes place in a calm and reasoned discussion. Rather the reverse: the capacity to understand what is really going on becomes available in the midst of the extremely violent and muddled turbulence of human social structures, and it is usually made available by people who stand up for the apparently unacceptable when it is in no way fashionable, and are prepared to risk their reputation and livelihood, and maybe even their life, to do so. What it invariably comes down to is people suspecting that potential victims may after all be entirely innocent, or at least no more guilty than anybody else, and that the whole unified voice to the contrary is nothing but ravenous wind. The cheap enlightenment and facile critique after the violence is over, to which we commentators are so prone, is, in a sense, even more despicable than sincere participation in the turbulence while it is afoot.

It is in this context that I want to talk about the Eucharist. Typically, Christian theologians talk about the Eucharist without a larger context of social violence, and in order to make sense of it, retreat into some of the sacrificial language which we have seen, language which tends to debase the dynamic presence which the Eucharist was always meant to, and does in fact, offer. If, however, the implications of Girard's thought into which I have been sinking, are true, then something much more exciting begins to emerge. The Eucharist is always in a sacrificial context as the antidote to that context. In the midst of a constant world of seething build-ups to near or actual lynches, it is the quiet presence of Yahweh himself as not-a-sacrifice-at-all, or as the one-and-definitive-sacrifice. This presence is designed to feed us with the capacity to work our way out of being moved by the winds of victim-aimed desire (the 'however you may have been moved' of 1 Corinthians 12:2 with which we started), and instead to teach us how to stand up against that and begin, however tentatively, another way of living together. In other words, it only makes sense as the beginnings of the gathering of semi-penitent former participants in the violence of the world, who, on a day-to-day basis, are learning to live in a way which does not require sacrifice.

I have nothing at all against highly sacrificial-seeming liturgies, provided of course that their highly sacrificial trappings are not the vestments of some theory of 'divine order maintained through sacrifice'. If, instead of that, their pomp and ceremony are a way of reminding people of what this is *not* all about, of pointing up the extreme irony of God really being made present through the signs of bread and wine in the midst of a world which seeks much stronger and bloodier sacrifices to keep its order going, then this is indeed acceptable worship. Personally I have found that part of my own development as a member of the Catholic faithful has been the ongoing sense of being let down by the sheer banality of so much of Christian worship, the fact that nothing grandiose seems to happen. This sense of being let down has been in fact a wonderful training in the perception of what really is happening: the quiet, hidden, but continuous presence of the Lord speaking through the words of Scripture and opening up new ways in which my sacrificial mind can gradually be unbound. This process which makes the presence of the Lord and his teaching permanently contemporary is, for me, one of the ways in which Girard's thought has enabled the hidden dynamic of the Christian faith to be made alive and find its way into living words.

What I am trying to highlight here is that the three-dimensional, deliberate presence of Jesus is not merely the presence of the Creator, God himself, reaching out to us, but that creative presence is in our midst as a deliberate and ongoing project of enabling us to detect, and analyse, and render into language, a critique of the sacred mystifications by which we fool ourselves and snarl up God's project of creation by engaging in exciting-seeming constructions of the sacred which turn against us with a heavy hand and demand sacrifice. I think that this is something of what the Second Vatican Council meant when it made the distinction between the Church and the Kingdom of God, such that the Church is not the Kingdom of God, but is the sign or sacrament thereof. What the living presence of the risen Lord enables us to do, little by little, and with an awful lot of false steps, is to discern when and where our gatherings are in fact signs of the Kingdom which is the always contemporary outbreak of creation in our midst, and when they are in fact the 'leaven of the Pharisees' – the pious disguise of the sacrificial world which we are so tempted to seek to restore.

reading texts and telling stories

My fourth point concerning Girard's thought is apparently at a slight remove from my concentration on the density of God's presence in Christ, though not for long. Girard's thought is, above all, shown in the reading of texts. Anyone who has read any of his books, whether on myths or the Bible, Shakespeare, Proust or Dostoyevsky, Freud, Lévi-Strauss or Nietzsche, cannot but see that what Girard does is read texts. Most of those of us who attempt to learn from his thought do likewise. Again, it is not just that there is an idea, and that the idea needs texts in order to show itself. I think that there is a more profound point here about the nature of truth-seeking: the idea can only be made present as the undoing of the various forms of sacrificial cover-up to which our texts and stories are prone. The idea just *is* the gradual, and contingent, undoing of lies. There is no 'idea' without the contemporary putting of it into practice as a detection of sacrificial structure and the learning to tell a different story.

I think that for many of those of us who have followed Girard's thought, there is a hugely exciting initial period, when we grasp what he's on to, and start to be able to detect the scapegoat mechanism everywhere, in every text and in every news bulletin. This is, genuinely, very exciting, and is the incentive for sticking with the thought. However, in my experience, this eventually yields to a huge and heavy boredom. I don't mean a boredom at Girard's writing, I mean a boredom at the tirelessly repetitive melody which grinds on and on everywhere. There just are no fresh stories anywhere, none which, at root, are not structured by the same, tedious patterns promising to create something interesting, and turning out to be just more of the same – a mood Girard caught particularly in his treatment of 'Hamlet's dull revenge'.[6] There are the Scriptures of course, but even these are so often overlaid with a telling stuck within the rhythms of sacrifice . . .

This is, for me, the stage at which something much more interesting can begin to occur, or we can just buck out of thinking about such things at all. This is the stage at which our reading can become self-implicatory. And that means we can be spoken to, challenged, subverted and built up by the Spirit. For none of us is a mere reader of texts, or listener to stories. All of us are tellers of stories about ourselves: that is what all our relationships are about. We tell stories to ourselves and to others about our childhood, about our parents, about our schools and our churches, about our political involvement or abstention therefrom, about our nations' histories and so forth.

There is something peculiarly subversive about this stage of living with Girard's thought. We find ourselves ever less able to be happy with telling lies about ourselves. Precisely because we can detect the deep structure of the sacrificial melody, we are less and less happy to reproduce that in our own little accounts of our marital difficulties, our dealings with our employers and so forth. This is, I think, when the really challenging aspect of Girard's thought begins to become apparent: how are we to tell a different,

---

6. Ch. 30 of *Shakespeare: A Theater of Envy* (New York, OUP, 1991).

a sustainedly non-sacrificial, story? How is there to be found on our lips 'a new song: praise of our God' (Ps. 40:3)?

I want to say that, for those of us who have the pretension of being theologians, for whom our calling is, in the apostle Peter's words, 'If any one speak, let him speak as the oracles of God' (1 Pet. 4:11), this is a moment of particular importance. What we are being challenged to do is to hear the residues of the sacrificial melody in our own voice. And this means that we are being called to undergo a very particular process of learning to tell the truth. To what extent is what we say, and what we attribute to God and the Gospel, not coloured by our own grasped belonging? Do we find ourselves speaking in a way which allows us to keep our jobs or reputations, to hold on to our grievances and perceived victimary status, but not to communicate oracles of God? To what extent are we part of the problem, not part of the solution?

There is, for me, at least, a terrible stripping away involved here. In the degree in which we start learning to tell the new story, sing the new song, we find that we cannot do so except from being contemporary with, and that means being involved in, the emergence of truth in the midst of the violent lie. And there is no way of being involved with that from the position of the wise and serene spectator. As we learn to read texts and tell stories from the point of view of the random victim, so we have to learn actually to inhabit the violence of the movement, involved alongside, and in solidarity with such people. And we have to do so without ever losing the sense that the violence is random, and thus that it is not because we are 'special' that we are undergoing it.

This, of course, is terrifying. The whole point of stories told from the position of the random victim is that they can't be heard, at least initially, and for a long time. Neither can they be associated with God. Usually they are simply off the radar screen of those who think they are interpreting God's word. Take this passage from John's gospel:

> 'You search the scriptures, because you think that in them you have eternal life; and it is they that bear witness to me; yet

you refuse to come to me that you may have life. I do not receive glory from men. But I know that you have not the love of God within you. I have come in my Father's name, and you do not receive me; if another comes in his own name, him you will receive. How can you believe, who receive glory from one another and do not seek the glory that comes from the only God?' (John 5:39–44)

This is the terrifying thing: belief in God and the ability to tell the story which comes from the victim, despite our own involvement, automatically implies learning how not to receive glory from one another. And this means losing one's reputation, being considered mad, obsessed, not professional and so on. Yet unless the story we are learning to tell is not simply a clever method for the detection of victims, but is rather the bringing to life of the new story of truth in the midst of real circumstances of victimage, then we are not really being theologians at all. To detect victims from a position of intellectual clarity is one thing, to start to sing the new song as we lose credibility, support, belonging, livelihood and reputation is quite another.

There is a passage in Girard's most recent book *Je vois Satan tomber comme l'éclair*[7] which brings this out:

> While Captain Dreyfus, condemned for a crime he hadn't committed, was 'paying his debt to society' on the other side of the world, there was on the one hand the 'anti-dreyfus' faction, very numerous and perfectly serene and satisfied, for they had their collective victim and were delighted to see it justly punished.
>
> On the other hand were those who defended Dreyfus, only a handful at first, and they were for a long time considered to be manifest traitors, or at least professional malcontents, obsessed people, always busy banging on about all sorts of grievances and suspicions the bases for which no one around them could see. Personal psychological problems or political prejudices were

---

7. Pp. 224–6, my translation.

alleged to be the explanation for the behaviour of those who defended Dreyfus.

In reality, the 'anti-dreyfus' belief was in the most exact sense a myth, a false accusation universally assumed to be true, kept alive by a mimetic contagion which was so overexcited by anti-semitic prejudice that for years no fact managed to break through it.

[. . .] If Dreyfus' defenders hadn't struggled to impose their point of view, if they hadn't suffered, at least some of their number, for the truth, if they had accepted, as is done in our time, that the very fact of believing in an absolute truth is the real sin against the spirit, Dreyfus would never have been rehabilitated, and the lie would have triumphed.

Here we have what it looks like to inhabit a different story, what it means to learn to tell the story from the position of those who receive no glory one from the other but, on the contrary, have found their way, whether knowingly or not, into seeking the glory that comes from the only God.

I suppose my fourth point is this, then. What Girard offers us is a reading of texts, and that means the gradual ability to begin to see through our own stories, and start to see the terribly discomfiting implications of starting to learn to tell the emerging, new story, which is not going to be a money-spinner, which doesn't back up anybody's ideology, and which is not going to bring respect, fame or a good reputation. The whole point of the story of the innocence of the victim is that, for the longest time, it is not believed, and this means that, if we are to tell it, that we will not be believed.

I have tried to set out the gradual process of learning to say 'Jesus is Lord' as Girard's thought has helped me learn about it. This final point of mine doesn't seem to be directly related to that, but it is. Coming to perceive the deliberate presence that I have described, making available the critical dynamic that opens up creation, is never done coolly. It is not a serene activity. As we sink into the boredom of the old story, and find ourselves having to learn our way into the new, I think we find that we are

not serene participants gliding in to a new theological and ecclesiastical elegance. It is with something of the whimper of
'professional malcontents, obsessed people, always busy banging
on about all sorts of grievances and suspicions the bases for which
no one around them could see' that we speak, if we are real.
And this means that, for the longest time 'personal psychological
problems or political prejudices were alleged to be the explanation
for the behaviour' of those of us who discover ourselves learning
to describe the strictly unbelievable, learning to imagine the truth
of what all around us tell us is a lie.

The ability to inhabit the darkness patiently and not despair,
but, by learning to tell a new story and using texts, to help ourselves and others reimagine a goodness that we never thought was
available to us, is not the least of what the Spirit makes possible
with the tools which Girard has elaborated. It is also, I think, what
brings us to be able to say 'Jesus is Lord': not as a deduction, nor
as a simple affirmation of presence, but as a non-serene recognition
of an unbracketable power, gasped at from the underside by the
Spirit who is teaching us not to lie.

an irrelevant coda

One of the criticisms that is levelled at Girard and at those of us
who have come to be called 'girardians' is that we are too
univocal, too one-track-minded in an obsessive approach to intellectual life which is just not pluralistic enough to deal with the
complexities and subtleties of life and theology. I doubt whether
anything I've said will have allayed the fear that that criticism is
on target. I suspect that it is true that 'the hedgehog knows one
big thing', and that to go on saying it, in different ways, is what
we do.[8] It may be that Girard's thought has a particular attraction

---

8. The reference is to the line by the Greek poet Archilochus 'The fox knows
many things but the hedgehog knows one big thing' as expounded by Isaiah
Berlin in 'The Hedgehog and the Fox: An Essay on Tolstoy's View of
History' in *The Proper Study of Mankind: An Anthology of Essays* (Pimlico,
1998).

for those of us who, in any case, tend to be obsessive or paranoid in our approach to intellectual life and to theology. In any case, what I would like to suggest is that, for these strange people, one of whom I am, the question is: does Girard's thought pander to our obsession, or help us break out of it? In my experience, what Girard's thought really hints at is a widespread, though often well-disguised, paranoia concerning a 'them' who are out to get an 'us'. It is not surprising, then, that the thought which enables us to get out of the paranoia, and think free of its parameters, looks very like the paranoia which it in fact helps to overcome. The real question is not: 'Are we obsessive?', but 'Are the hard-won fruits of our understanding still locked in the obsession which many of us have experienced, or have they come to yield what is, in the best sense, a catholic breadth of sympathy with, and love of, the human condition?'

I cannot answer this directly, and it is in any case only for those looking on to say. But I would like to end by pointing to a source in my own thought that has nothing at all to do with René Girard, and nothing at all to do with the mechanisms that I have been describing, and which has yet been, for me, of incalculable help in reimagining the world. I'm referring to the writing of a nineteenth-century Italian, none of whose works I have ever read, and the same, I suspect goes for almost every one of you. By allowing myself to be permeated by the fruits of this man's creativity for something like twenty-five years I have learnt something which not even Girard's thought, nor I suspect that of any great thinker, could teach me. I have learnt what my own circumstances of life, and the theological enclosure in which I was brought up, actively impeded me from seeing. Slowly, and imperceptibly, because this man consistently shows signs of actually liking being human, I have been taught one of the hardest lessons any of us can learn: actually to like the human condition, find it funny, tender, capable of moving sighs, without needing the stimulant of deep tragedy or great drama; to appreciate its delicacy and quirkiness and its moments of unexpected exuberance. I have allowed myself to be brainwashed by about thirty-five of this man's forty-something works, and if anyone is capable of offering up hint after hint of what the new song might sound like, one far removed from the repetitious burden of sacrificial drudgery, it is he. Great thought is not, of itself, much given to facilitating tenderness of heart, gentle and pointless frivolity, a ludic which is neither sacrificial or ludicrous, even though really great thought may understand how little is there when these are not. It has been given to me to start to learn these lessons, vital complements to any other, from another vastly underrated master, Gioacchino Rossini. If you can think of a stranger marriage than that between the thinker with whom we began, and the one with whom we end, then I look forward to hearing about it!

on not being scandalised

introduction

In July 1999 the Congregation for the Doctrine of the Faith, the Vatican body charged with the oversight of doctrinal orthodoxy, issued a Notification regarding Sister Jeannine Gramick and Father Robert Nugent. The Notification indicated that it was bringing to an end a complex and time-consuming ten-year process of investigation into the pastoral work and published writings of Jeannine and Bob in the area of 'homosexual persons'. And it pronounced sentence against these two labourers in the vineyard. They were permanently prohibited from engaging in pastoral work in that area and they were temporarily made ineligible for office within the religious congregations of which they are members.

In the year following the Notification both Bob and Jeannine obeyed very exactly the terms of the prohibition. However, both of them publicly raised questions, not about the prohibition itself, but about whether or not due process was violated in the investigation which led to the Notification and the sentence. These are questions which any judicial system should be able to handle, and if necessary review. It is an increasingly normal presumption in any institution, nation, corporation or society which has respect for the rule of law that whatever harm an individual or group may be seen as doing to the fabric of the institution, that harm is as nothing compared to the deleterious effect on the whole body of the perception that the organs charged with watching over the well-being of the body are acting in dishonest ways to achieve predetermined results. Think of the scandal caused to the possibility of law enforcement when internal investigations into alleged police malpractice simply cover up for those accused and treat those questioning the culture of cover-up as enemies to be subjected to harassment and threats. The normal way in which this deleterious effect is avoided is by the appointment of an independent commission, composed of people other than those who conducted the first investigation, and who are susceptible neither to pressure from those investigators, nor to the sort of 'group think' from which those investigators might have suffered without being aware of it. This commission looks into the complaints to see whether or not due process was in fact followed.

Sadly, in May 2000, Jeannine and Bob were summoned to Rome again to be expressly prohibited from airing their questioning of the transparency of the process which led to the Notification. This definitive prohibition was backed up by the relevant Vatican authorities ordering their respective religious congregations, which had offered them support during their ordeals, to enforce this silence with the threat of expulsion.

In July 2000, the English Catholic weekly *The Tablet* reported Cardinal Francis George, Archbishop of Chicago, as having said, in a closed meeting with a group of religious superiors, that the whole thing had been 'very badly handled'. It is a pity that this remark had to be smuggled out of a closed meeting, rather than immediately aired in public. The one thing which can begin to diminish the damage caused to the credibility of Church authority by behaviour like an official foreclosure of due process is the public perception that people who might normally be regarded as 'party men', and thus more likely than not to go along with the Central Office line, are in fact capable of public and candid disagreement with Central Office. I suspect that it is against Catholic faith to believe that Nietzsche was simply right when he said 'Of necessity, the party man becomes a liar.' But what is against Catholic faith is the little phrase 'of necessity', not the generalised presumption that party men become liars. And the Catholic response to Nietzsche should not be to rubbish the generalised presumption (which is in any case affirmed by our doctrine of original sin), but to challenge the 'of necessity' by producing party men who show themselves publicly able to distinguish between the truth and the tendency to toe the party line.

In the face of this sorry situation in which we, as a Church, are involved, I would like to offer a tribute to Bob and Jeannine by examining some of the issues raised. Bob and Jeannine have been subjected to extremely painful treatment, have had their life work treated not so much as of no value, but as something harmful to the Church and to the eternal well-being of those to whom they have ministered. They are now threatened with a loss of home, livelihood and financial security when they are both of an age at which it would be impossible to start again for themselves and prepare for anything like a comfortable retirement, unless they agree to go along with a procedure which even a somewhat conservative Cardinal reportedly describes as 'very badly handled'.

However, I do not think that I would be doing either Bob or Jeannine a favour by harping on about their being 'victims'. They know, as do any who profess the Christian faith, that those who find themselves pursuing the truth and challenging the lie, casting light on dark places, must be prepared to face persecutions and loss. And this does not make those persecuted 'victims', people who use their status to accuse 'victimisers'. Jeannine has explicitly warned people against using her case to demonise Cardinal Ratzinger. The Christian faith enables us to inhabit the space of being victimised not so as to grab an identity but, in losing an identity, to become signs of forgiveness such that one day those who didn't realise what they were doing may see what they were doing and experience the breaking of heart which will lead to reconciliation. This, I take it, is how Christ teaches us to read Zechariah's prophecy 'They shall look upon him whom they have pierced.'[1]

So, rather than contribute to the accusatory heat of victimage which this case has generated, which would simply be to stir the scandal, I would like to look at one or two of the theological and pastoral issues behind it.

---

1. Zech. 12:10; cf. John 19:37.

scandal and incorrigibility

There appear to be three different understandings of scandal at work in this matter. There is the official view of scandal, the scandal of the Gospel, and the public perception of scandal. Each of these understandings finds support in the frequent, but infrequently commented on, presence in the gospels of the word *skandalon* – stumbling-block – and its derivative *skandalizein* – to cause to stumble.

The official view of scandal is that the faithful must be protected from anything which might scandalise their faith. In itself, this is a perfectly good understanding. It might well be the case that people who have a straightforward faith in God, and Jesus, and the sacraments of the Church, can be scandalised if and when they come across evidence that those who should be upholding the faith in these matters either do not really believe what they are preaching, or believe it in such an unrecognisable form as to put into question the organic continuity between what they believe and what is believed by those to whom they are ministering. It may well be a proper part of protecting the faithful from scandal to take care that the loose talk of theologians, who may come up with provocative statements without showing the organic link between their faith and their statements, does not reach beyond those who are strong enough to understand what is really being said.

From the official perspective, the pastoral work of Bob and Jeannine was causing just such a scandal. The scandal was not that they were simply denying that the teaching of the Church in the area of 'homosexual persons' is true. They weren't. Neither of them, to my knowledge, has ever publicly labelled Church teaching in this area as untrue. The scandal was that they were suggesting, by implications both written and pastoral, that there might be other voices with different tones which might lead to the teaching being modified. In other words, and this does appear to be the substance of the Notification against them, they appeared, in the name of the Church, deliberately to be fostering an ambiguity which allowed people to think that the current teaching of the Church might not represent the fullness of God's voice as directed to the lives of those to whom they were ministering.

Such a suggestion obviously scandalises the faith of those for whom every particular of current Church teaching must be true, if any of it is to be true. In just the same way, those whose faith in the inerrancy of Scripture holds that every word of the Bible must be true if any of it is to be true, are scandalised by the suggestion that Genesis does not mean what it clearly says about the creation of the world in six days.

However, this is not the scandal which the authorities were seeking to avoid by their prohibition of the pastoral work of Bob and Jeannine. They were seeking to avoid 'homosexual persons' being led into believing that the voice of God might be saying to them something other than what official Church teaching claims it is saying. This is the scandal (a bad thing) of people being fed a teaching which does not, in the eyes of the guardians of the faith, present to them fully the scandal of the Gospel (a good thing) as it applies to their circumstances of life.

So here we have a second understanding of scandal: the scandal of the Gospel. The notion that the Gospel is a scandal has a good pedigree. Paul refers to the preaching of Christ crucified as a scandal to the Jews and folly to the Greeks (1 Cor. 1:23). Jesus himself says 'Blessed is the one who is not scandalised by me' (Matt. 11:6). At least one possible inference of this statement is that the Gospel might normally be regarded as a scandal. The official interpretation of the scandal of the Gospel takes it to be referring to such hard sayings as 'if any one would come after me, let him take up his cross daily and follow me', and in fact this very phrase is adduced in official teaching aimed at 'homosexual persons'. The faithfulness to the Gospel of 'homosexual persons' would be shown by our understanding that neither having nor contemplating an intimate relationship with a same-sex partner is the sort of scandal with which Jesus presents us as a condition for following him. If we are not scandalised by the demand, but are simply able to follow it, then we are blessed. Anyone suggesting that maybe taking up a cross daily and following Jesus might after all be perfectly compatible with an intimate relationship with a same-sex partner (and it is after all clearly compatible with a sacramental relationship with a partner of the other sex), would be scandalising the faith of the 'homosexual person' in question by failing to present him or her with the scandal of the Gospel.

Then there is the third sense of scandal, one which is not covered by official teaching, because official teaching is implicated in it. This sense of scandal cannot be predefined, but only measured by the depth of dismay which it causes when it arises. This is when those who have been charged with upholding the Gospel behave in ways which are so manifestly at odds with the Gospel which they teach that they cast into doubt the possibility that the Gospel might be true, or livable in the institutional form which is claimed to be truth-bearing.

Curiously, the faithful are remarkably resilient in the face of badly behaved ministers. After all, it is, as St Augustine says, penitence, not innocence, which God requires of all Christians, and anyone who gets something wrong and can admit it ceases to be frightening.

What really scandalises is incorrigibility, the inability to undergo correction. This is the spectre which has been raised by the way in which the Vatican authorities have treated Bob and Jeannine. Their silencing is the result of the authorities reckoning that Bob and Jeannine are causing a scandal to the faithful by publicly raising the question of whether or not they underwent due process. The spectre this raises is that the institution charged with protecting people from scandal is oblivious to the ways in which it acts scandalously, that its only understanding of scandal is a self-serving, and never a self-critical understanding. The effect of such obliviousness is to put into doubt the truth which in theory was being protected. After all, as it becomes clear that someone has got something wrong, there are two possible outcomes. Either I can be transparent about how the current situation arose, and join in an exploration about whether or not the claim that something is wrong is really true. In this case it will gradually become clear whether I got something wrong or not, and where I was right and where I was wrong, and I will be able to accept the consequences and continue in healthy life. Or I can refuse the possibility that I could conceivably have got something wrong. In this case, I very rarely let the matter rest at that, but typically compound my error, justifying it with new arguments and insisting more and more loudly how right I am, and how everyone else is wrong, and how I am the victim of people ganging up against me. The bystander watches with amazement at how a small mistake grows and grows into becoming a defining part of the personality of the person or institution in question. What is terrifying about this process is the perception that the person, or institution, in question is so utterly scandalised by the very possibility of being wrong that they lose their ability to reason. Instead they start casting around for all sorts of sacred justifications (and to claim 'victim' status is one such sacred justification) which, by being sacred, are beyond the possibility of rational discussion. This sort of incorrigibility is the very reverse of the gift of infallibility. In fact it looks like a terminal disease.

I confess that I am tempted to wonder whether the treatment of Bob and Jeannine, their silencing with what is simply a naked use of power, is not a sign that we are dealing with a body which has retreated into a world of sacred justifications for indefensible actions, actions which *of themselves and without the need for further commentary* raise the suspicion that the positions being defended are indefensible by any other means and thus untrue. What fuels this suspicion is, it must be said, a history by the authorities in question of the use of a particular understanding of scandal in order to refuse discussion. So, when a few years ago an Irish bishop said that he publicly welcomed discussion of the possibility of opening the priesthood to married men, he was silenced by a curial cardinal who claimed that he was scandalising the faithful. Well, it is quite clear that the bishop was not scandalising the Irish faithful who, whether they agree with a married clergy or not, are at least not shocked at the question being raised and show their understanding of these matters in opinion poll after opinion poll. But what is frightening is the possibility that the bishop may indeed have been scandalising the faith of people in the curia, raising the possibility that their faith is so weak, and so utterly dependent on people flattering their sense of the perfection of their system, that they cannot tolerate open discussion. In short, it is the authorities' use of 'causing a scandal to the faithful' that has become scandalous.

And we saw the same sorry story in diocese after diocese where it emerged that those harmed by paedophile priests had been told to keep quiet so as not to scandalise the faithful. As patterns of abuse and cover-up emerged, the faithful were treated, with far too few honourable exceptions, to a thoroughly defensive attitude which sought to protect the institution before making amends to those harmed. Nowhere were the authorities more incorrigible than in facing the suggestion, which seems increasingly plausible, and certainly worthy of examination, that there is a systemic element in the clerical culture which led particularly to this form of misbehaviour, and this form of cover-up. For to discuss that possibility would scandalise, not the faithful, but themselves.

To yield to the temptation of believing in the terminal incorrigibility of the authorities would be to lose the Catholic faith. In the struggle between the infallibility with which Christ endowed the Church and the incorrigibility which is merely the current hallmark of a mutable system which we have not yet learned to transform, I do not doubt that infallibility will eventually triumph over incorrigibility. Nor do I doubt that infallibility takes the form of remaining in the truth by being able to discern where we have been wrong, where we have been telling other than the truth to ourselves and others. Peter, after all, made the one indisputably infallible Petrine pronouncement which we have on record, after, and as a result of, a process of discovering himself *to have been wrong* about the binding nature of the entire purity code of his own religious background. This meant recognising that he had been wrong about his own entire set of cultural presumptions and presuppositions with their consequent categorisation of gentiles as impure and profane. When I label this the one indisputably infallible pronouncement which we have on record, I mean that, as a matter of fact there is no Christian, of whatever denomination, who does not accept without argument, and usually without even thinking about it, that here the Petrine ministry was exercised infallibly. This was the pronouncement by which Peter said to the gentile Cornelius 'God has shown me that I should not call anyone profane or impure' (Acts 10:28), and consequently added the baptism of water to what God had already baptised with the Spirit. That is, having discovered himself wrong, he gave official recognition and welcome to what God was already working independently of him. Every gentile Christian is the direct beneficiary of this pronouncement and the dynamic which led to it.

Having said this, there is no doubt that the appearance of incorrigibility is scandalous, and I suggest that one of the ways we can begin to recover rationality, which means a capacity for sane, nonscandalised fraternal discourse, in this area is by having a look at the second of the three types of scandal which I indicated, the scandal of the Gospel.

a closer look at gospel scandal

Jesus did indeed say 'Blessed is the one who is not scandalised by me.' However, it is not at all clear that the scandal in question is directly related to the 'hard sayings' in the way that official usage has suggested. In fact, the obvious reading of the gospels suggests that the real scandal is the possibility that when God himself becomes present in the midst of a particular human group, those who are scandalised are not scandalised by the heaviness of his demands. On the contrary, they are scandalised by the fact that God himself does not fit into the scheme into which, according to them, God should fit. It is not that God is too sacred for ordinary people to be able to bear it, but that he is so *little* sacred that *religious* people find it impossible to bear it. It is they who find it scandalous, and seek to retreat into old wineskins. The heavy demands which certainly do follow from this scandalising presence are not the heavy demands of scrupulous religious observance. On the contrary they are the existentially heavy demands of letting go of the sort of security and belonging which good religious people may find themselves aspiring to, and setting off into something which will look markedly atheistic, which is to say, into the heart of God. These existentially heavy demands will include running the risk of being persecuted, even to death, just as Jesus was, especially by religious people who think that they are serving God

by persecuting people of unbound conscience and bold speech.
This is, after all, what happened to Jesus: God was 'counted
among the transgressors'. That is the scandal of the Gospel. It is
above all a scandal to those who have a lot invested in whatever
passes as 'good' in their society, and it is notably less scandalous
to those who have found themselves living the shadow side of that
goodness: prostitutes, tax-collectors (i.e. 'collaborators') and so
on. Thus has it been for nearly two thousand years.

When Jesus said 'Blessed is the one who is not scandalised by
me', he was sending a message to John the Baptist, who wanted
to know whether Jesus' mission really was in continuity with his
own somewhat severe penitential preaching, and who had begun
to doubt it. The implication of Jesus' reply is that by following
Jesus we can learn to move *without being scandalised* from a world
of heavy religious demands and apparently sacred structures into
a world where those structures no longer bind us, but where we
are with comparative ease able to fulfil whatever was authentically
of God in them. Sure, our freedom of conscience may scandalise
others who need a sacred structure to give them being, and we
must try to avoid scandalising them. But it is blessed *not* to be
scandalised by this process, including not being scandalised by the
violence which will be meted out to us. In other words, the
scandal of the Gospel is not the heaviness of religious demand
made on weak individuals, but the fact that the collapse of what
seemed sacred is a collapse produced by God himself.

Now we Christians have very cleverly managed to short-circuit
Jesus' impact here by limiting the collapse in question to a critique
of 'Judaism'. We can tolerate Jesus scandalising 'Judaism', and
then we cunningly transform his teaching on scandal into something as bad as our very worst caricature of the 'Judaism' which
Jesus scandalised: we make Jesus into someone who demands sacrifice! However, if, as our faith rightly teaches us, the same Jesus
is alive in our midst, teaching us and producing discipleship among
us, then his transformation into someone who is stern of heart,
and whose yoke is hard and his burden heavy, is a sign that we've
got something wrong in our understanding of the scandal of the
Gospel.

I propose that living with the scandal of the Gospel means refusing the option of explaining away the passages in which Jesus demonstrates a systemic understanding of the way religious people especially create and shore up a false 'sacred' which makes God complicit in something terrible. Normally we explain them away by reading those passages as 'Jesus overcoming Judaism'. On the contrary: living with the scandal of the Gospel means accepting with joy Jesus' making available for us the chance to participate in universal Judaism by learning ourselves how to undo our own tendency to create and shore up a false sacred which makes God complicit in something terrible.

If we do this, then various things come into immediate focus: scandals are sure to come, and blessedness involves being able to live with them without losing faith in God being bigger and better than the messes we make of things. Keeping alive this faith means that religious authorities, who are, on the obvious reading of the gospels, the ones most likely to be directly challenged by the scandal of the Gospel, need, for their own sakes, to develop and keep alive constantly and publicly a watchfulness over their own teaching and practice. In other words, to develop the self-critical habit of the sort which asks 'Are we succumbing to the institutional tendency to bind up heavy burdens on people's backs and not lift a finger to help them?' 'Have we been trapped by our own arguments into systemically straining out gnats and swallowing camels?' 'Has our insistence on a certain sort of continuity of teaching led us to confuse the word of God with the traditions of men?' 'Mightn't the vineyard be being given over into the hands of others, who produce its fruit?'

And this constantly alive self-critical habit probably needs an attempt to develop a self-critical institutional instance – though what form that might take is seriously difficult to tell at this point in history. We have become so used over the last few centuries to the tiresome spectacle of an 'incorrigible' religious authority being pulled kicking and screaming into what turns out to be something like conformity with its own teaching by the force of civil law that many of us simply imagine that civil law, for all its blunders, is the providential corrective device. The idea that we should do for ourselves now what others will eventually force us to do seems unthinkable. Yet, anyone who begins to be aware of the effect of 'group think' on his own thinking is very serious indeed about seeking outside opinion lest he make a terrible mistake unawares. John Paul II seemed to be conscious of this when he called for outside help in coming to understand what might be the proper significance of the Petrine ministry for all Christians. Anyone who is not aware of the effect of 'group think' on his own thinking can only become more and more scandalised as he becomes aware that his voice is perceived to be institutionally self-interested and not taken seriously.

The blessedness of those who are not scandalised by Jesus also means not allowing ourselves to be terrified by the intransigence of those who do appear to be scandalised by the Gospel. It means our learning not to imagine God as associated with things which appear to be sacred, but are not sacred, merely frightening. The blessed who are not scandalised by Jesus understand that in each generation there will be attempts to shore up the sacred violently – that is just how things are in our fallen planet. And in each generation, the real 'sacred' of the Gospel will emerge quietly and gently, usually at the hands of those whom the strongest supporters of the sacred regard as especially inimical to faith and good customs. That is how it is. We have the blessing of not being scandalised by Jesus when we realise that the intransigent are more to be pitied than feared. We would be right to fear gods who demand sacrifice. But there are no gods. And God is not in the image of the gods.

Furthermore we show that we are not scandalised when we patiently refuse to regard as definitive what seems to be wrong, and develop ways of talking about it which show that we respect the rightful function of religious authorities, do not want to frighten them more than they are already frightened, but insist, patiently and gently, on participating in the fraternal task of keeping the Gospel dynamic alive.

It is with this background in mind then, that I would like to turn to a closer examination of the Notification regarding Jeannine Gramick and Bob Nugent with which I began.

the question of ambiguity

To believe in the corrigibility of religious authority is to believe that we are *not* simply faced with people who are being driven unawares into madness by a dangerous system which has enveloped them. It is to believe that, appearances notwithstanding, 'what they do' and 'what they say' are not so intimately bound up with each other that we are dealing with a package which must either be accepted or rejected in its entirety. When our Lord taught us to make this sort of distinction (Matt. 23:3) he was not giving us a special new divine command. He was teaching us how not to be scandalised by religious authority, but instead to learn to treat it on the same sort of fraternal level as we hope would be applied to ourselves. One of the ways I can tell the difference between my friends and those apparent interlocutors who don't really want to talk to me at all is that the former make distinctions of this sort when talking to me, while the latter regard what I say and what I do as part of a single package which is taken as removing me from the realm of rational discourse. The lack of a loving ability to talk with distinctions indicates that someone is not a friend. This is true whether the ability is absent owing to an attitude of condemnation *or of adulation* on their part. In both cases, it is not 'me' they are talking to, but they are projecting on to 'me' something which affirms them in unchallengeable righteousness.

So, let us try to avoid projections and instead have a go at fraternal talk by making a distinction between the scandal of the practical mishandling of the Gramick/Nugent case and the content of the Notification. I very much hope that between my writing these words and their being published, voices like that of Cardinal George will have been raised in such a way as to cause the process to be re-examined, the various strictures on Bob and Jeannine lifted, and the pressures on their religious congregations to act against conscience relaxed. Scandals should not be explained away, they should be investigated transparently and undone.

Having said that, I would now like to do something which you may find surprising, but which is consistent with what I have attempted to say about not being scandalised by religious authority. I would like to offer the Congregation for the Doctrine of the Faith (hereafter CDF) thanks for its Notification concerning Bob and Jeannine. I think they are on to something important, and if only they can learn not to sully their insights by persecuting people, then what they have to say might help all of us in the Church towards adult discussion of a complex and painful area.

Let me make it clear that I am saying this as a Catholic who has come to find it necessary to dissent publicly from what the Congregation claims to be the 'clear and constant teaching of the Catholic Church in this area' (a series of paragraphs from ecclesiastical documents ranging from 1975 to the present day). I do not believe that that teaching is in fact consistent with the revelation of God made available to us in Jesus Christ. I have come to consider that the Congregation's teaching in the area of what they call 'homosexual persons' makes God inappropriately complicit in the traditions of men.

I may be wrong, and I certainly couldn't be right without running the risk of being wrong. However, it is not my purpose here to debate how to make the expression of the Church's teaching in this area more adequate to the Word of God. The issue of truth is the only worthwhile discussion in this area, but it can only be conducted publicly when circumstances permit. Those circumstances are only now beginning to come into existence and will take some time to flourish appropriately. My purpose here is to point out how much better, and how much more bracing an ecclesial document, the CDF's Notification is than most responses would indicate. As a member of the faithful who strongly disagrees with what they take to be the truth in this area, I nevertheless find myself strongly resonating with, grateful for, and desirous of pursuing further, their desire to clean up the ambiguity and hypocrisy which surrounds this area in the Church. I find that the Notification shifts the ecclesial discussion and the resulting ecclesiastical ambience in very interesting directions.

I would like to highlight three of these directions with gratitude. The first (and most startling because best hidden) is that of the recognition of the delicacy and yet of the relative unimportance of the issue; the second is the recognition of the ecclesially deleterious nature of deliberately fostered ambiguity; and the third is the insistence on interior assent to accompany teaching.

The first point becomes evident at the end of the Notification, with the pronouncement of punishment. The Notification sets out a lengthy apologia for itself, indicating how long the process has been grinding on (over ten years), the various commissions which have pored over all the literature involved, and so on. Manifestly the CDF was acting as a shock-absorber to filter out some of the rubbish spewed out against gay people or those brave enough to take our side in the eighties and nineties. So, there has been a certain delicacy here, and a desire to avoid easy accusations and condemnations. What is more remarkable is that this delicacy is accompanied by a recognition that, for all the time and energy spent on the case, the matter is not, objectively speaking, a very important one.

Frankly, and without wishing to minimise the pain caused to Bob and Jeannine by their run-in with a powerful institution, by comparison with the anger and fear that this issue has aroused in our own and other churches, the punishments are very low grade. There is no excommunication – an indication that for the CDF the matter involved is simply not a communion-breaking issue (which is to say, a Church-dividing issue). There is no suggestion of heresy – an indication that for the CDF the matter is not one of a serious defect from the faith. Being 'wrong' in this area does not imperil the integrity of the theological virtue of faith. In Bob's case there is no suspension from the priesthood, and in neither of their cases was there, at the time of the Notification, any attempt to have them expelled from their religious congregations. Neither priesthood nor religious life are limited to those who assent to Church teaching in this area. The punishment consists in a permanent prohibition from engaging in pastoral work among gay and lesbian people, and a temporary ineligibility for office within their religious congregations. These are harsh indeed, but seem somewhat different from the rhetoric of the discussions of these matters in some Christian circles, both Catholic and non-Catholic, where it does seem that the gay issue is communion-breaking, one where dissent from the party line is thought to imperil the integrity of the theological virtue of faith, to make one a non-Christian.

Now, please excuse the kitsch, but for those who enjoy fantasising about the CDF as inquisition, then consider the wonderful picture this conjures up: a magnificent auto-da-fé in some dusty Spanish city, a huge procession bearing Bob and Jeannine to the pyre, throngs of delirious right-wing Catholics rejoicing at the long-awaited triumph of the faith of their fathers, a few disconsolate gay people huddled behind closed doors scarcely daring to watch. Ashen-faced Cardinal Ratzinger (for it is he) advances, flaming torch in his hand, grim Hickey and Bertone not far behind, fully clad in El Greco robes. Our Inquisitor comes up to the pyre, raises the torch, and then, with a slight gesture, hands it back to Hickey, and solemnly proceeds to gag Bob and Jeannine and spit in their faces. Nasty, yes, but a bit of an anticlimax really.

Camp aside, Cardinal Ratzinger seems to have pulled off (and not for the first time) a remarkable sleight of hand. While seeming to throw meat to the wolves (and I do not forget that that 'meat' is two human careers) he may in fact have managed the feat of rationally downgrading the importance of the whole issue. This is very significant, since it means that the arena in which the truth of the matter is from now on to be worked out might be a much less drastic one than many of us feared, and the discussion likely to be that much less unpleasant. If only the enforcers could now be called off, we might find that the temperature has gone down, and Cardinal Ratzinger will have done his job by helping us navigate through what was always going to be a very complex and painful issue with much less hysteria than might have been expected. That would surely be worth a cheer.

My second grateful cheer for the CDF concerns their attitude to ambiguity. The clear and overriding intention of the Notification is to put an end to deliberately fostered ambiguity in the area surrounding homosexuality. The CDF thinks it quite wrong that a Catholic pastoral work, while claiming and appearing to be Catholic, should give its participants the impression that Catholic teaching is something other than what it is. I strongly welcome this. Whether or not Bob and Jeannine have in fact deliberately fostered ambiguity, as is claimed, I doubt. That they have laboured generously in a severely harassed vineyard at a time when ambiguity seemed the only pastorally sane option is clearly true.

But the Catholic faithful do, as the CDF indicates, deserve better than ambiguity: we deserve truth. Deliberately fostered ambiguity in this area has been the enemy of truth because it has suggested that we can get by without having the serious discussion about whether the teaching is true or not, and if not, what is true, a discussion in which the participants face the consequences of their positions. Ambiguity hints instead that there are nice parts of the Church under whose friendly umbrellas we can shelter, so long as we don't rock the boat by raising the question of truth and thus putting those wicked Vatican bureaucrats on the alert.

This is silly. If the Church's teaching is true, then of course it should be insisted on without ambiguity. And of course, the CDF, which is a bureaucratic office for the maintainance of doctrine and not, in theory at least, a fount of new doctrine, does not have open to it the option of saying that it is not true. It has to insist that it cannot enter into debate about the matter, because for it to concede that there is a debate about the matter is effectively to abandon as untrue one of the poles in the debate. Given their starting point, they are quite right. Until it has become self-evident that the constructs which shore up the CDF's position are not of God, and until a fuller, richer and more whole appreciation of the matter becomes available and effectively supersedes their position in the minds of the faithful (as has happened frequently enough in the past with other issues), they must hold on to it. They knowingly run the risk of looking like Pharisees and fools in the eyes of history, a burden some of them bear with considerable grace and patience, and they do so as a service to us. We are not Catholic if we refuse the possibility that Pharisees as well as free spirits share in the Spirit's keeping alive of God's revelation in Christ.

So, truth must be upheld unambiguously. I disagree with the content of what is held to be true, but that the faithful deserve unambiguous truth is quite right. Now, very interesting consequences flow from the CDF's position, and it must have cost them a lot to arrive at it. For ambiguity in this area has not been the preserve of a few named pastoral agents. It is in fact a tone which permeates the ecclesiastical sphere in at least the three continents where I have worked, and is a serious danger to the moral and spiritual health of those who inhabit it. In countless seminaries, houses of formation, religious communities, curias and so on, an endless game of ambiguity is played which goes something like this: 'We will turn a blind eye to the obvious so long as you don't rock the boat by talking about it.' The result is swathes of the clerical caste engaged in a continuous game of internal emotional blackmail, for this issue can always mysteriously be raised in order to threaten or expel. To the surprise of no one at all and the scandal only of those who salivate for scandal, the Roman curial employees who published *Via col vento in Vaticano*[2] documented that the Vatican itself is not exempt from this ambience.

The consequences of this perverse lifestyle are terrible: on the one hand, expulsions, loss of career, livelihood, reputation and, in some cases, loss of life by suicide, and, on the other hand, promotion, security and so forth for those whose consciences allow them to flourish at the expense of honesty, of solidarity with their brothers and sisters, in short, of their capacity to be witnesses to the Gospel.

To their credit, and within their logic, the Vatican has tried a visitation of seminaries to deal with this matter. They made a distinction between those seminarians whose homosexuality was 'egodystonic' (i.e. who don't accept their being gay as part of their 'I', but are troubled by it), and those whose homosexuality was 'egosyntonic' (i.e. for whom saying 'yes I'm gay, and it is as a gay man that I'm called to serve God in this way' is non-problematic). The former were deemed acceptable for the priesthood, and the latter unacceptable. However, few people in their right minds were able to go along with this borrowing of psychological jargon to back up the CDF's a priori of the disordered nature of the homosexual inclination. So the visitation was

---

2. Milano, Kaos edizioni, 1999.

something of a damp squib and the culture of nudge-nudge, wink-wink, and the turning of the blind eye triumphed once again.

The Vatican's logical but unreasonable attempt to deal with ambiguity by insisting that only non-self-accepting gay men might make good priests, for only they accurately reflect the teaching of the Church, seems to me to compare favourably for sheer consistency with a different emerging voice in seminary formation which sounds 'reasonable' but is not half so candid in recognising its own a priori. This voice recognises that there is a gay majority in most seminaries, and observes that this has a destabilising effect on the vocations of the straight minority who feel out of place.[3] Now I do not doubt the observation, but it is much less clear that the destabilising effect is owed to the simple fact that the majority is gay. Most of the gay majority in a Catholic seminary or house of religious formation are typically living with some or other degree of fear of expulsion, of officially sanctioned self-hatred, of bad consciences over any relationships they might find themselves in, of severe self-questioning about whether or not they are being hypocritical in living at the expense of, and becoming the public representative of, a body which acts in public as though it hates them. Never mind all the gossip, backbiting, intrigues, power games and delations which go along with such states of mind. That at least has been my experience in living in, teaching in and visiting houses of formation and seminaries in three continents.

Might this somewhat-less-than-honest ambience not have something to do with the destabilisation? The ambience which Donald Cozzens accurately reports[4] as more 'Truman Capote' than 'Spencer Tracy'? What sort of a surprise is it that it be destabilising to live with a majority of gay people who are officially committed to believing that being gay is not a normal part of nature? Not only straight people, but also gay people who prize honesty

---

3. For an example of this see Donald B. Cozzens' in many other ways excellent *The Changing Face of the Priesthood*, Ch. 7 (Minnesota, The Liturgical Press, 2000), with supporting references to articles, signed and anonymous, in *The Tablet*.
4. 'Telling the Truth', *The Tablet*, 5 August 2000.

are thoroughly destabilised by living in such an environment. To point to the destabilisation without questioning whether this isn't caused by factors other than being gay, like maybe having to live under an erroneous official characterisation of the nature of same-sex desire, seems to me less than candid.

I very much suspect that it is only when seminary formation is indifferent to whether seminarians of either orientation are married, or in partnership, or aspire to one or the other, but is seriously concerned that they be searchers after honesty, learners of responsibility, and lovers of the weak and poor, that the current ambience will become more healthy. In such circumstances, just as in lay life, healthy celibacy will flourish as God calls it forth. I also suspect that the Vatican authorities are perfectly aware that to drop the insistence on clerical celibacy for straight priests while maintaining it for gay priests would be untenable for long. Thus, in practical terms, the issue is not only one of the recognisedly mutable Church discipline concerning clerical celibacy. Practically inseparable from that is the issue of what the authorities regard as a divinely ordained prohibition of same-sex intimate partnerships. Not to treat these two together is to play off straight against gay in a less than fraternal manner.

In the meantime, and until we pluck up the courage to face these questions squarely, the CDF are surely right to try to alter the destabilising climate of ambiguity which permeates our Church. While subtlety and discretion may well be Christian, these should be part of letting 'your Yes be Yes, and your No be No, for anything else comes from evil'. Ambiguity in this area is a way of saying neither yes nor no, but of nailing a rainbow flag firmly to the inside of the closet door, and of making cowards of us all. No one advances towards truth while the rules of the game are 'We'll leave the nasty bit up to the Vatican which is a long way away, so don't worry. You'll be OK with us provided you don't rock the boat, though of course we reserve the right to mistreat you should we feel threatened, and will dissociate ourselves from you if you get into trouble.' So, the CDF is to be congratulated for trying to spur us into being a little braver and seeking truth and thus beginning to clear up this canker in the life of the Church.

There is, of course, a second source of ambiguity in the ecclesiastical ambience concerning homosexuality, but it is one not deliberately fostered by cowards, and it may well be a highly positive force towards the emergence of truth. This is the ambiguity caused by the tension between the Church's new-found human rights teaching, which condemns unjust discrimination against gay people on the one hand, and the official characterisation of the homosexual inclination and acts on the other. As the momentum to take the former seriously grows, and hierarchs find themselves having to take positions on changes in civil legislation city by city and country by country, the latter becomes increasingly arcane and irrelevant. In point of fact, it no more helps the emergence of truth in charity when the pursuit of the former is taken as an excuse for avoiding discussion of the latter than when insistence on the latter is used as an excuse for not recognising the demands of the former. However it is at least possible that the ambiguity produced by the creative tension between the two nudges us towards Catholicity.

We are in the early stages of what appears to be quite a serious shift in human self-understanding. As so often in the past, part of that shift involves the gradual emergence of what created reality really *is* from beneath the tatters of violent and superstitious moralising characterisations of what 'ought' to be. This is, it seems to me, an authentically Christian dynamic. The scandalous movement from a 'sacred' which imprisons to truth which sets free was breathed upon us by the man to whom the terms 'one counted among the transgressors' and 'Very God of Very God' both apply. It is, furthermore, a movement the contours of whose outcome are, thank heavens, not possessed by any of us. I suspect that the CDF would join me in cheering to that.

And so to my third grateful cheer, the cheer for interior assent.

The CDF's Notification goes further than simply seeking to remove ambiguity. It specifically raises the question of interior assent to the teaching. Only those people who believe the CDF's teaching in this area to be of God should exercise a pastoral ministry towards gay and lesbian people. The CDF's insistence on interior assent in a judicial process of this sort has been much commented on as something of a novelty, and its legality questioned.[5] If this is a novelty and if a way has been found of combining respect for conscience, due process, and manifestation of interior assent, I welcome it. It goes to the heart of the way we deal with the gay issue in the Church, because it is insisting that there be no hypocrisy in this area.

The CDF is right again, for it is hypocrisy in this area, not gay sex, which is the real moral and ecclesial problem, a matter which destroys lives and may well damn souls. By comparison even habitual failures of chastity seem laughable. In demanding both a lack of ambiguity, and interior assent to the Church's teaching in this matter as of God, the CDF is taking rather a brave and radical step. It is effectively demanding that the hypocrisy which surrounds this matter in the life of the Church now come to an end.

This is not some direct and terrible blow to Bob and Jeannine, who have manifestly and honestly struggled with the issues over the years, and suffered the consequences publicly in a way which is anything other than hypocritical. But what the CDF have demanded of Bob and Jeannine is what any of us should demand from each other, especially from those who have a teaching and pastoral ministry over us. How many of us have not met priests and bishops who try to reinterpret, or put a good spin on, Church teaching in this area, but end by upholding it? Some of us may even be the people whom we have met! The same people 'off the record' are thoroughly kind, decent and broadminded, and manifestly do not give interior assent to the teaching. And we gay Catholics have far too often been pathetically grateful to such people. The CDF is right. We should not be. They should either uphold the Church's teaching because they believe it to be true, or they should indicate dissent from it, and face the consequences.

The matter becomes more complicated when we consider one of the obvious reasons behind this culture of ambiguity and

5. This is one of the areas in which it is alleged that due process was not followed in the investigation of Jeannine Gramick.

hypocrisy, which is that so many priests and bishops are gay, and yet so few are 'out'. Bizarrely, the only chance that the CDF's teaching has of demonstrating its truthfulness convincingly is when someone is able to give witness to it. This means someone living in a way which makes clear that by accepting that their homosexual inclination is an objective disorder and that any homosexual acts they might commit or desire to commit are intrinsically evil, they are thereby more closely configured to Christ. It is not at all clear to me what a personal witness to this teaching could possibly look like.

Appearances aside, being a closeted gay man is no less public a way of being gay than being 'out'. It is only the quality, and not the fact, of public relationality which changes. However, the closet has the disadvantage of crippling a person's capacity to give witness. To give witness in this area would require a gay man or lesbian woman who is able convincingly to tell a life story and develop relationships which manifest the Christlike nature of their assent to this teaching and the godliness of the transformation it produces in them.

Let it be clear that the issue here is not that of bearing witness to the goodness of chastity. The issue of chastity is a separate one from the issue of assent to the teaching. You can be chaste without accepting the CDF's teaching, and you can assent to the CDF's teaching without being chaste. The CDF is not, in this case, demanding chastity, it is demanding assent to a teaching. But if the teaching is to be believed, some healthy witnesses to the effects of assent to the teaching are required.

I have, myself, yet to encounter such a witness. But if you can't witness to it, you shouldn't teach it as of God. The CDF is right again. More follows: it is a maxim of Roman law that one who is silent thereby consents. This is in fact an accurate assessment of complicity in a group dynamic. If I do not object to a movement in my group, I consent to it. If I consent because I believe in it, all well and good. But if I consent by my silence because unwilling to face the consequences of being in the minority where I strongly suspect the truth to lie, then I am very probably a coward and a hypocrite. For evil to triumph it is only necessary that the good do nothing.

The consequences of the CDF's insistence on interior assent begin to become clearer: little by little colours are going to have to be nailed to masts. They should only teach who genuinely believe the teaching to be from God. If this is despite themselves, they should say so, and so give witness and be prepared to be scrutinised by the faithful for the healthiness of the lived consequences of what they teach. If the matter is for them a grey area, then they should say so: a grey area cannot be imposed on anyone as of God. If they do not assent, then they should say so and face the consequences.

And the CDF might even be consistent with the overriding intent of its own Notification and offer practical help in the clearing up of this climate of ambiguity and hypocrisy by making quite sure that the consequences of dissent are less terrible than many fear. If ambiguity is fostered by cowards, then the merciful thing is not to shout at the cowards, but to give us signs that we need not fear honest speech. If ambiguity is fostered by a learning process of being pulled between two teachings, then it needs to be sat in patiently as we find our bearings and learn to tell the truth from the midst of the sad history of murder, muddle and mendacity which has characterised our faith's relationship with same-sex desire. In that case also, the best way to overcome ambiguity is by finding ways of encouraging the development of truth-tellers, which means people who are not frightened of being wrong, because they know that it is being loved, not being right, that matters.

The Gospel promises us a sign of contradiction which reveals the thoughts of many hearts. The very same Gospel promises us that what is whispered in secret will be shouted from the rooftops. I am sure that the CDF's Notification seeks to contribute to this dynamic, and I have indicated why I think that it in fact does so. I merely wish that the Congregation's practice were more consistent with its best intentions, which is what it prayed for in the Jubilee Year ceremony of asking for forgiveness in St Peter's Basilica, and which is what I pray also for myself.

on finding a story

introduction[1]

If someone had told me ten years ago that I, an English Catholic theologian, would be invited to make a presentation as a gay activist to a highly educated audience within a stone's throw of San Francisco, a city I knew only through Armistead Maupin's 'Tales', I would have laughed like the aged Sara when she overheard the angel telling Abraham that next year she would be with child.

What extraordinary tectonic upheavals have gone on in our countries, our forms of social belonging, our churches and our souls to have made this sort of conversation possible! What amazing shifts in perception of what it is to be human, to be Christian, to be rational do we find ourselves working through! I would like to start by asking you to inhabit the very strangeness of this exchange, how bizarre that it is possible at all.

I have been asked to help develop a conversation among you centring on the theme of violence and the gay question, a conversation which has acquired some urgency in the wake of a number of murders, some not far from here.[2] Our imagination has been

---

1. This chapter originated as a talk given in Woodside, California in October 1999 as part of a series of discussions on violence. My host informed me, apologetically, that he had billed me as a 'gay activist' so that my talk would fit in with those of the speakers at the other events: an African American theologian and a rabbi. Some are born gay, some achieve gayness, and some have gay activism thrust upon them!

2. A gay couple had recently been murdered in nearby Redding, California, their murderers apparently convinced that to kill them was to be about God's work.

caught both by their brutality and by the repeated hints of a package of self-justification on the part of the murderers, a self-justification which in some way or other reflects a sense of lost bearings, of flailing around for an identity, of inability to live with, rather than resolve, ambivalence.

I would like to suggest that one of the ways in which we can repeat the murderers' gesture of resolution is to crystallise the issue into the neat format of 'violence and the gay question', in which we understand that violence is a bad thing, that gay people are basically decent co-members of civil society, and that what is at stake is how we stop, or at least limit, the violence. This resolution lines us up together in indignation, gives us a sense of being the good guys, and enables us to begin to cast around for causes of the 'problem'.

Now that's about as certain a formula for violence as you can get — the righteous looking for someone to blame. So, rather than go down this path, I'd like to try something a little different with you, something which you may feel disqualifies me both from my pretension of being a Catholic theologian, and from the role which I have found ascribed to me, of gay activist. I'd like to stand back from the terms of the discussion, and see if we can advance together by learning to perceive the issue anew. Rather than talking about violence and the gay question, I'd like to talk about creation and cowardice.

Gomes' challenge

A couple of years back, I was struck by a comment of Peter Gomes, the Preacher to Harvard University, in his *The Good Book*.[3] He commented, almost wistfully, while showing how to read the Bible well, and how not to be trapped by taboo in the gay question, that he felt that the movement of gay liberation, or whatever you might like to call it, has lacked something important. Whereas the Civil Rights movement, the struggle and dignity of African Americans, was fuelled and empowered by a wonderful set of

---

3. New York, William Morrow & Co., 1996.

biblical images and stories, principally linked to the Exodus narratives and God's ineluctable 'Let my people go', so far there has been nothing comparable within the gay groundswell, and this is an important lack. In other words, African Americans were able so to inhabit the biblical story of liberation from slavery that the truth of their lived experience and their moving on became unanswerable. Pharaoh has been left speechless, first with rage and then with shame, and where he has recovered his speech, it is as a brother that he has had to learn to talk.

I think Gomes' comment is absolutely right, and I would like to take it up as a challenge. We gay people have as yet been unable to inscribe our lives into the biblical story, inhabit the biblical universe. And that means that we have fragmentary stories, of coming out, of standing up against hypocrisy, of surviving and growing through AIDS, of discovering that we really can love after all, of peaceful partnering and husbanding of each other, of learning to invent new forms of family bond, of asserting civil rights, of withstanding religious violence, of becoming socially acceptable. None of these is despicable, many are astounding, all of them reach deep into our souls; but while they remain fragmentary, they also remain reactive. And this means that there is something as yet limping and breathless about our story. It does not yet have eagle's wings.

Before I go further I'd like to make a point, what you might call the believer's point. I'm not talking, as I'm sure Gomes is not talking, about a strategic matter: 'Hey guys, the Bible has some good stories. If we can learn to tell our story in Bible terms, we can turn the table on our enemies by occupying the high moral ground.' That would be a cynical exercise in marketing: finding the right story. No, I'm talking about something rather different. My conviction is that there is only one Bible story, and that it is the story told by God, and it is within this that we are invited to inscribe ourselves. In other words, God calls us into being through giving us the gift of story, and that uncompleted story is one in harmony with, and nourished by, the fragments of biblical nudges towards it. To make the point another way: it is not a question of us searching for a story, but of us discovering, slowly, painfully, and through endless muddle and losing the thread, that we are being invited to inhabit a story which is one not of reaction, but of being called into being and rejoiced in. It is much more a question of discovering ourselves to have been dragged into an unimagined story than of us sitting down after some crime and working out how best to sell ourselves when the cops come by.

What I'd like to do with you is have a first shot at accepting Gomes' challenge by exploring why it is such a heavy demand on gay people that we find ourselves within the Bible story, a bit like Babylon demanding of the exiles from Jerusalem that they sing one of Sion's songs; but then I want also to suggest that there are in our midst hints of an emerging capacity for story, a capacity which can enrich us all, straight and gay alike.

from 'no story' to 'coming out'

To understand the heaviness of the demand, let us dwell on the absurdity of an openly gay man talking to you about the things of God. Not so long ago, this conversation would have been unimaginable. The reason is simple. The very fact of being a gay man would have put me outside the bounds of what could be talked about at all, let alone talked about within a sharing of theological discourse. And this is not because non-gay people were stone deaf, or gay people too shrill to be heard except by dogs, but because the universal assumption would have been that everything to do with God is fundamentally opposed to everything to do with being gay. And it is not only non-gay people who would have thought this, but gay people as well.

I cannot emphasise this strongly enough: there were not words with which to talk about these things, let alone a story within which to inscribe them. Being gay was associated with shame, with deception, with denunciation, with blackmail, with disease, with abnormality, with suicide and, floating freely among all these, with sin. And these associations were not merely held by the majority, while all along gay people themselves knew better. Gay people were at least as likely to have found ourselves inhabiting lives and relationships which were structured by these associations;

or *more* likely, since what were trivial and unimportant attitudes among the unaffected, were burning existential matters among those for whom these associations coalesced around and in an 'I'. Where an 'I' is only an 'I' as annihilated, how can it tell a story?

Furthermore, the mother and fount of all stories, the biblical world, was resolutely and absolutely closed to gay people, or so it seemed. We were clearly enemies of religion and of God, even when we were, often enough, brought up and educated within the bosoms of deeply religious households. How on earth to hold on to what is good, and righteous, and pure, while discovering ourselves, to our devastation, and without any sense of having chosen it, to be enemies of God? How easy to agree with the definitions given us, to mull over the fact that we must, in some deep sense, have chosen this awful abomination, and to line up with the discourse and denounce ourselves and those like us, killing ourselves by consent when not in deed!

It was common sense that the biblical world, the language of God, and the life of our churches seemed only to offer the hard face of rejection, or of acceptance along with the demand for self-rejection, which is only a subtler and more cunning version of the same thing. In the face of all this, it is scarcely surprising that the development of words, of stories, of all that leads to life, could not flourish within the religious ambience. Instead it poked forth in ghettos, with help from humanistic discourses themselves in scandal at the whole Christian and biblical 'thing'. It developed with help from protest movements, from psychology, from philosophies of political liberation. Those who were able to develop with it were brave people. They were often doubly detested by those of us who cowered in the midst of religions to which we maintained a perverse loyalty even when they hated us and made us hate ourselves. It developed in the midst of a terrible epidemic which forced upon us both a collapse of façades and the emergence of eternal questions in an unimaginably urgent form.

One of the key elements of story developed during all this is the story of 'coming out'. Apparently this term originally derives from 1950s talk where a group of friends would celebrate the emergence into honesty of a gay friend, borrowing the language of a young lady who might have a 'coming out party', where she would be presented to society. It was only later that the storyline shifted from 'girlie party talk' to something less light-hearted and more critical, with the notion that one was coming out 'of the closet' – in other words, leaving behind a world of furtiveness and double-life to start to be what one is.

It is interesting how this shift has caught the popular imagination, so that the language of 'coming out' and 'the closet' is now simply part of mainstream discourse which can be applied to almost any sphere where someone stands up for, and publicly identifies themselves with, a position thought to be unpopular – admitting one likes Tchaikovsky in a social circle governed by highbrow Wagner fans, or whatever. However, there's more to the notion of 'coming out of the closet' than meets the eye. The suggestion is that there was something private and hidden before, and now this is 'up front' and public. The result is that someone 'coming out' gets a clean slate, rather like an evangelical conversion experience. There is a 'before' and an 'after'.

Now, I don't want to belittle the coming-out experience, which is, for many of us, a very important spiritual moment in our lives. Yet my Tridentine[4] instincts are wary of evangelical conversion experiences! In a couple of books published in 1993, by Bruce Bawer[5] and Michaelangelo Signorile[6] respectively, both of whom hold very different positions within intra-gay debates, I noticed a coincidence both curious and very moving. Each of them mentioned in his book, entirely independently and en passant, a moment in his life, long after he had 'come out' and was publicly identified as a gay figure, when he had happened across someone who had known him before, who had been at college or university or some such place with him before he came out. At that time, these unnamed people were already identified as gay, whether

---

4. 'Tridentine' is the adjective referring to the city of Trento, or Trent, in Italy. It was there that the Council of Trent deliberated over several decades in the sixteenth century, producing a series of doctrinal documents which mark the Catholic Church's response to the Reformation.
5. *A Place at the Table* (New York, Simon & Schuster).
6. *Queer in America* (New York, Doubleday).

because of some visible attitudinal trait, or whatever. And in each case, they had at least suspected that our as yet undisclosed future gay author was gay. These people, in a school or college atmosphere of very great stress and violence, had borne the heat of the day at a time when our authors had been stuck in the closet. These people really could have done with solidarity at a time when neither of our authors was prepared to stand up for and identify with the object of mockery. They didn't receive the solidarity.

Now what each author reported separately was the experience of an unidentified gay contemporary from his past coming up to him and telling him how glad he was that the author had come out, and how pleased that he had become a gay opinion leader. Hats off, ladies and gentlemen: we are in the presence of great-heartedness, of spiritual grandeur! The labourer in the vineyard who started early in the morning was not jealous that the master was paying the same wage to the latecomer, but was just delighted that the latecomer made it to the vineyard at all, and in a senior capacity!

Now apart from thrilling to this moment of grace, I'd like to use the coincidence to make a point about 'coming out' which is not often part of the story we tell, and yet is, to my mind, a very important access road to the real story which we might be able to tell, and which would bring us closer to meeting Gomes' challenge. The point is this: the coming-out narrative imagines an individual's move from troubled potential gay man to flourishing actualised gay man, and that is that. First I was a sinner, then I knew Jesus, and now I am saved. End of story.

However, the encounter with the past should not be an incidental coda to the story. Rather, it is a vital part of the story, and without it, we are not going to be able to move into the richer pastures of a non-reactive, but a given, identity. Wherever a coming-out story is real, it also includes what I would call a penitential element: how I was a coward and failed to stand up for my brothers when the heat was on, but am now being given the grace to stand up and risk the opprobrium.

This is, dare I say it, one of the critical points in the relationship between the gay groundswell and ecclesiastical Christianity.

Where the coming-out narrative is able to be trivialised by those telling it as well as those rejecting it, as an individual conversion experience akin to a form of self-indulgence, a grabbing of a too easy and belittling identity, we don't get anywhere. It is too easy to say: 'But being gay shouldn't be the centre of anybody's existence, therefore I won't come out and run the risk of being trapped in too small an identity.'

But that is not the point: the point is 'if I don't stand up for my brothers, then I am consenting to their treatment.' The real drama of the coming-out experience is precisely that it is the beginning of a taking of positions in the midst of something like a lynch mob, and the discovery that by taking position I become not 'a gay man', whatever that might be, but a real participant in the life of the human race, just as I am, warts and all. But it is also the realisation that my previous failure to stand up for the weak was not simply neutral, but left me in collusion with violence.

It is, I suspect, this gradually dawning and terrible realisation that is really shaking from the inside the clerical establishment of our churches. No amount of doctrine, of theological learning or of canon law can hide for ever from preachers who expound texts like 'take up your cross and follow me' or 'are you prepared to drink the chalice that I must drink?' our shame at our own failure to practise what we preach in an area which touches so many of us intimately, and where there are already so many examples of moral fortitude among our non-clerical brethren.

from 'coming out' to 'being created'

Now please allow me to continue in my bigoted, partisan, Tridentine approach to this question. I say Tridentine, since I think that, in theological terms, what we are talking about is exactly the difference between the understanding of original sin, conversion and new life espoused by the sixteenth-century Reformers, and that insisted on with astounding perspicacity and depth by the fathers of the Council of Trent. I think that the key element is the link between conversion and creation, in some wise sundered by the Reformers, and obstinately held on to by the Catholics.

I would like to look at some of the factors which stand in the way of the shift from a dead-end coming-out narrative to what I would like to call a catholic narrative. Most of the gay commentators over the years have come round to the view that coming out is not a one-off experience, but is rather a process over time, already a shift towards Trent – my brother in the faith and compatriot Andrew Sullivan has written of this in a number of different essays.[7] I would like to look at that process and suggest that one of the things that has hampered it is precisely the inability to discover the link between penitence and creation.

It is easy, and inebriating, within the confines of a discotheque to sing along to such gay anthems as 'I am what I am'; and yet, really to believe that I am loved as I am is, for most of us, a journey which is only partially under way. And here I suspect that we come across one of the cruellest barriers to our being able to meet Gomes' challenge, and inhabit the biblical story. The last bulwark of theological obstination against our being able to tell our story is the official view of the doctrine of creation. This is true whether in its Protestant form, dependent on a reading of Genesis which can be reduced to the famous 'God made Adam and Eve, not Adam and Steve', or in its Catholic form, with talk of God's eternal law being written into the natural law in a way detectable only in reproductive creation.

Let me reduce this to two voices: first there is a voice, proclaiming with apparent pride, but underlying fragility 'I am what I am' – already, if we consider it quizzically, an astounding biblical claim, for this is the very name of God, and behind the name, the realisation that it is 'I am who I am' who makes all things to be. Then there is what I might call the ecclesiastical voice: 'You are not'. Let me be clear that it is not at all the ecclesiastical prohibition of sexual acts between people of the same sex that is really problematic, but the justification for that prohibition, the deep voice which booms beneath it, claiming to be of God: 'You are not. I didn't create you. I only create heterosexual people. You

---

7. Cf. *Virtually Normal* (New York, Random House, 1996) and *Love Undetectable* (New York, Alfred A. Knopf, 1998).

are a defective heterosexual. Agree to be a defect and I'll rescue you. But if you claim to *be*, then your very being is constructed over against me, and you are lost.'

Now, I can scarcely find words to tell you how powerful that voice is, and how much and how deeply it informs the lives of even apparently self-accepting gay people. This is a voice which, within the ecclesiastical sphere, makes cowards of otherwise brave and splendid leaders. If I had the time and means to write a book, it would be one aimed at facilitating the unbinding of conscience in exactly this sphere, for it is when we get this right that we'll all be able to move on.

I know of only one story able to reach these depths, offering both to affirm 'I am what I am' in its brave fragility, and to empower people to move beyond the fragility in discovering ourselves being loved into being. And that is the story of one who was quite clear that what the politico-theological establishment of his time took to be the eternal law of God tended to make God into the whisperer behind the lynch, the scatterer of the weak and frightened, the lover of sacrifice rather than mercy, one who rejoiced in breaking bruised reeds and snuffing out smouldering wicks. In the face of this, he made the astounding statement that only he knew the Father, and only the Father knew him, a claim that his 'I am' was held completely and gratuitously in being by the one who calls all things into being, without any fragile grasping at being over against anything at all.

That statement, and its corollary, that the only access to the Father is through him, has as its effect an extraordinary anthropological consequence – either it was simply blasphemous, and God is the upholder of eternal and binding laws which drive us all eventually into the ground, and Jesus was a silly protester hurling abuse at the immutable, or *that* god is an idolatrous projection of human paternity on to God, and the real paternity of God is only discoverable by creating a new sort of fraternity with Jesus on his way to being cast out by the forces claiming to stand for the divine paternity.

It is the centre of our faith that on the third day, the Father of our Lord Jesus Christ revealed that Jesus was right to trust in his

Father, and that he is the God who brings into being and holds in being even what is nothing, even what has been killed, such is the hugeness and vivacity of his creative power.

Let me try and stammer through this again. The only real narrative of creation we have is the narrative of the collapse of an idolatrous picture of creation linked to an order which tends to crucify, and the birth of an entirely gratuitous notion of the Creator who calls his sons and daughters into being, out of nothing, in such a way that death itself is not even the enemy of creation, since the same gratuitousness which brings into being, sustains in being through death.

Yet this is exactly what we celebrate every time we celebrate the Eucharist – my beloved Trent once again! We celebrate the real presence of our crucified and living Lord breathing among us the power to become penitent, to undo our ways of being bound in by the powerful paternity of the world, and to become able to relate to each other as weak brothers and sisters, ones of no account, who are coming to be held in being by the apparently weak, but ultimately unimaginably powerful creative love of the Father who is.

What I want to claim, and I think that this is at the centre of our faith, is that the doctrine of the creation and of the resurrection are the same doctrine, the same doctrine as God's fatherhood of Jesus Christ, one counted among the transgressors. And this doctrine is simply not existentially available by any sort of theological a priori. It is only existentially available as we undergo the experience of sharing in a kind of death at the hand of the false paternity to which we gave credit for far too long, and discovering ourselves, when brought to nothing and become the offscouring of the world, held in being in an unimagined and unending identity as children. It is, in short, a doctrine only able to be discovered by undergoing just the sort of process that gay people have found ourselves undergoing, and always and everywhere, if it is a true discovery, it will seem to be off-beam, disordered, heretical.

Listen to the half-crazed heretic holding firm to the weirdness of the truth:

Remember Jesus Christ, risen from the dead, descended from David, as preached in my gospel, the gospel for which I am suffering and wearing fetters like a criminal. But the word of God is not fettered. Therefore I endure everything for the sake of the elect, that they also may obtain salvation in Christ Jesus with its eternal glory. The saying is sure: If we have died with him, we shall also live with him; if we endure, we shall also reign with him; if we deny him, he also will deny us; if we are faithless, he remains faithful – for he cannot deny himself.

(2 Tim. 1:8–13)

Are we not in the same narrative world as the one I have been describing to you?

What happened to Paul, and the other disciples: cowards, hypocrites and traitors when not persecutors? They were enabled to stumble out of the old paternity into the new, following Jesus into the apparent atheism which turned out to be the hidden paternity of the Creator of all things from nothing. They must have undergone something very much like the shift from the timorous 'I am what I am' which was OK when Jesus was around to shield them, to the collapse of what looked like a fragile boast in the face of the crucifixion, when it must have seemed as though the official voice of God, the 'You are not!', the 'Cursed is the one who hangs on a tree!', had triumphed again.

Yet all the evidence is that within a remarkably short time of this collapse, these cowards had been made brave, and were able to stand up to the trumpet-bearers of the old booming tone, because their 'I am what I am' had been touched by something which removed all its fragility and turned them into the sort of brave men who would rather die than not speak the truth simply. These were people who had come to know where their paternity was, to rest in one who held them in being out of nothing, and thus discovered that they could speak out of an unanswerable boldness which was not in reaction to the authorities, but simply truth coming into being. The New Testament even has a special word for this curious new form of boldness: *parrhēsia*. Their consciences had been unbound from the false paternity of the world, and they were able to speak as created children relaxing into discovery.

Now I think that there are already signs of this among us gay people. I think that there are already signs of creaturely sonship being discovered as given to us just as we are. And there is nothing any earthly power can do to take it away, just as there was nothing any earthly power could do to unbaptise Cornelius when the Spirit of God had fallen on him (Acts 10:44). The real sign that this has come upon us will be when we are not even bothered or scandalised by church authorities, angry preachers, hypocritical politicians and so on, because we are too busy doing our own thing. And our own thing, if we really have learned to inhabit the biblical story, will be to see beyond the anger and the hatred and the violence in the hearts of those we once saw as our persecutors, over against whom we railed with similar anger, hatred and violence as we held on to our indignant and tense identities. Instead we will be learning to reach out to the brothers, hidden under the guise of hypocrites, cowards and traitors who do not yet dare to become unscandalised by the adventure of creation.

violence and the gay question

I have tried to shift the subject I was asked to deal with, from 'violence and the gay question' to 'creation and cowardice'. This is because I think that violence is not a 'they' question. Violence is the 'we' question, and it is a question of no interest at all in itself. Sound and fury, signifying nothing. Violence is the clinging on to old being when, in the midst of our world and giving it great birth pangs, the Creator is bringing forth the new creation starting from those who are not. We are all formed by, and tempted to, violent belonging, violent association, violent loyalty, and we are all masters at hiding it from ourselves. I've talked about cowardice, because that has been my problem, my way of holding on to the old paternity and not daring to allow myself to be held in being by the new. But in as far as unwittingly gracious persecutors have conspired to push me in directions I would never have dared to tread by myself, I've started to look at this not as an issue to do with violence and gay people, but as one where faith in the Creator has begun to make possible an equal-hearted fraternity which defies all definitions of identity.

To come back to the occasion of our conversation. Think of those murders. What do you see? I see Matthew Shephard, the Redding couple, Billy Jack Gaither, Scott Amedure and the other victims, all in the hand of God, beyond the need of our ministrations. But in whose hands are their murderers? And how will we use those hands? I've seen something of the guys on television, in news articles and so forth. What do I see? I see trailer parks, dusty pick-ups with gun-friendly bumper-stickers, worn-in jeans and cheap white underwear. I see heads filled with kooky bits of bible-talk, dwellers in conspiracy theory and all the intellectual dead-ends of resentful poverty. I see kids silently howling for manhood, when everything of manhood except its cheapest and most vulgar accoutrements is permanently, grindingly denied them. If I can't beat up on a faggot, then who the fuck can I beat up on except myself? The sort of world that only a great soul like Flannery O'Connor could do justice to with both realism and a respect bespeaking love.

But I see more than that. I see the same kids that I have been and I have known in gay clubs, in dark rooms and bath-houses, fumbling for a fix of manhood, a sense that in the middle of all this shit I may have some value, be of some worth, be able to be loved, just be. I see kids scandalised by a changing world with upside-down values, where we all try to find an identity, and all feel our failure. We too flail around in relationships which we don't know how to sustain, we write off our aggression in articles, we look for a 'politically correct' pack with which to hunt, we deplore guns as violently as others defend them. I'm learning to see brothers: straight, gay, what the hell, scandalised brothers who have to grab being from each other since we can't let go and learn to receive it from the only giver.

And beneath and in the midst of that I see the Sacred Heart of Jesus, palpitating and bleeding with pain and love because these are his brothers: the weak ones, the fatherless ones, the shepherd-less ones, the murderers and traitors and the simply confused, who can, oh yes who can, be nudged into a story of being held in being beyond all the flailing around, the bravado, the cover-up of a life out of control. And he's saying, and it cuts me to the quick: Feed my sheep, feed my sheep, feed my lambs.

CHAPTER TEN

Nicodemus and the boys
in the square

introduction

As a student of theology, part of me has always wanted to have
'a serious discussion about the Truth' concerning the relationship
between God and matters gay. I have constantly been disappointed. And I discover that it is right that I should have been.
Discussions about truth privilege debaters. They also privilege pre-
agreed terms of discussion. For example, framing the discussion
as one concerning 'homosexual acts'. Or 'Church teaching'. Or
'Gay lives'. But they will only debate who think they have a good
chance in the arena in question. In any case why should debaters
be privileged? Why should anyone stay within someone else's
terms of discussion rather than embark, for instance, on a sustained
journey of training the imagination towards a massive recasting of
concepts?

The realisation that there is no level playing field on which my
longed-for debate is going to happen has made it difficult to work
out to what voice I should aspire. There are certainly theologians
who live rich gay lives, and plenty of gay people who live rich
theological lives. But there are few of either who seek, as a matter
of vocation, to speak both languages as one. And even if we were
to pull off this linguistic feat, with what tone should we speak?
Contrition? Anger? Delight? Mourning? Dismissive superiority? My
attempt has been to give words to the voice of complicity speaking
the reverse of vengeance. This requires no small act of imagination. Tales of revenge follow the easiest storyline in the world,

and lead precisely nowhere. Consistently to undo the whole woof and warp of the structure of threatened or actual revenge is perhaps the most difficult work a storyteller can undertake. To make of forgiveness a sustained anthropological reality, rather than a deus-ex-machina resolution, is perhaps our imagination's greatest stretch.

I'm not sure what form the Christian discussion about matters gay will take in the future. I'm confident that the dynamic which has been at work since Pentecost will continue. This is the dynamic by which we discover the truth about *what is* in the degree to which we learn to step aside from our involvement in lynching. In the degree to which discussions about being gay take place outside the shadow of the bonfire, in that degree will we discover what it is all about, and learn to behave accordingly. Understanding starts to flourish where people refuse to put torches to pyres. If anything is meant by the phrase 'natural law' it is this: that *what is* gradually becomes available to our understanding as what God has always lovingly intended for us, in the degree to which we step out of the darkness of our own moralistic solutions to what we do not understand. Moralistic solutions create and shore up false understanding by victimage, and are the strict reverse of the journey towards truth proposed by the Paraclete, the counsel for the defence.

Because of this, I'm not sure that ecclesiastical discussion is interesting or important. The steps away from the bonfire are mostly being taken elsewhere, and where they are taken, there understanding comes. Yet charity demands having a go at creating a conduit between the paralysed world of ecclesiastical half-truth, within which I have heard and continue to hear the Gospel, and the possibility of living in the light. The idea is not mine, but comes from John's gospel, where this very role of conduit between paralysed half-truth and living in the light is fleshed out. If there is to be genuine ecclesiastical discussion of matters gay, it will not be because the 'enlightened' and the 'obscurantist' shout at each other, or because inalienable human rights clash with unalterable divine decrees, but because Nicodemus is learning to speak the truth.

los jóvenes de la plaza

A few years ago in a medium-sized city in a medium-sized Latin American republic, a friend of mine, another foreign priest, started to befriend some of the boys in the main square – los jóvenes de la plaza. These boys – in their late teens and twenties – hung around the main square towards nightfall, and were what people from another culture, and little by little, they themselves, would call gay. Their emotional centres and sexual experiences were with people of the same sex. Sometimes money would change hands, sometimes not. Among themselves there was considerable honesty, and considerable discretion, as to with whom, outside their own group of friends, they had 'been'. My friend, a self-accepting gay priest was (and is) not a predator. He was interested in talking to these young men, giving them a sense of dignity, allowing them to understand that their lives and stories of love were not fragile and silly, but of worth and interest. He was (and is) confident that it is in the degree to which people feel loved and worthy that we learn to avoid self-destructive emotional patterns and forms of behaviour.

It did not take long for my friend to discover something which in retrospect should not have thrown him as much as it did. He was by no means the first priest known to the boys in the square. On the contrary, some of the priests of that city were well known to one or other of the boys. And these priests tended to know the boys more as customers than as friends. What the boys also knew, but shrugged off with a certain world-weariness, was that it was the priests they knew under these circumstances who were the strongest in denouncing the evil and sin of 'homosexuality' from their pulpits – in fact the only ones who bothered to mention the issue. Little by little my friend found himself in an increasingly dangerous position. That of knowing far too much about the relationship between desire publicly condemned and desire privately unleashed.

And of course, the knowledge travelled both ways. From my friend's point of view what he was doing was (and is) honest pastoral work. For the clerical clients of the boys, it was intensely threatening that someone, let alone one of their own number, should be able to talk in an open and friendly way with the boys, and be well received and able to share their stories. What was threatening was that this priest was not paying the price of having a guilty secret in order to enjoy the boys' company. Thus he was not subject to tacit blackmail, and so was not safe.

You do not need to be a genius to know how this story ends. Several of the priests of that city, along with colleagues in another city, managed to orchestrate a campaign to discredit my friend, making quite clear that he was *persona non grata*. All too easily, I'm afraid, they managed to persuade his superior from a far-off land to have him removed from their country. So impressed was the superior with the gravity of the charges that my friend was sent for psychological evaluation and therapy. Mercifully the supervisor of the centre in question, accustomed to dealing with genuinely disturbed patients, immediately saw that there was no reason for my friend to be there, besides that of preventing other people losing face. My friend now exercises, very fruitfully, the same ministry, in semi-anonymity in a much larger – and thus more anonymous – city, in a different country.[1]

Of course the scenario is familiar. We all know that in the gospels Jesus delights in the company of 'sinners', while the 'Pharisees' were only able to approach him very tentatively, and were constantly being scandalised by his unscandalised proximity to those whom they regarded as outside the Law. It would be easy to use the story of the boys in the square to say 'hooray' for the boys and 'boo' to the priests, and of course part of any of us should want to say just that. But that was not the lesson that I began to learn as I accompanied the story.

The interaction between the boys in the square and the priests in their pulpits taught me instead something about Jesus and the integrity of human desire. Behind the stories of Jesus' easy table-fellowship with sinners something began to come into focus, something of the social dynamic which is what is really explosive in

---

1. This is not disguised autobiography. My friend has read, corrected and consented to my telling of his story.

those stories, and which very rarely emerges in their telling. What Jesus was doing then, and what his presence constantly tends to do now, wherever his story is told, and wherever his disciples imitate him, is to undo a social construction of goodness. It is not that there were some good people, for whom Jesus had little time, and some bad people for whom he had a great deal of time. Rather he moved in a world, just like our own, in which goodness tends to be captured and hedged around by some people and turned into a goodness which produces its own counter-image, badness. In other words, the world of the 'Pharisees' and the world of the 'prostitutes' are worlds which imply and constitute each other – a self-reproducing system. Jesus moved in this world with what clearly seemed to some of his contemporaries to be something remarkably like atheism: he didn't attribute anything divine at all to this system or the divisions which it produces. Which means that he didn't attribute anything divine at all to the system of religious 'goodness', and thus didn't see the divine as in any way at all condemning religious 'badness'.

Jesus seemed to think that God's goodness was to be found in quite other ways, and that falling short of it looked quite different from what was previously imagined. He also made it clear that he thought that the access to that goodness was far more easily to be found by those who inhabited the 'bad' part of the picture than by those who inhabited the 'good'. Naturally! Those who have less to lose will find it easier to let go of a 'bad' social identity as they are given something which makes them aware that they have worth. Those who have a lot to lose will prefer the worth which they are given by the current system of goodness and badness. For the 'good' to discover themselves in the same need as the 'bad' of being given the love which humanises, involves travelling a far more painful road of dispossession. There may well be those who prefer to lose their life by holding on to it, rather than to gain their life by losing it. So, the first will be last, and the last first.

Now Jesus did not simply look at this world from the outside and give us a theory to enable us to understand group sociology. He dwelt and dwells within it. And the world I'm talking about is the hugely complex world of human desire. It is people like us who are frightened of our desire who create and help to shore up this world of goodness and badness. In other words, back in the city where we started, Jesus dwells in the world both of the boys and of the priests, which is the same world, without being scandalised by the desire of the boys, or the desire of the priests. For he knew and knows that this is the same human desire in both cases. This is what I, as both a gay man and a priest, started to find alarming and challenging. Jesus is not scandalised either by the gay world or the priestly world. He does not condemn either the world of repetitive and loosely relational sex, or the world of compulsive and ritualistic goodness, let alone the many who struggle in a world shot through with elements of both. The bondage of desire in our night clubs and the bondage of desire in our curias are the same bondage, the flip sides of the same distortion.

That some priests are 'lace by day and leather by night' (in a phrase I wish I'd invented) is mystifying only to those who share their scandal. Jesus knows that they are both the same world, and that any of the priests could have been any of the boys, and any of the boys could become any of the priests. For him, there is no underground: everything is in the light of day. From any point within the spectrum of socially constructed goodness and badness any of us can move into becoming someone loved who can learn to love honestly and openly and speak and perform creative words of love into the heart of another human being. The sad thing about the story of the boys in the square was not that the priests had dalliance with the boys, or the boys with the priests. The problem was not that money did or did not change hands. The sad thing was that the priests were trying to exorcise the boy within themselves, and the boys in the square were not receiving the Good News that they need no longer go along with this degrading perpetuation of good and evil. And when my friend made an attempt to break down this wall, only the wonder of air travel could prevent outrage from leading to crucifixion.

The tragedy is when we take our goodness and badness so seriously that we ontologise them. So we create a sacred goodness, thinking that thus we can cut out the painful business of working through the same patterns of desire that we would have faced if we had stayed in the square, rather than merely cruising it furtively by night. And we create a sacred badness as well, as much a phoney cult of unredemption as the other is a phoney cult of redemption – a certain pleasure in being 'bad'. And of course it is true that those in the square are much more likely to find themselves, with no great loss, moving off into the beginnings of responsible adult relationships, gradually discovering that what seemed like a casual pick-up has turned into a man who has spoken words into their hearts which enable them to relax into being loved.

For the priests, this is more difficult, since priestly goodness is officially ontologised by both Church law and what many take to be divine decree. What we are likely to discover is that the words which enable us to relax into being loved may well also make it impossible for us to live within a structure which claims that that love can only be a sham. So, we may be tempted to settle for the structure and the furtive sex which give each other support, rather than the love and a life. And what better way to keep the structure alive than to repeat our scandal at our desire by condemning that desire, thus holding tightly on to what is 'good' and what is 'bad', and desperately hoping that we won't be caught. One of the most effective ways of keeping that structure alive is by insisting theologically that there is something in the nature of same-sex desire that makes it ontologically incapable of unscandalised fruition. If we can hold on to that, read our scandal at our own desire back into the very nature of things, then there is just a chance that we'll make it through our careers without being ambushed into the messiness of love.

But the extraordinary stature of Jesus, who is able to move between the world of sinners and the world of the righteous with an effortless integrity not shared by the denizens of either, is a sign of the possibilities of unscandalised human desire. Jesus did not feel a need to run away from the world of sinners. He does not feel threatened by the world of rent boys, nights on the heath, dark rooms, saunas and so on. He doesn't need to, since he is at peace with human desire, and thus able to see those worlds for what they are: worlds in which people are capable of being reached and touched by a love which may not even pull them far out of those worlds. It may teach them careful and responsible brotherhood for others in the same world, a gradual and non-scandalised unbinding of their desire where they stand.

In the same way, Jesus was not scandalised by the world of the righteous. He understood its dangerousness well enough to be able to side-step its attempts to lynch him until his hour had come. And he was very clear in warning his followers against allowing themselves to be deformed by what he called 'the leaven of the Pharisees' – their way of causing the social and religious culture to 'rise' and acquire consistency and system. However, he was perfectly able to imagine people within that world being very close to the Kingdom of God, able to be but a short step from leaving the security of that world and following him.

Just as there is nothing intrinsically disordered in the desires of 'sinners', so there is nothing intrinsically disordered in the desires of the 'righteous'. No one is terminally incorrigible, but everyone, starting exactly from where they are, can undergo that relearning of desire which is what it takes to become a disciple of the Kingdom. Jesus was neither a sinner nor a Pharisee, but an imitable model of healthy human desire who is able to draw some more easily, some less easily out of our systems of 'goodness' and 'badness' and into the Kingdom of God. To follow one who is neither Pharisee nor libertine is to learn the extraordinary stature of being able to bestride the world of 'scandalous' desire by night and the world of 'sacred' desire by day without being scandalised by either, but to become aware that both are essentially the same deformation of desire, and that from within that deformed desire, if only we will not sacralise it, fruition is possible.

by night

Nicodemus appears only three times in the apostolic witness.[2] He scarcely says anything at all. Yet what he does say, and the road

---

2. John 3:1–21; 7:50–3; 19:39–42.

he travels between his first appearance and his last, bespeak a huge and hidden transformation of heart. Nicodemus' first appearance is by night. He is 'a man of the Pharisees, a ruler of the Jews', and does not want to be seen to be consorting with Jesus by day, for that would get him into trouble with his brethren. Or maybe his brethren are happy for him to go to Jesus by night, they simply don't want 'the people' to know about it, lest they be given an ambiguous message. Nicodemus presents himself to Jesus as a spokesman for a group of potential disciples within Pharisaism:

'Rabbi, we know that you are a teacher come from God; for no one can do these signs that you do, unless God is with him.'

After this, Nicodemus scarcely gets a word in edgeways, except to ask a couple of questions which make him look foolish. Jesus does not seem to do what I am trying to do in these pages, which is to try and be gentle with the closet. On the contrary, he launches into a radical account of quite how different it is to be born of the Spirit than to be part of the order of the 'flesh' – meaning in John's gospel not sex and food, but the whole of mendacious and fratricidal human cultural life. Jesus does not pander to Nicodemus coming to him by night, allowing himself to be flattered by the attention. He knows that to have desires by night which are in contradiction with desires of the day are signs that both are distorted. He gives it to Nicodemus straight: there is no such thing as a closet disciple. Those who are born of the Spirit are moved in ways which are simply incomprehensible to those who live within the flesh. There is a radical rupture between the two modes of existence. When Nicodemus questions this rupture Jesus tells him:

'You are a teacher of Israel, and this you do not know?'

The implication is that the distinction between the flesh and the Spirit, the religious world of the authorities and the true cult of Yahweh is something which has always been available in Israel, and that any real teacher within Israel could make such a distinction, could learn to detect what in their own teaching was of the flesh and what was of the Spirit.

After this, Nicodemus doesn't say anything more, and in fact Jesus doesn't even talk to him as a singular individual. He ignores Nicodemus having come to him by night as an individual and talks to him as part of a plural 'you', addressing him as one of the group of Pharisees who do not receive Jesus' testimony concerning who God is. Nicodemus has after all presented himself as representing a 'we'. Thus it is his daytime persona whom Jesus is addressing, not his night-time one, even though his night-time persona looks to us like the better of the two. Yet it is who Nicodemus is happy to be by day that determines who he is, not his tentative sortie from that security into a risky night-time visit, where he may feel that he is being much more honest, much more himself. And it is by day that he will have to face the challenge of deciding whether he believes in the Son of Man.

After having delivered himself of the most famous verse of the New Testament –

> For God so loved the world that he gave his only Son, that whoever believes in him should not perish but have eternal life

– Jesus draws out its consequences. If you believe in him, then you are not frightened to come into the light because of it. If you do not believe in him, then you prefer the darkness which does not reveal what your deeds really are.

> For every one who does evil hates the light, and does not come to the light, lest his deeds should be exposed. But he who does what is true comes to the light, that it may be clearly seen that his deeds have been wrought in God.

Poor Nicodemus! He had thought that it was possible to give witness to belief in Jesus by night. Instead he is assured of the absolute incompatibility between his daytime practice and belonging, and his night-time confession. He gets told that only if he is able to act on what he claims he believes in the broad light of day will he really show that he has believed it. He must have gone home with a heavy conscience. For what he had said in the dark would have to be heard in the light; what he had whispered in private rooms would have to be proclaimed upon the housetops

(Luke 12:3). In the next chapter of John's gospel Jesus will not scandalise the woman he meets at midday by the well of Samaria. But here he has scandalised Nicodemus into silence.

The next time we see Nicodemus, he has begun to pluck up some courage to step tentatively out of his closet (John 7:45–52). Following an incident in which the Temple guard have managed to fail to arrest Jesus, who was speaking openly, and thus scandalously, in the Temple, the Pharisees get seriously annoyed. The enforcers really should not allow themselves to be led astray by this man's fine-sounding words.

> 'Have any of the authorities or the Pharisees believed in him? But this crowd, who do not know the law, are accursed.'

At this stage, and with considerable courage, Nicodemus dares to break the angry unanimity which can only anathematise those with whom it disagrees. He raises a legal, procedural question to defer the violence:

> 'Does our law judge a man without first giving him a hearing and learning what he does?'

The Pharisees are not fooled. Due process is unimportant when the truth is already known. Anyone who speaks up on behalf of such a person is probably 'one of them':

> They replied, 'Are you from Galilee too? Search and you will see that no prophet is to rise from Galilee.'

In other words: only 'one of them' could take him seriously, and the unanimous voice of Scripture is against the possibility that 'one of them' could tell the truth. Nevertheless, Nicodemus does seem successfully to have thrown a monkey-wrench in their works, for he breaks their conspiratorial unanimity and 'they went each to his own house'. Nicodemus has run the risk of stepping outside the 'flesh', and has lived to tell the tale.

What went through Nicodemus' head as he went to his own house? He had just witnessed the other side of what Jesus had said to him: the absolute incompatibility between flesh and Spirit. The Pharisees were even clearer than Jesus had been about the radical nature of witnessing, however half-heartedly, to the possibility that there might be a discussion about Jesus' presentation of God. But where Jesus had simply confronted him with being consequent, the Pharisees had instantly detected what his failure to join their unanimity said about him, had seen that it gave him away. The closet is a place in which you are safe neither by night, nor by day. By night you face the threat of coming clean and thus losing your daytime belonging; by day you face the threat of being found out, and thus being expelled. Which is the more frightening, to take your chances with the living God, or to see whether you can negotiate survival in the midst of violent men?

Well, we know that Nicodemus made it in the end. The last time we see him (John 19:38–42), he and Joseph of Arimathea, another closet disciple, 'a disciple of Jesus, but secretly, for fear of the Jews', join together to bury Jesus. Joseph gets the necessary permission from Pilate, and Nicodemus turns up with a heavy mixture – a hundred pounds weight – of myrrh and aloes. John reminds us that Nicodemus was the one who had earlier come to Jesus by night. But here it is day, just. And Nicodemus and Joseph get Jesus buried before nightfall ushers in the Day of Preparation, when such activity would have rendered them impure. So Nicodemus, no doubt prepared by his own near brush with a lynching, had not been swept away by the unanimity against Jesus, but had found himself able to honour one who, in all scriptural rigour, had died under what he should have regarded as God's curse. Maybe Nicodemus' act was still timid. Maybe, like some of us who have accompanied those terminally ill with AIDS at a time and in places where it was assumed to be a particularly gay disease, he found it possible to honour in death what he was not brave enough to honour in life. Even so, the richness of his tribute bespeaks a genuine freedom of conscience, a having broken out of the world of 'flesh' and an emerging into the world of Spirit.

'you are a teacher of Israel, and this you do not know?'

Now I do not think that Jesus was gay, or that Nicodemus was a closet gay ecclesiastic. I do think, however, that the way in which 'the Jesus question' erupted in first-century Palestine and the way 'the gay question' is erupting in contemporary Christianity are so structurally similar that we would be foolish not to allow the gospels to help us find our way to understanding what really is of God.

Between Nicodemus' night visit to Jesus, his introducing a legal monkey wrench into his confrères' conspiratorial unanimity and his full-hearted tribute to 'one counted among the transgressors', a huge change had taken place. We can take it that Nicodemus, being an educated religious authority, was not simply swept by volatile emotion into swapping one allegiance for another. The very timidity and carefulness of his conversion speaks against that. It is not unreasonable to suppose that he had, indeed, been challenged by the central question with which Jesus had confronted him: 'You are a teacher of Israel, and this you do not know?' In other words, he had started to reread his own religious tradition in order to try and distinguish between what in it was of the 'flesh' and what of the Spirit. This had caused him to undergo a self-critical process of learning to find himself to have been wrong about a whole number of presuppositions and teachings which he had regarded as sacred. And not wrong because someone new had come along and said something new. Wrong because the person who had challenged him had pointed him in the direction of uncovering a number of elements in his own tradition which were of far greater weight and importance than his contemporary orthodoxy, and which made clear quite how far that contemporary orthodoxy was in contradiction, or even overt enmity, with the deepest melodies of his own tradition. He started to become something like what Jesus says in Matthew's gospel:

> ' . . . every scribe who has undergone discipleship for the kingdom of heaven is like a householder who brings out of his treasure what is new and what is old.' (Matt. 13:52)

What Nicodemus certainly knew, as a good Pharisee, is that there is no such thing as a simple rupture of tradition. Scribes, Pharisees, priests, theologians – we are all champions of continuity, of trying to keep alive what we have received by casting it into new words, new styles. Nicodemus was being challenged, just as we are being challenged, not simply to break with his tradition, but to rediscover and make alive within his tradition whatever points to God enabling us to break out of the order of 'Egypt', of 'this world', the order of 'flesh', and to correct in its light whatever closes down that enabling, and traps us into making God a function of 'flesh'. In fact Nicodemus did exactly this when he broke the unanimity of his group by raising a legal question. He was using the Law to defer violence, against a reading of the Law which seemed to be demanding it. In this he was engaging in that most noble of Jewish practical interpretations: reading the Law against sacrifice, making the Law point to Spirit rather than allowing it to become the instrument of the 'flesh'.

It was clear to him, from the evidence we have, that it was no merely intellectual challenge with which he was being faced. He was also being faced with the existential task of working out for himself where he stood in relation to the socially constructed world of goodness and badness of which he was a part, and of acting accordingly. It was this world that Jesus was challenging on a daily basis both by his teaching and by his freedom of movement within it. Nicodemus knew that to read his tradition as Spirit could not be done in a vacuum. It involved either deciding that there was no further work of interpretation to be done, and going along with the pharisaic maintenance of good and evil, the world of those who knew the Law, and those who did not and were 'accursed'(John 7:49). Or it involved taking steps to put into practice the undoing of that world, whatever the consequences. And, it was this, however tentatively, that he began to do.

back to the square

Uncertain of what the rupture between flesh and Spirit towards which Jesus had pointed might look like, Nicodemus wandered down to the square. He was going against his normal practice of retiring early and knew little of what went on there after dusk. To his surprise he found something like a carnival getting under way. The tropical night was cloudless, and the elegant colonial plaza with its well-spaced trees and cast iron benches was filling by the minute. People of all sorts and ages milled about, some dressed casually, some in costume, some watching over gently stumbling infants. Different groups of musicians were playing at different corners. In the middle was a large bonfire waiting to be lit, and not far from it a group of people were setting up a battery of fireworks.

One particular piece of fancy dress gave him a momentary start. In the far corner of the square sat a figure who was dressed up as the Grand Inquisitor. It looked as though he had borrowed the costume from the local Opera's massacre of *Don Carlos* earlier in the season. As Nicodemus drew closer he could see resting on the Inquisitor's knee a mask with a pointy beard and severe, but slightly silly-looking, spectacles. Nicodemus was irked. Fiestas are all very well, but don't mock the Church! Wishing away his residual puritanism about such things, Nicodemus pushed past a group of people dressed as Harlequin and company, side-stepped a gesticulating couple whose difficulty with high heels suggested that they were unaccustomed to their drag, and came up to the Inquisitor. The figure turned slightly and caught Nicodemus' eye as he drew close. 'You!' said Nicodemus, with surprise and outrage. 'You! You have spent two thousand years trying to convince people that you are not the Grand Inquisitor, and now you descend to this?' The Inquisitor held a finger to his lips, and began to adjust his mask over his face. Then, with a nod, he pointed towards a group of revellers moving through the crowd.

Four young men were propelling towards them what can only be described as a Duchess. As they drew close, the Inquisitor adopted a stern pose on the end of the park bench, elegantly avoiding some dried bird-droppings. The Duchess was obviously a man, of medium build and spreading girth. He moved forward, part pushed, and partly under his own steam, pretending to resent being dragged before the Inquisitor. The boys, it pained Nicodemus to notice, were, one might say, pretty, and obviously knew the Duchess well. A couple of them added to the mixture of judicial drama and hilarity by pinching her bottom. A hint of a wink between one of the young men and the Inquisitor flashed 'mission accomplished'. The Duchess had successfully been lured to a prearranged tribunal. She came to a halt in the position of the penitent before the judge with a gesture of annoyance that there was no prie-dieu in place for her to kneel. Overcoming her mock dissatisfaction, she drew herself up. 'Ecce Homo' she announced, with suitably exalted intonation, to laughter from both boys and Inquisitor.

The Inquisitor gave a judicial-sounding cough and intoned: 'Let the hearing begin. With what heresy is this maiden charged?' The Duchess gave a little curtsey, as if of gratitude at the ludicrous gentility of 'maiden'. 'Sentence first!' cried one of the boys, who'd obviously read his *Alice*, pointing to the yet-to-be-lit bonfire in the centre of the square. 'Sins against dress sense, sins against dress sense' piped in another, whose own outfit was a testimony to the zeal and purity of his religion. 'Unfair, unfair' squawked the Duchess. 'Anyone over 28 years of age and with more than a 28-inch waist is absolved from that heresy. I know my catechism!' Nicodemus couldn't help noticing that her tone sounded as though it too had been borrowed from some of the less satisfactory moments of *Don Carlos*. 'Stinginess' shot out another of the boys, and then, slightly maliciously, and amidst a flurry of raised eyebrows, 'Only twenty pesos an hour.' The Duchess caught back a response which suggested that the boy was overvalued at that, but not fast enough for everyone to see what she meant to say, and even the accuser laughed at himself, and gave the Duchess a little hug and a squeeze. The least noticeable of the boys said 'Envy. She stopped me joining the seminary because I'm the boyfriend of another of the priests.' The Duchess didn't quite know how to react to this outbreak of sincerity, but the other boys turned on the accuser with a chorus of 'ahs', pushing and punching him gently and made as if they were playing sobbing violins.

'Enough!' barked the Inquisitor at the boys. 'I asked for a charge of heresy. All you have given me are grave acts of sedition against this kingdom, for which I may have to relax Madame to the secular arm.' 'Yumm' said the Duchess, forgetting her falsetto and rolling her eyes at one of the young men, whose khaki pants, military boots and toned muscles, obligingly flexed in response, hinted that playing the secular arm was not beyond his possibilities. The boys whooped with delight, and even the Inquisitor had to adjust his mask. Round to the Duchess.

'So,' said the Inquisitor, regaining his composure. 'Given that you incompetents can't muster a charge of heresy, I will have to proceed myself, with the authority duly invested in me, to the Ordinary and to the Extra-Ordinary Question.' He pronounced the last words as if to make sure that an imaginary scribe would not fail to add capital letters.

'First, the Ordinary Question. Madam, in the presence of these witnesses, I conjure you, profess your faith in the clear, constant and unchanging teaching of Holy Mother Church concerning Homosexual Acts and the Homosexual Inclination.'

'With great pleasure,' said the Duchess, who didn't often get the chance to show off as a professor in front of the boys. She drew herself up and raised her hand solemnly. On a moment's reflection, this seemed a little more Boy Scout than Duchess, so she clasped her hands together regally and rested them on what passed as her bosom. Then she intoned, mostly keeping the operatic voice with which she had started: 'I truly and firmly hold that homosexual acts are always objectively evil.' She exaggerated the 'o's in 'homosexual' with refined disgust. 'On the solid foundation', she continued, 'of a constant biblical testimony which presents homosexual acts as acts of grave depravity, Tradition has always declared that homosexual acts are intrinsically disordered. The homosexual inclination, though not itself a sin, constitutes a tendency towards behaviour that is intrinsically evil, and therefore must be considered objectively disordered.' She ended her aria *rallentando* so that it sounded a little like Mrs Thatcher driving home a point.

The boys all applauded wildly, except for the one who had raised the charge of a heresy against dress sense. He had been brought up in a pentecostal church, just knew that it was all wrong, and didn't get the Catholic stuff about tradition. The boy who had protested stinginess clearly knew the script, since he pulled off a few dance steps, keeping time to the elegant cadence of 'must be considered objectively disordered'.

'Very well, Madam,' said the Inquisitor, inclining his mask with a gesture of condescending approval. 'Since I cannot fault you on the Ordinary Question, let us now pass to the Question Extra-Ordinary.' He paused as a loud cheer and applause greeted the lighting of the bonfire further down the square. 'Please profess your faith in the clear, constant and unchanging teaching of Holy Mother Church concerning concupiscence, as defined by the Council of Trent. And I might remind you', he said, emphasising his sixteenth-century robe with deliberation, 'that I myself played a small, but not, I hope, an unimportant role in that august assembly.'

The Duchess paused, slightly taken aback by the question, since he taught the course on Trent and original sin at the seminary. Was all this leading to some extravagant vengeance, planned by someone who knew him too well? Like maybe his confrère whose boyfriend he had kept out of the seminary?

Drawing himself up, and slightly conscious that his Duchess persona was slipping, he recited: 'I firmly believe and hold what the Council of Trent taught, namely that if anyone says that the guilt of original sin is not remitted through the grace of our Lord Jesus Christ which is given in baptism, or even asserts that all which pertains to the true essence of sin is not removed, but declares it is only rubbed out and not attributed: let him be anathema. For God hates nothing in the reborn, because there is no condemnation for those who are truly buried with Christ by baptism into death, "who do not walk according to the flesh" but putting off the old person and putting on the new person created according to God, become innocent, stainless, pure, blameless and beloved children of God "heirs indeed of God and fellow heirs with Christ", so that nothing at all impedes their entrance into heaven. The holy council confesses and perceives that in the baptised, concupiscence or a tendency to sin remains; since this is left for the struggle it cannot harm those who do not give consent but, by the grace of Christ, offer strong resistance; indeed "that person will be crowned who competes according to the rules". This concupiscence the Apostle sometimes calls sin, but the holy council declares that the Catholic Church has never understood it to be called sin in the sense of being truly and properly such in those who have been regenerated, but in the sense that it is a result of sin and inclines to sin. If anyone holds a contrary view: let him be anathema.'

By the end the Duchess, having started with her accent, was speaking quite normally, and with a hint of pride at the archaic majesty of her script. No applause greeted this rendition, and the boys looked slightly uneasy, as though they'd been left out of a somewhat long joke, if joke it was.

Nicodemus, however, was stunned. He had quite forgotten that Trent was so uncompromising in holding to the absolute lack of hatefulness, the absolute lack of condemnation, which had gone along with baptism ever since Peter poured water on Cornelius. But also Trent's freedom in insisting that there was no such thing as intrinsically evil desire, only intrinsically good desire, in however distorted a form.

'Well,' said the Inquisitor, meditatively. 'Well what?' said the Duchess, reverting to camp in an effort to revive the atmosphere.

'Well, which of the two do you believe?' asked the Inquisitor 'What do you mean, which do I believe?' snorted the Duchess, her indignation becoming her costume. 'Why both of course! Surely Your Eminence can see how beautifully crafted the teaching on the homosexual inclination is, so that it coincides exactly with this very teaching on concupiscence.' The boy in the military pants was fumbling in his pocket to extract a pack of cigarettes from the keys and condoms amongst which it nestled. He produced it, offered one to the boyfriend of the seminary priest and took one for himself. The Duchess cast a disapproving glance at both of them, but the Inquisitor beckoned for one too, and, realising that his mask would make smoking difficult, tucked the cigarette behind his ear. 'Go on,' he said.

'Well,' said the Duchess, now speaking only in his own professorial tone, 'Trent teaches that human desire is intrinsically good, but is always and everywhere experienced by us as accidentally disordered, so that there is no human who does not start from a life that is moved by disordered desire. But it is also true that there is no human who cannot, from within that disordered desire, learn to desire what is good.'

'Bravo!' said the Inquisitor, and the boys applauded politely. Encouraged, the Duchess continued with a flurry, as though especially proud of his point: 'You see, there's all the difference in the world between teaching that God loves us just as we are, and it is because of that love that we find ourselves becoming something even more wonderful that we could not have imagined ourselves, and teaching, with the Reformation, that God does not love us as we are, but has kindly agreed to pretend that we are something else. It is the difference between saying "It is you that I love" and saying "It is not you that I love, but I will love you if you become something else." Not that I think that the Reformers really meant that,' he said, casting a patronising glance at the Pentecostalist, 'but that was what Trent thought that they meant.' The Pentecostal boy looked slightly embarrassed, as though caught between not knowing how to defend his heritage, and not really thinking it was his heritage to defend anyway.

'Go on,' said the Inquisitor. 'Well,' said the Duchess 'so the whole argument concerns what good desire really looks like. And we know what good desire looks like objectively.' 'We do?' asked the Inquisitor. 'Yes of course,' replied the Duchess hurriedly, not certain whether the question was asked with respect or with irony. 'Let's take a case that has nothing to do with sex, to make it easy. Someone who is grasping and even dishonest about money can gradually learn to become someone who is utterly honest and even generous. They can learn to put their own finances at risk so as to attend to those who are needy, instead of putting their own security before their ability to create friends.' The boy who had claimed being underpaid grinned and gave the Duchess a little squeeze. If the truth be told he'd never been sure whether the money he'd received had been payment for services rendered or a token of friendship from someone who just wasn't very good at showing it.

'And another example of movement towards objectively good desire,' continued the Duchess, glad at the squeeze. 'Someone who consistently uses fine words to cover up the truth, a liar who uses words to protect himself and his position, can gradually become someone who learns to speak the truth, even when to do so puts him at risk from people who maintain the status quo out of self-interest.' The boy whom he had prevented from entering seminary was giving him a steady look, and the Duchess coughed and said in an aside, 'Well, maybe that was an unfortunate example.' The boy smiled wryly.

'Well, go on,' said the boy in the military pants, crushing his cigarette butt with his boot, 'get to the sex bit.' 'As I was saying, if you'll give me half a chance,' said the Duchess, 'my point was that we know what good desire looks like objectively. Anyone, whatever their sexual desires start out as, can become someone who is chaste according to their state of life. So, if you are single, "chaste" means ordering your life and friendships so that they are without sex. And, if you are married, chaste means ordering your sex lives so that sex is never deliberately closed to the possibility of having children, which is what it was obviously intended for by nature. It's that simple. Any sexual desire that does not fit into that pattern constitutes a tendency towards behaviour that is intrinsically evil, and is obviously, therefore, objectively disordered. *Et voilà.* That is how there is no discrepancy between the teaching of Trent and the Church's teaching on the homosexual inclination and acts.' He finished with a deep bow towards the Inquisitor, as if to say 'Didn't think I could pull it off, did you?' The Inquisitor showed no sign of movement.

'Wait a second,' said the Pentecostal boy, with a hint of annoyance. 'Dizzy Protestant fashion queen I may be, but even I can see that there's something not quite right here. For your position to be true, it would mean that there's no difference at all between straight people who don't buy your Church's teaching on birth control, and gay people. I mean, what's the difference between a married couple who practise birth control, or my brother and his girlfriend having sex, and me and my boyfriend.'

'There's no difference at all,' said the Duchess, glowing. 'That's the beauty of the Church's teaching. It's absolutely even-handed with regards straight and gay. And it means of course, that any church which does not accept our teaching on birth control has no logical position at all from which to forbid gay sex. Once you have accepted a rupture between the procreative and the unitive aspects of sex, the only barrier to complete acceptance of gay couples is prejudice.'

'Whoa!' said the would-be seminarian, caught between pride at his own Church's logic and a desire to come to the rescue of the Pentecostalist, with whom he too had been a theological sparring partner in the past. 'But that's not what it's like in practice. I mean, if what you say is true, then the Church would have no objection to our having civil rights, being able to register our unions, even having partnership ceremonies in church, because its teaching about sex would have exactly the same impact on our lives as it has on the lives of straight people! And that would mean that, in practice, we would be accepted as couples, and whether or not we are having sex would be up to us and our consciences. But that's not how it works. I mean, straight couples aren't asked to swear to uphold the Church's teaching on contraception in order to get married. In other words, the stability of their lives is given priority over whether or not they buy the line about contraception. With us, it's just the reverse. Only if we first buy the line on sex are we even allowed to hold meetings together on church premises. When Father John tried to set up a Mass for gay people in his parish, you all fought against it on the grounds that it wasn't specifically aimed at promoting the Church's teaching on the "evil of homosexual acts". In other words, with us your even-handed logic has the reverse effect of what it has in the lives of straight people: the purity of the teaching takes precedence over the stability of our lives. And if you're so keen on maintaining your logic and avoiding prejudice, why do you so happily join forces with a whole lot of churches, none of which buy your line on contraception, in order to lobby against civil rights for us, whenever the issue comes up? If you were consistent, you would refuse to ally with them, and say that since your teaching on straight sex and gay sex is even-handed, you can take no part in any legislative campaign which doesn't put both straight and gay on the same footing. In practice, your teaching for all its logic, leaves our Church being every bit as prejudiced as the other churches you so grandly dismiss. It also means that your bit about "God loving us as we are" is reduced in practice to the same as what you said about the Reformation: God only loving us if we agree to become something else.' He finished breathlessly to nods of approval from the others.

'You know,' said the military-looking boy, slowly. They all turned to look at him since he was not much given to talking. 'I've been thinking about this. Actually, about my parents. They knew I was gay before I did. I only discovered that several years later when I told them who I was dating. That was when I discovered that they'd worked it out for themselves – not just the gay bit, I mean, but the prejudice bit. I always thought they were just a bit innocent and hadn't worked out what the sleepovers and the nights out meant. What they told me when I came clean to them was that they had always known, and at first had been shocked. But they had thought about it, and reckoned that if they had backed up my brother and my sisters as they grew up and started to date, and had listened to the stories and shared the heartbreaks and dried the tears – well, that was more my Mum than my Dad – then they couldn't do any less for me. They actually wondered whether it wasn't against the Church to be so tolerant, and asked a priest, and he said it was against the Church, and that it was their primary duty to teach me that "intrinsically evil" stuff and to stop me having sex. So they sat down and tried to work out how they would have wanted to be treated if they had been growing up gay, compared it with what the priest told them and decided to ignore him.' Nicodemus smiled, as something about 'Which father among you, if his son asks for a fish, will instead of a fish give him a serpent?' meandered through his mind.

'It wasn't that they were innocent about the sleepovers and the nights out,' the boy continued. 'They deliberately played along, actually insisting that my regular friends stayed over, getting to know them and hoping that one day I would be able to share my stories and the sob stuff, just like my sisters and my brother, so that they could be involved in my life and help me get ahead. One day, when I was about fourteen, my Dad gave me a stern lecture about being responsible and using condoms, and I played along, made as if I were glad to be told how to be a careful straight boy. Only much later did I discover that it had been *he* who was playing along with *me*, telling me how to be a careful gay boy without making me ashamed, but also letting me know that no one was going to kick up a fuss if condoms were found in my room. Well, the day that I came out to them, like five years later, they started to cry, and I thought "Oh no, this is going to be awful." But hey, they were crying with relief that their risk had paid off. Actually it was embarrassing, since they insisted on my date coming to dinner, and he was ever so jumpy about not having to pretend.'

'So that was what he meant by asking which of the teachings you believed in!' They all turned as the Pentecostalist referred to the Inquisitor in the past tense. And indeed the park bench was empty, and the retreating robes and a hint of cigarette smoke showed that the Inquisitor had tired of his mask and moved on. The boy continued, 'You showed the beautiful logical consistency between the teachings, but in practice, if you believe in the teaching about the homosexual inclination, you don't believe in the teaching about desire, because you make the homosexual inclination the enemy of growing up and becoming human. And in practice, if you were to believe in your Church's teaching about desire, you wouldn't believe the teaching about the homosexual inclination, because it would be an irrelevant consideration in the midst of guys growing up and learning to love each other. Now that there's no Inquisitor here, come clean, say you're wrong, say his parents were right to ignore their priest.'

The Duchess was silent. Now that there was no Inquisitor there, the game was over. No one before whom to protest a purity of teaching. Only young men who seemed to understand both too much and too little. Too much, since the practical questions were the only questions. And too little, since for him, the only practical question was surviving the gap between purity of teaching and the messiness of his desires, and thus holding down his job. The boy who had claimed underpayment moved closer to him, sensing his sadness, and rubbed his arm. Actually, the priest knew that the boy liked him a lot, and if the truth be told, he liked the boy –

no not a boy, a man thirteen years his junior – more than he knew what to do with.

'You know what I've seen,' said his friend, making sure that there was no accusation in his tone. 'I've always wondered about the payment bit. You remember how it was when we started. I insisted on payment, because I was trying to convince myself that I was straight, and so it was OK if I got paid for it, because it meant that I was only doing you a favour, and it wasn't the real me who was doing it. But after a bit, I got over that, and realised that it was the real me, and felt cheap that I was getting paid. So I stopped asking for cash, but you carried on giving it to me anyhow. Well, now I see that you're just like what I was, but the other way round. You need to give me money because that makes you able to believe that it's bad. If you're doing something bad, then you keep the purity of your teaching. But, can't we just drop the cash bit, and be . . . well, be what we are?'

The Duchess was shaking as his barriers against his friend's forgiveness began to crumble. In his first non-theatrical move of the night he clutched at him to steady himself. 'I'm sorry,' he said. 'I'm sorry.' And the tears started to wreak havoc with the make-up. 'I'm sorry,' and he could say no more, just sobbing and leaning and trying to hug, in as far as the dress would allow it, and fussing to avoid getting make-up on the other man's shirt. The man in military drag suddenly looked his thirty years. He knew, as one who had not been shamed when he might have been, about avoiding shaming others, and moved to protect the priest from curious passers-by, shielding his face from the light thrown by the bonfire. The fashion-conscious Pentecostal boy overcame a momentary hesitation about running make-up defiling *his* clothes and lent a hand to prop up the couple at the centre of the group as they hobbled off across the square.

The bonfire was at its apogee, and two small girls were throwing little crackers on it and then clutching their ears as they went bang. As the men holding up the weeping figure walked past, a couple pushing a pram and walking a small boy looked up and the wife laughed gently. The husband crouched down and pointed his five-year-old at them and waved. The military escort waved back as he moved between their smiles and the priest. The would-be seminarian, who seemed to have worked out that anyone who could say 'I'm sorry' and cry couldn't be all bad, took over the task of shielding the priest's emerging face from further attention, apparently unaware that there was no need. As the first of the fireworks burst upon the night, they headed off the square and towards a bar where they could sit away from prying eyes, if any there were. A bar whose owner was not at all discriminating about who used the ladies' room to adjust faces before returning to other lives, other roles, and braving the day.

Nicodemus shrugged with perplexity as he watched them leave the square. Could the teaching on gay people be a de facto defection from the very teaching on desire that it had so clearly tried to link up with? Is this what was meant by 'for the sake of your tradition you have made void the word of God'? What was Flesh and what was Spirit? How could he tell? Who would tell him? And if it were so, what would it look like, for someone as cautious as he, to lift a finger towards unbinding a heavy burden from the shoulders of men like the Duchess, let alone the boys, from whose shoulders it seemed to be slipping without his help?

He walked slowly towards the other end of the square and the route that would take him home. On the corner a street preacher, blue suit, crisp white shirt, blue tie and large black Bible, was haranguing anyone who would listen about the destruction of Sodom. The preacher paced, and waved his book emphatically, pausing every so often to intersperse his warnings with readings from the text. People moved by, some nodding at him good-humouredly, and a few stopped to listen. Among the ones listening, apparently raptly, Nicodemus saw the Inquisitor. As Nicodemus came up to him, the Inquisitor turned and tugged at his sleeve. 'Look, look!' he exclaimed, pointing down the square between the preacher and the bonfire. Then, with an elation somewhere between pride and an almost infantile radiance: 'The same old words, but no one on the fire! No one on the fire! You will work it out for yourselves! You will work it out for yourselves!'

Nicodemus stumbled off into the night with goose-bumps, uncertain whether he had just heard a prophecy, or been given a command.